5-12 (6)

D1234674

Donut Dolly

Joann in steel helmet and armored vest on the way to Bear Cat, December 1966.

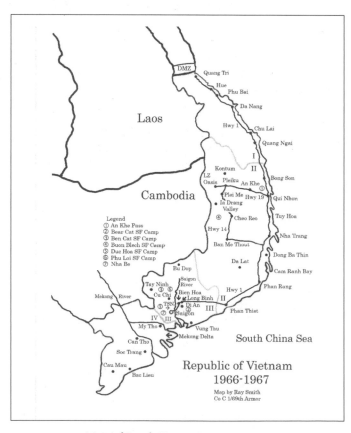

Laos

Cambodia

Legend
① An Khe Pass
② Bear Cat SF Camp
③ Ben Cat SF Camp
④ Buon Blech SF Camp
⑤ Duc Hoa SF Camp
⑥ Phu Loi SF Camp
⑦ Nha Be

DMZ
Quang Tri
Hue
Phu Bai
Da Nang
Hwy 1
Chu Lai
Quang Ngai
I
II
Kontum
Bong Son
LZ
Oasis
Pleiku
An Khe
①
Plei Me
Hwy 19
Qui Nhon
Ia Drang
Valley
④
Cheo Reo
Tuy Hoa
Hwy 14
Nha Trang
Ban Me Thuot
Da Lat
Dong Ba Thin
Bu Dop
Cam Ranh Bay
Saigon
River
Tay Ninh
③ ⑥
Bien Hoa
Hwy 1
Phan Rang
Cu Chi
Long Binh
II
Mekong River
⑤ TSN
Di An
Phan Thiet
⑦
③ Saigon
III
IV
III
My Tho
Vung Tau
Can Tho
Mekong Delta
South China Sea
Soc Trang
Cau Mau
Republic of Vietnam
1966-1967
Bac Lieu

Map by Ray Smith
Co C 1/69th Armor

Map of South Vietnam ca. 1966–67.

Donut Dolly:

An American Red Cross Girl's War in Vietnam

By Joann Puffer Kotcher

Number 6 in the North Texas Military Biography and Memoir Series

University of North Texas Press

Denton, Texas

10 9 8 7 6 5 4 3 2 1

Permissions:
University of North Texas Press
1155 Union Circle #311336
Denton, TX 76203-5017

The paper used in this book meets the minimum requirements of the American
National Standard for Permanence of Paper for Printed Library Materials,
z39.48.1984. Binding materials have been chosen for durability.

Library of Congress Cataloging-in-Publication Data

Kotcher, Joann Puffer, 1941–
Donut Dolly : an American Red Cross girl's war in
Vietnam / by Joann Puffer Kotcher.—1st ed.
p. cm. — (Number 6 in the North Texas military biography and memoir series)
Includes bibliographical references and index.
ISBN 978-1-57441-324-3 (cloth : alk. paper)
1. Kotcher, Joann Puffer, 1941– 2. American Red Cross—Biography. 3. Vietnam War,
1961-1975—War work—Red Cross. 4. Vietnam War, 1961–1975—Women—United
States—Biography. 5. Vietnam War, 1961–1975—Personal narratives, American.
I. Title. II. Series: North Texas military biography and memoir series ; no. 6.
DS559.63.K68 2011
959.704'31—dc23
[B]
2011028208

Donut Dolly: An American Red Cross Girl's War in Vietnam
is Number 6 in the North Texas Military Biography and Memoir Series

Dedication

To single out any individual or group of people for special gratitude would be impossible. Too many people contributed key facts to make this book a complete picture of a small piece of a war that will forever be controversial.

Nonetheless, this work is dedicated to our veterans, past, present, and future. Those who have not served can never understand their sacrifices and heroism. Particularly because of the nature of the book, most of my information came especially from combat and Vietnam Era veterans. We should sincerely honor them. They were my sources who have become lifelong colleagues, and who have accepted me into their *Band of Brothers.*

Contents

Preface

Donut Dolly: An American Red Cross Girl's War in Vietnam[1] is my personal view of the early days of the war. I kept a journal for a year while a program director for the American Red Cross. I wrote what I saw and did, what I felt and thought—a faithful representation of that time. The comedian Jeff Foxworthy said, "The best stuff is not stuff you make up. It's true stuff."[2] This book is based primarily on that diary and other confirmed sources. The story unfolds day by day as I lived it. What happened on one day usually had no connection to what happened on the next. I included only information that I experienced first-hand. Later I expanded the original diary into a book-length narrative. I hope this book will convey the twists and turns of a turbulent time. While filling in the notes of my Vietnam diary I used the internet extensively. My searches led me throughout the country to renew friendships with people I knew well or casually. These people were good representatives of the 2.6 million who served in the war. More about my old new friends in the chapter, "Whatever Happened To . . . ?" however. Through our shared experiences we are forever young.

Before I went to Vietnam, my mother, a well-published writer, told me, "Keep a diary. You think you will remember, but you won't." She was right. More than once when reading the diary years later, I found a story in my handwriting that I did not recall.

Ernie Pyle, the World War II Pulitzer Prize-winning journalist wrote, "I haven't written anything about the 'Big Picture,' because I don't know anything about it. I only know what we see from our worm's-eye view, and our segment of the picture consists only of tired and dirty soldiers who are alive and don't want to die. . . ."[3] Most of the time, I didn't reflect much on why anything happened. I was too busy keeping my head down and trying not to get anybody killed. A senior Army officer who served with me in Vietnam advised, "Focus on *your* experiences. People have written about the *soldier's* view. Your story should be the way you saw it, as *you* lived it."

I served in Korea for 14 months and in Vietnam for a year, from May 10, 1966, to May 10, 1967, in the American Red Cross Supplemental Recreation Activities Overseas (SRAO). The first Vietnam SRAO unit opened at Danang in September 1965.[4] Military Assistance Command Vietnam (MACV) ordered that we could take recreation to the military anywhere in the combat zone, with permission of the local commander.[5] No one acknowledged that this was the first time any women had been formally allowed in a combat zone. Eight months later I was the 45th Donut Dolly of 627 in the program's seven-year Vietnam history.

Early in the Vietnam effort, the Red Cross drew its resources from the SRAO program in Korea. Most of the girls had served there. Our recreation activities were designed for able-bodied soldiers, not hospital patients, and to allow the men to interact with the girls.

In Korea in April 1965, at the 1st Cavalry Division, I had written a program about numbers with simple problems and geometric shapes. Other topics that were popular with the men included sports, dogs, history, and not surprisingly, women. Another girl and I gave the numbers program one day to a group of about 30 men in a mess hall. The mess sergeant had coffee ready. We served each man a cup and gave him two donuts with a smile and a friendly word. We made small talk as we set up our props. I started the program with a paper and pencil game of several "Pick a Number" activities. The men loved the mysterious results. We followed with trivia about numbers and their history, and then we played a quiz game of story problems. The men tackled the challenge with amazing speed. Ironically, when I was a Math teacher, my students hated story problems. But outside the classroom, numbers became relevant. The program had a couple of other activities that kept the men enthusiastic, competitive, and mentally sharp. When the hour ended we reminded the soldiers that the program next week would be about women. That brought a cheer. We talked with several men who stood around while we packed up our props, and then set out for our next stop.

The Donut Dollies didn't have donuts in Vietnam because, according to one mess sergeant, "It was too damn hot." We set up recreation centers and made mobile visits wherever commanders requested, including Special Forces Teams in remote places in the jungles. Our job was to remind the soldiers of home, or to be like their sister or the girl next door.[6] Officers would ask us to take risks, because they felt our visits meant so much to the men.

We gave recreation programs wherever we could; there were few mess halls in Vietnam. We often met men coming off an operation or going out to one, sometimes served an item in the mess line, or ate with the men. Our military cooks occasionally supplied cake, muffins, or cookies. We usually took envelopes of pre-sweetened Kool-Aid powder and paper cups with big red crosses on them. When we visited troops, we would request a five-gallon can of water, dump the powder in, ask one of the guys to shake it up, and ladle it with a cup. Sometimes we had nothing to give out. We walked around and greeted everyone or sat with them and talked. We never went off duty. We smiled 24 hours a day and waved at everybody we saw. They always waved back. Sometimes they whooped and hollered. I never felt more appreciated in my life.

I departed Vietnam on May 10, 1967, one year after arriving. I stopped in Japan to go shopping, detoured to Korea to see my pen pal, and then returned to teaching in my home town, Flint, Michigan. The Vietnam Clubmobile program ended five years later in May 1972 when the girls at Bien Hoa (pronounced "Ben Wah") made a final visit to Fire-base Bunker Hill.[7]

Two Red Cross men and three women lost their lives in Vietnam and one woman was wounded.[8]

I have heard that some veterans believe the nurses were important in Vietnam, but that the Donut Dollies were a distraction. Some soldiers saw us as a tease, a reminder of a home life they couldn't have. In 1967, a tease meant "to worry or irritate . . . often in sport."[9] Or, as one man put it, "A tease is a girl who flirts with you, but has no intention of going any further." When we reminded men of home, we made sure it was a good memory, not a tease. During my 26 months overseas, at seven duty stations, the soldiers always thanked us for coming. One veteran recently said to me, "You lovely ladies put some sunshine in our lives at a not so good time! THANK YOU! Sure there was a bit of ogling, but I would think that it would have been stranger if it didn't occur what with us young guys being so far away from home."[10] We appreciated the soldiers' gratitude as much as they appreciated what we did for them.

The soldiers felt the same about us as they did about Bob Hope, the attractive women he brought, and all the other United Service Organizations (USO) entertainers. Nobody ever said, "I think Bob Hope is a tease." Everyone was thrilled to see him. Everyone I met during my service, and in the 40 years since, has been grateful for our part in the war. A few months ago a veteran remembered, "Seeing an American girl after ten or 11 months in the field was like seeing an angel walking."

I have not talked to all of the 2.59 million personnel who served within the borders of South Vietnam,[11] but, I'm sure anyone could find enough people who felt we irritated them, to make it seem like the majority view. They would have to look hard. You can find a quote in the Bible to say anything; you can probably find someone who thought we were a torment to them.

We smiled, waved, spoke to everyone, and were always friendly and professional, always careful not to give a false impression. We were pleasant and attractive, always fresh and modest. Petti-pants were in fashion. They stayed in place better than under slips if a helicopter blew our skirt up. One girl noticed that when the light was behind us, you could see a shadow of our legs, so we went back to half-slips, no matter how hot it was. The Red Cross rules said skirt length must be modest, we always had to wear the uniform belt, and long hair must be off the collar. Some of us thought we looked dowdy.

Ever since the Civil War and centuries before, young women have gone among the soldiers to care for the wounded or to provide comfort. The Red Cross knew the score. If the men and their commanders thought we were bad for morale, they would have banned us, because commanders always had the last word. The reason everyone loved the Army nurses and believed they had an important purpose was not solely because they provided medical care. It was because they were women. Men could do their medical job. Some did. I dated one in Korea.

It was traditionally a woman's job to care for the sick. Men did the fighting. When they were wounded, women cared for them. Everyone loved women for it. And so, nurses did two jobs. They were nurses, and they reminded men of home, and the smile and scent and form of a woman. I doubt anyone ever thought, "Nurses should all be men because having women around is distracting."

Trainers in Washington, D.C. told us that the Red Cross tried sending young men to do able-bodied recreation, as our job was called. The idea died fast. Why? I couldn't say it any better than Ernie Pyle:

> One nurse was always on duty in each tentful of twenty men. She had medical orderlies to help her. Most of the time the nurses wore army coveralls, but Colonel Bauchspies wanted them to put on dresses once in a while, for he said the effect on the men was astounding.

The touch of femininity, the knowledge that a woman was around, gave the wounded man courage and confidence and a feeling of security. And the more feminine she looked, the better.[12]

. . . The usual bunkhouse profanity was strangely absent from those tents, for there was always a nurse around.[13]

Ernie Pyle summed it up:

More than anything else, [our men] miss women. Their expressed longings, their conversation, their whole conduct show their need for female companionship, and the gentling effect of femininity upon man is conspicuous here where it has been so long absent.[14]

A veteran recently told me in an email: "Come on girl. You're a Vietnam Veteran too. I think every G.I. in Vietnam fell in love with a 'Donut Dollie.' You brought a bit of the world with you to Nam."[15]

So, yes, nurses were at war to provide essential medical care, an important job, but they did our job, too. Actually that was the real reason they were there. It could be argued that the job of being a woman was more important than being a nurse. The male nurse I dated told me he was often assigned to isolated places where they only needed one nurse, and it wasn't appropriate to send a woman. He laughed, "Once they sent me on one of those assignments. After I had been there for a while the guys told me that, when they got the news they were going to get a nurse, they were all excited. They could hardly wait. Then, when I showed up, they could hardly believe it. They were so disappointed."

Nurses didn't associate with Donut Dollies; they were jealous, we thought. Heads turned when we were around because we looked more feminine. The nurses had to wear green fatigues and combat boots. We wore a blue dress and loafers. Girls stand off a little from another girl who is prettier. The nurses knew they were there to be women, too. It's just that nobody ever said it.

I asked some veterans and Donut Dollies if they ever encountered anyone who thought we were a tease, a distraction.

Jennifer Young responded: "I can understand the 'not liked' position about DD's in Vietnam. There were times when our presence was an extra hassle—such as when weather caused us to have to stay on a fire-base where there were NO facilities for females. Often this was during some sort of 'alert,' adding frustration for the Commanding Officer. . . . We were not bimbos meddling where no one wanted us. 1) The military REQUESTED our presence and 2) one had to be a college graduate."[16]

John Ahrenberg aired his bad experience: "After hitting a mine and destroying my tank I was back at base camp (hill 29) making repairs. I found out the Donut Dollies were up at the mess hall, so I decided to go see an American girl again and just maybe get to talk awhile with her. What a joke! I never got to say more than Hi. They were all too interested in the officers. I guess a lowly Specialist-5 was not good enough. I got the cold shoulder. I wasn't expecting her to jump in bed with me just to talk with her and find out how home was and where was home? It took nerve for them to travel to the base camp. It's too bad they didn't have time for us combat soldiers. I remember after that the guys tagged them with the name Pastry Pigs!! That's not fair. There could have been others that visited with the real combat soldiers."[17]

Bill Conboy expressed a view that our training anticipated: "I remember my first reaction when I first saw [Donut Dollies]. I said to myself, 'What the hell are they doing here? This is a war zone, it's bad enough we have to worry about the Vietnamese civilians in this mess.' It wasn't right. I read stories from WW II about nurses at Bataan and Corregidor and what they went through. I didn't want these ladies to go through those ordeals. We soldiers were busy watching each other's backs and we'd have to worry about looking after the Donut Dollies too."[18]

Richard Morris had another view:

> I served in RVN on 2 tours. Both times as an advisor and not with US units. Tour #1: Central highlands 1st Lieutenant, without another American. I had no opportunity to interact with Red Cross except when out processing in Saigon in 1963 which was a wonderful morale boosting experience. Definitely no "tease" just service, please. Tour #2: In the Delta, Major, 3 officers, 3 NCOs, 1 PFC. No road access, mail was air dropped. The "Doughnut Dollies" did make one visit to our 7-man team house, after "Tet" in 1968. This was a hostile environment with daily incoming mortar fire and the Red Cross visitors showed courage in coming out there by chopper and staying a few hours. What a boost to morale! Our young PFC was especially moved and grateful for this breath of fresh, perfumed air from "home." Of course, we all were appreciative of the brave commitment these ladies all had to this mission. One of my team said, "People actually care enough to send these angels into our midst, that's just amazing."
>
> There is no adequate way to express how great an impact the Red Cross had on improving the attitudes and morale of the soldiers serving the cause of freedom. The courage and dedication of the Red Cross "Dollies" was unparalleled and vastly unrewarded, but not unappreciated!
>
> With respect, my thanks and admiration.
>
> Richard C. Morris, LTC, US Army, Retired.[19]

Whether anyone thought we were a tease, a burden, or a reminder of home, I present the facts. This book is a time capsule. It uses the politically incorrect vocabulary, beliefs, and assumptions of the time, and it is human. It describes only what happened, without an agenda. I follow Ernie Pyle, who gave readers a window to another war. I invite them into that world, a realistic view of war, not a screenwriter's view, written for entertainment. That version was all I knew in the beginning, but I soon learned there was much, much more.

Among the 627 Donut Dollies to serve in Vietnam, three lost their lives, and one was wounded. We followed the traditions of women who volunteered for combat zones in every war. They served along side conscripted men until 1973. Then President Nixon signed into law voluntary military service. We visited the soldiers anywhere and any way we could. I can understand why Bob Hope, James Garner, and other celebrities kept returning to Southeast Asia. The soldiers appreciated them beyond anyone's expectations.

I was scared all the time when I first got to Vietnam, as much for the soldiers as for myself. I thought most of them would be killed. Soon, I learned which areas were safe and which were not and that few of the soldiers would die. I relaxed and tended to business. Later I learned that danger hid in some places that everyone thought were safe. Often, I didn't know that I had been in danger until long afterwards. I found that war is not constant explosions, as the media portrays.

My four assignments spanned the country from the Central Highlands to the Mekong Delta and from the South China Sea to the Cambodian border. Each location was a different job, a different living situation, a different climate and terrain, a different war, different people, a different experience. Each unit I visited had its own pride, characteristics, and germs. Every time I ate in a new place, about once a week, I got sick. I saw many different lives of the soldiers, and I was privileged to see many faces of Vietnam. Most soldiers saw one location, one unit, and one job. On the other hand, I was there for only one year of the many years of the war. As the years passed, the conflict changed, the people changed, hemlines changed, and the attitudes, both civilian and military at home and in the war changed. I know the year I was there, and that is what I describe. Likewise, I did not meet nor did I share experiences with the women who have chronicled their tours in Vietnam. None was there at the same time or at the same place as I was. I cannot comment on what they saw or have written.

I dodged bullets with the soldiers. I flew with them into "hot" areas, visited them in hospitals, and walked lines of foxholes.

Soldiers are pawns in what goes on around them. They are like us, ordinary people, but sometimes events call on them to perform extraordinary acts of courage. I learned the power of fear from our soldiers. I learned myths and legends of war, and lessons I still treasure. Vietnam showed me places both terrifying and awesome. The dangers I faced were those of a soldier, and real peril followed me more times than I liked. The war showed me what a hero and bravery are, and why a soldier will suspend the most basic instinct, self-preservation. I did it, myself, and experienced how people react when they are brave. I called on latent resources to copy the heroism those around me showed. I came to understand what they thought and felt about being in the war. It's difficult to comprehend the sacrifices and selflessness the war required of the typical soldier. Theirs is a story of common bravery. When I came home I found that people were confused about Vietnam. Time and distance have changed little.

We who served remember. We look back to a time that tested courage. We are proud of what we saw and what we did. In Vietnam people told me, "You never know what you're going to do until it happens." We learned early that we had courage. We knew that for the rest of our lives we could call on that courage. We built up a reservoir of self confidence.

Author's Note

Almost all facts and accounts in this book come from my direct observations and experiences as recorded in the journal I kept while serving in Vietnam. Some accounts in the book, I heard second hand. In order to maintain the absolute integrity of hearsay stories, conversations or events, I personally verified with at least one primary source who had direct knowledge or actual documentation. In some cases, an event required verification from several sources. When stories, conversations, or events appeared to be obvious or highly likely, but could not be verified, I did not include them in this book. Most of my sources were veterans, because they gave me eye-witness unpublished experiences. Without the telling, these stories would be lost. Sometimes, I referred to people by names other than their own. I did this mostly by their request.

The medals listed for each veteran are as that person reported to me. These military men must be honored for their heroism. Yet, there are others equally as heroic, who, for whatever reason, refused their award or had no witness to the display of their courage.

Joann Puffer Kotcher

✦ CHAPTER 1 ✦

On My Way to the War

During the Civil War neighbors would load up a wagon with quilts, food, and any other supplies they could spare for the soldiers. Sometimes a young, unmarried woman went. Someone, maybe a grandmother, would risk her life to drive the wagon as close to the fighting as she dared. The young woman would stay to help in the hospital. The wagon would return with wounded to be cared for at home.

The Donut Dollies were part of that tradition. Clarissa Harlowe Barton, or Clara Barton, was one of those women.[1] When she was 60 years old she founded the American Red Cross on that legacy of volunteer service. She ran the charity for over 20 years until she retired in 1904 at the age of 83.[2]

In World War I my grandmother's sister was a Red Cross nurse in France. Her diary records that she attended a dance at a Red Cross Center. In 1917 the Red Cross started canteens where 55,000 volunteers served food and snacks to servicemen around the world.[3] In 1918 the Red Cross began hospital recreation in the United States. The ladies wore gray dresses and veils. Patients called them "The Gray Ladies." Almost 24,000 Red Cross nurses served the military. By war's end, nearly one-third of the US population was either a donor or volunteer. The Red Cross suffered 400 killed; of these, 330 were women.[4]

During WW II the Red Cross Nursing Service recruited 212,000 nurses for the Army and for civilian service, where there was a shortage of doctors. Of these, 71,000 made up over 90 percent of all the nurses who served the military during the war, at home and abroad. The Red Cross also ran recreation facilities around the world, employing at its peak 5,000 workers and approximately 140,000 volunteers.

The Red Cross introduced Clubmobiles in Great Britain in 1942 and later deployed some to the continent. These were converted pick-up trucks and single-deck buses operated by three American Red Cross women and a local driver. They were equipped for making and serving donuts and coffee and other small items. The girls passed out donuts to long lines of soldiers. The men called the girls "Donut Dollies." "The women staffing them [Clubmobiles] were allowed to move through combat areas with more freedom then many soldiers or journalists, as they brought coffee and doughnuts right up to the GIs in camps and sometimes in foxholes. . . . But most of the Red Cross women who died overseas in World War II were killed in the course of this dangerous kind of work."[5] "Red Cross girls often reported that every moment of their work and life at war seemed infused with meaning and depth that belied the auxiliary, or sometimes even trivial, surface appearance of the duties they performed."[6] In wartime service 52 Red Cross women and 34 men lost their lives.[7]

Everything the soldiers received was free or at cost. The Allies required their soldiers to pay for everything, and pressured the United States to charge. The uproar at home was so great that the Red Cross petitioned the government to let them stop. Now, the Red Cross gives out everything free or at cost.

During the Korean War two Red Cross men lost their lives.[8] Two months after the Cease Fire in 1952, at the request of the military, the Red Cross set up Clubmobiles for isolated areas in Korea. All Donut Dollies were US citizens, single, female, college graduates between 21 and 25, and were screened in Washington D.C. I volunteered for that program and arrived in Korea in 1964. Korean bakers made our donuts at night on the Army installations, ready for us in the morning. We scheduled weekly visits to military units where we passed out donuts and gave one-hour recreation programs of games and stories in the mess halls. Our job was to remind the soldiers of home. We represented their sisters or the girl next door. We also visited hospitals. The Clubmobile program in Korea ended in 1973; 899 women had served.[9] I finished 14 months in Korea in October 1965, had about six months of rest in the United States, and then shipped to Vietnam.

How did I get into the Red Cross and volunteer to go to Vietnam? I always had a sense of adventure. When I was little our tablecloth had pictures of airplanes with big teeth. My mother said, "Those are the Flying Tigers, heroes who fought in China on the other side of the world." I wanted to see China.[10] My father was away working in a war factory, and I lived on a farm with my mother, Lela Puffer, and two sisters, Phyllis two years older, and Karen 18 months younger.

The Korean War started when I was nine.[11] The war became one day old, two days old, a week old, and then, like World War II, it became part of our lives. During summers and vacations my family visited every state except Rhode Island and North Dakota. We followed the St. Lawrence Seaway to Nova Scotia and saw the forts at Montreal and Quebec City. Guides in period uniforms told about the battles between the United States and Canada. Later I learned that a Puffer was in those battles.

In 1961 I went to the University of Michigan, 20,000 students, eight men to every woman. I was a Math major, which impressed everyone. Both Phyllis and Karen went on to graduate school. They weren't going to be one-degree women. Phyllis joined the Women's Army Corps (WACs) after graduation. I was the maverick. I didn't like school. I wanted to travel.

The three of us girls were active in church youth groups. My sisters became less active during college, but I continued. The pastors emphasized pacifism. "For the price of one airplane, we could fund much-needed social programs. We should protest war. It takes two to fight. If we refuse to fight, we will have peace." Nobody argued the other side, and I became a committed pacifist.

During August of 1962, after my junior year, I went on a three-week Peace Seminar in Berlin on a church scholarship. Students from all over Europe attended the seminar. The first anniversary of the Berlin Wall came around. We learned that one year before, shortly after midnight on Sunday, August 13, 1961, armed East German soldiers began to construct the Berlin Wall. The people tore down that wall 28 years later, on November 9, 1989.[12] On that first anniversary of the wall, while everyone else went to a protest rally, I went to East Berlin alone early in the morning to Communist headquarters. I wanted to find out what Communists were really like. I talked to them for a little while and decided they were screwy. Afterwards, on that Monday, at noon, I walked through deserted streets, crossed to the West at the American Check Point Charlie, and re-joined my group. The West teemed with crowds of noisy protesters.

Later that afternoon, someone asked me, "The East is full of people protesting the Wall, too, isn't it?"

I answered, "No. They don't have that right."

After I graduated in 1963 with a degree in mathematics, I visited my sister, Phyllis, a WAC lieutenant, at Fort McClellan, Alabama. She asked, "Why don't you get a job?"

I found that in 1963 a woman newly graduated from college, could be a waitress, a telephone operator, or a teacher. Our opportunities were limited. But I discovered another job, one more exciting. My sister's roommate had a brass plaque with a striking, enameled red cross. She told me, "It was a going away gift from a job I had in Korea before

I joined the Army." I had been writing to a pen pal in Korea since tenth grade, and still do. I didn't care what the job was, just that somebody might pay me to go someplace exciting. The Red Cross invited me to Atlanta for a whole day of interviews, and hired me for a recreation program in Korea. I stored my belongings in my parents' attic, sold my car, wrote a last will, and flew to Washington, D.C. in July 1964.

I trained for two weeks with 15 new college graduate girls. We heard lectures on the history of the Red Cross, its organization, its accomplishments, and projects. Our job was called "able-bodied recreation." We served military people stationed in isolated areas. The Red Cross would not assign us to work in hospitals or with wounded, though we were to visit them when we were able. Some of our recreation activities could be used with patients, but we must never sit on the beds. I was too busy trying to remember everything to think to ask why. Trainers never told us how to do our jobs or how to write an able-bodied recreation program. They instructed us to be creative, but not to humiliate anyone: "If you tell the men to stand on their heads for an hour, they'll do it. Don't make them look foolish." Some of the games we made up may have been simple, but they reminded the men of home and gave them a chance to talk to an American girl. That was what the soldiers looked forward to.

Many of the rules we had to follow were for our safety. We had to know where the dangers were in our new environment. Other rules were preventative, to keep the men from misinterpreting why we were there, and what we were doing, to set the ground rules for our recreation programs. We had to know what the misunderstandings might be and how to minimize them. The Red Cross said they would move us often to keep us fresh. That worked. Every time romance began to bloom, I got transferred. Most of my dates were like going out with my brother. I never knew a man long enough to get more than just acquainted. I never thought that was a coincidence. We had training lectures on

Korea, its history, geography, climate, and customs, and about military courtesy. Trainers emphasized that we represented America to everybody. I felt the burden and remembered it. We learned how to behave as the only western women among thousands of men: "Don't let anyone push you around. One girl was at a party. She felt someone pinch her on the behind. She turned around and drew back her arm to slap the perpetrator. She was looking at a star. A general had pinched her. Later she asked her supervisor, 'What should I have done?'

"The supervisor answered, 'Follow through.'"

At that time in 1964, and especially a few years earlier, men would whistle at or pat a pretty girl. Depending on the circumstances, girls took it as a compliment or an insult. No one considered it particularly polite, but it was accepted. I never got that kind of treatment from the people I knew, but where we were going, we had to be able to handle all situations. A Donut Dolly in World War II reported, "En route to the town, we passed a crowded compound of Nazi prisoners. We disdainfully ignored their cat-calls and wolf whistles."[13]

An iron rule that I saw play out later, concerned romance. If any of us got married, we would be sent home. Another caution was, if you fall in love and want to get married, don't do it overseas. Wait until you get home. The man might look perfect to you over there, but when you get home he could look entirely different. Trainers warned us to be cautious about whom we dated. We would enjoy the married men because they were more at ease with women, knew more about what women liked, and missed the company of women more than single men did. Therefore, we shouldn't spend too much time with married men. It could be dangerous. At best, it would be a waste of time. The trainer explained a phenomenon called the S.S.R., State Side Reject, an unattractive girl who can't get a date State Side, so she goes overseas where the men are so desperate she can be popular. I shuddered, but I got the point.

We learned that we were civilian non-combatants. We could not be armed and we could not fire a weapon. The men would be proud of their firearms and would want to show them to us. We might be invited to pose for pictures with arms and artillery pieces. We could not pose holding weapons, but we could pose beside an artillery piece. Sometimes the men invited the girls to pull the lanyard to fire an artillery piece; we could not. It would violate our non-combatant status. I thought, *That's easy. I'm a pacifist.* Unarmed, we were vulnerable. It was our responsibility to stay out of danger. Otherwise, the men would concentrate on protecting us and not on doing their job. We must not let that happen. I thought, *That's fine with me.*

We met the important people in the Red Cross, and toured all the major sights in Washington, D.C. We got dog tags and shots at the Pentagon, and received uniforms that were hand tailored. We looked sharp. Rules for wearing the uniform were flexible. We wore it when we were on duty or traveling. Sometimes we got instructions to wear the dress uniform instead of the work uniform, with either high heeled shoes or flats instead of loafers. Officially, we never went off duty, but outside working hours we usually wore civilian clothes. Beyond that, each unit made its own decisions. In training we learned that we would have officer status so we wouldn't have to sleep in the soldiers' barracks; that idea was a shocker. We could eat in any mess hall; and we would have priority for transportation because we had to travel to work.

Young women in isolated areas like Korea and Vietnam raised questions about our behavior, so the rules helped us preserve our image. We assumed a woman's virtue in spite of the gossip dribbling from men's locker rooms. When I was in college, girls snickered about "the Pill." Many looked at it not as women's freedom, but as a license for sex. It was not legal in some states, especially for unmarried women. The early and mid-1960s held on to some of the strict values of the previous generation.

The Red Cross demanded that our conduct be above reproach, and to *appear* to be above reproach. That was for our safety and to prevent misunderstanding. As paid national staff of the American Red Cross, our salary was about the same as that of a first-year teacher. The previous year, as a Math teacher, I received $3,600, or about $18,000 in today's money. The Red Cross strongly prohibited us from accepting any other money for *anything*. Our payment was in knowing we were doing something worthwhile for the soldiers. The rules said we must never be alone with a man. Moreover, we must never give the appearance that we were alone with a man. As my father had taught me in second grade, we traveled with another girl. We knew that people watched everything we did and knew everything we did. We "lived in a goldfish bowl," and we acted accordingly. We also knew that people would make up rumors about us, no matter how proper we were. We all felt responsible for the reputation of the program. Of all the girls I served with in Korea or Vietnam, I never knew one, or even heard of one, who behaved improperly. Virtuous girls went overseas, and virtuous girls came back. That's the kind of girls the Red Cross recruited.

Our honor was probably more protected than anything in Vietnam. Trainers told us that each man would want to make advances. He knew he couldn't, so he would make sure no other man did. We found it was true. Once in Vietnam, one of the girls, Lori, and I visited an isolated radio relay station. The sergeant sat beside us in the mess hall and scrutinized everything. One man said "Damn." The sergeant exploded. "Watch your mouth. Jesus Christ, there's ladies present!" The men made it their top priority to protect us, even above their own safety. In Korea I overheard one man say, "Those girls could get married right this minute to anyone here, if they wanted to."

Hugh Hefner had just opened the first Playboy club. Girls in scant bunny costumes waited tables. In 1966 it would not be unusual for a man to pat or pinch a waitress. Hefner's new rule was customers could

"Look, but don't touch." It was a unique idea, but the Red Cross had long conveyed that message. We girls made the men understand. If a man wanted sex, he could buy it. Korean and Vietnamese prostitutes were everywhere. We Donut Dollies didn't use sex to be popular. We knew that when men were interested in us, it was because we had sisterly qualities they appreciated.

*   *   *

My class of 15 girls flew to Korea on July 25, 1964, with 190 soldiers. We arrived at Kimpo ("Kim poe") Airport for a week of training in Seoul (pronounced "Sole"). On my first free time on July 31 I went to visit Cho Dong Song for the first time. She had been my pen pal for eight years. Her friendship would become priceless. She would show me the popular and hidden Korea. Dong Song would introduce me to the foods, the customs, and the private lives of a Korean family. Getting to see her, though, wasn't easy. It was a cultural adventure. Traveling by taxi with a driver who didn't speak English, I didn't know where I was or what I would find. That evening my ancient, tiny vehicle crept along a muddy, one-lane alley between tile-roofed, walled houses.

After about half an hour of feeling lost, three young people, a woman and two men wearing suits, ran toward the taxi, yelling something I couldn't understand. The taxi stopped, and I heard the strangers say, "Jon Poopa, Jon Poopa." They were attempting to say my name. My own name, "Joan Puffer," became cryptic. Dong Song, her brother, Cho Dong Gun, and her husband, Kim Ke Chul, had flagged down the taxi. They ushered me into a new world, the home of successful Koreans. My girlhood dreams of seeing China and the other side of the world were close to being real.

I arrived at my first assignment the following day. On August 1 I joined the Flying Nine at Army Support Command (ASCOM) southwest of Seoul, at Bupyong (pronounced "Boo pyong"). Anticipating new experiences, I didn't pay any attention to the news. In the first days of August 1964 the Gulf of Tonkin Incident, off the coast of North Vietnam, ignited the Vietnam War. Years later I heard people talk about the incident, but I didn't know anything about it.

Joann's first day in the ASCOM Unit, EUSA (Eighth US Army) Depot. Army Public Information Office photograph, taken Saturday, August 1, 1964, one day before the Gulf of Tonkin Incident. The five in uniform are the new arrivals. Top: Penny, Becky, Nella, Mary; Center row: Carolyn, Grace, Cathy; Front: Edie, Joann, Pat, Jane.

Historians still dispute what took place on August 2 and 4, 1964. Most observers believe that the confrontation never happened as reported. The National Security Agency (NSA) asserts that on August 2, the USS *Maddox* (DD-731) encountered three North Vietnamese torpedo boats. They were approaching at attack speed. Three warning shots failed to stop them. Both sides exchanged ineffective fire. An hour later, planes from the aircraft carrier *Ticonderoga* (CVA-14) had crippled one of the North Vietnamese boats and damaged the other two. On August

4, the *Maddox* returned to the area, supported by the destroyer *Turner Joy* (DD-951). The US ships detected electronic signals and acoustic indications of a likely second attack. They requested US air support. That second incident compelled President Lyndon Johnson to declare war in the name of the United States. The Gulf of Tonkin Incident and the Vietnam War defined the direction of our country for the next decade, and guides American foreign policy to this day.

A series of errors, maneuvers, and escalating tensions on both sides had led up to August 2.[14] It was a situation waiting to explode. If the Gulf of Tonkin Incident had never happened, it wouldn't have been long before something else did. Strategists at the Pentagon have contingency plans written for every situation. Unlike in other wars, the United States had a primed military and abundant materiel. To discuss the complex and disputed history of the conflict between these two countries is outside the intent of this book. I know more of the nature of the war itself, during that one year, than someone who has read it in a book, but not as much as the combat veterans I quote. The standard history of the Vietnam War was written before and after I was in Vietnam. This book is about my time in that country. It is what I saw and what I did in Vietnam, taken from my diary. An archeologist excavates and records every detail of what he finds. Then he takes his data back to a research facility, where people pore over it for years to glean its meaning. This book is my record of my personal excavation. Reporters pressed the World War II chronicler, Ernie Pyle, to give his opinion of the war. He refused, saying he knew nothing about it. I agree with Ernie.

Back in Korea, like a kid in a candy store, my dreams of travel came true. I visited my pen pal again several times. At the large ASCOM unit, distance between stops took so long we only gave three or four programs a day. We had access to any military transportation available. Whenever we needed to, we hailed an Army vehicle and asked for a ride. Once, traveling by helicopter, darkness came quickly, forcing the pilot to make an unscheduled landing to avoid flying into Communist territory.

In September, Grace, the Unit Head, went home the long way around the world. I decided I would, too. In October we opened a travel run to a missile launch site, Sea Range at Kunsan ("Koon sahn"), in the south. The schedule called for two girls to stay for three days. On my first trip I went with Carol. We were supposed to return on Friday, but got weathered in on a missile site. Finally after dark, conditions cleared enough for an H-21, Chinook, to take off—the helicopter that looked like a banana. So many passengers and cargo had been delayed, that the big aircraft was overloaded. The commander told us he was taking a chance, but he allowed us on board. The ship labored. It lifted a few feet, got to the edge of the hill, and then, like an elevator, it fell. I gripped the seat and held my breath. The passengers tensed. Some gasped. The fall increased our airspeed. Finally, the ship leveled off and began to climb. We landed at the nearest base, Camp Humphreys, without our suitcases. Jim Heinl, an ASCOM Chinook pilot, finally got us our bags and brought us back to ASCOM on Saturday at noon. The Seoul office called on Wednesday, October 21 to tell me that I was to report to Camp St. Barbara for work on Monday, November 2, in ten days.

Jim was a chief warrant officer, a technical rank (CW2). While I was at ASCOM, he asked me out several times. I liked him because he was interesting, but I wasn't looking for a boyfriend. I was excited about traveling. When I was transferred, he was just about to rotate home. One day he took off his field jacket. "Here, take it, a going-away present."

"But, you'll be cold." I was shocked, but the look on his face told me I couldn't refuse.

"I won't need it." He was from the South. "Besides, your uniform coat doesn't look that good." Our coats were painfully out of date. Nobody wore them. All the girls had acquired other jackets and parkas, except me. I wasn't fashion conscious enough to notice.

*Joann with one of the two Clubmobile three-quarter-
ton trucks at St. Barbara, wearing the field jacket.*

Jim's field jacket is a lasting souvenir. The Red Cross bowed to peer pressure and authorized us to wear military coats. They required us to wear our first name on the right front, the Red Cross patch on the left shoulder, and our unit patch on the right. When I was transferred I took the 8th Army patch off and sewed on the new I Corp patch. I didn't want to throw the old patch away, so I sewed it on the inside. I did that each time I was transferred. People saw the patches and gave me their patches, rank, and insignia, gifts I couldn't refuse. I have three dozen mementos plus brass and even an air medal.

Camp St. Barbara, I Corp Artillery Headquarters, proved as exciting as ASCOM. It was north of the 38th Parallel, the boundary between North and South Korea before the war. Every morning and night a flag detail raised and lowered the colors and fired an artillery piece. The sound threw me out of bed on my first morning. By the time I left, I was sleeping through the explosions. Our home mess hall was the General's Mess. We dressed for dinner and ate off china on white table cloths with rows of sil-verware. The Army offered a judo class, there in one of the birthplaces of martial arts, under a Korean master. I had always felt vulnerable. I earned a blue belt, and under the Master's direction I gained confidence.

At Christmas we took decorations and Christmas music to the mess halls. It was the worst thing we could have done. The men were in a funk. We had to drag them from their chairs to participate. The music and decorations reminded them how far they were from home and made them lonelier.

Birthday cards were a hit. Each month we silk-screened a design, all of us signed it, and we mailed them to every man who had a birthday that month. Sometimes we would visit a unit and a 200-pound man would come up to us, reach into his pocket and bring out our card, all crumpled, and say, "It was the only mail I got all month. Thanks."

In January I went on vacation with two girls from other units. We spent New Year's Eve in Hong Kong, took a day trip on the Macao hydrofoil, and then flew to Thailand. The other girls worked on their tans, while I explored the temples and Buddhas in Bangkok. From Thailand's sun and sand we returned to Korea's Chicago-like winter on January 8, 1965. My single-engine military plane approached the runway at St. Barbara. The pilot announced, "Temperature on the ground is nine degrees."

Soon after my vacation Maren announced that she was engaged. Days later she was married in a tiny, surprise ceremony in a chapel at her fiancé's unit. We all knew that it was against the rules to be married. Seoul sent Marenie home on the next plane. No one thought there had been any impropriety. I thought she made a mistake. She should have stayed engaged. She could have been near the man she loved. When they got married, they were immediately separated. The last thing I wanted was to be in her place.

I have been asked, "Why did the Red Cross believe that it would not be proper for a married woman to do this recreation work? If the program had no overtures of sex, why did the program insist on single women?" There are many aspects besides making love in relationships between men and women, some obvious, some not. While I was at Dong Ba Thin ("Dong Bah Tin") in Vietnam a year later, my sister, by then a Women's Army Corp captain, came from Saigon to visit me for a few hours. I happened to be working at the recreation center for part of that time, and so, my sister sat in the center and read a magazine while she waited for me. Her uniform was made of the same material as mine, except that it was light green instead of light blue. Not a big difference. Her name tag said, "Puffer," her last name, instead of her first name, or a nickname, as the Red Cross girls' did. So, at first glance, she could have been another Red Cross girl.

One of the men sat down beside her and asked, "Puffer. Where did you get that name?"

Flustered, Phyllis stammered, "From my father."

The soldier took another look. He saw the captain's bars and realized his mistake. He apologized and beat a retreat. The Army's rule of no fraternization with officers was iron clad. It protected the nurses, but it didn't protect us. The same rule applies to married women. In the workplace, some unmarried women wear a wedding ring, just to keep interaction with men professional. Most men don't treat married women the same way they treat single women. They usually keep a distance from another man's wife. It has nothing to do with sexuality. It has to do with honor, and some might argue morality.

In February I got ten days' notice to report to 1st Cavalry Division. Headquarters said they moved us "to keep us fresh." I believed it was to keep us from getting too involved with a man. No use losing trained and experienced girls. It took me about three months to attract a male friend. At St. Barbara I had two. Suddenly, on February 28, 1965, as I departed, they came face to face: from Camp St. Barbara, a captain, a doctor from upstate New York; and from Camp Kaiser, a second lieutenant, incredibly handsome, from Shreveport, Louisiana. The moment was awkward, silent, and stormy. Both instantly assessed the situation. The lower-ranked man bowed out. The doctor wrote to me afterward. I couldn't read his writing, so I never knew what he said. The lieutenant was a Southern gentleman. He wrote every week, "How about a short note telling you how much your company has been missed. Wish you had been here this week to lighten and warm our [mess hall lunch] table with your eyes and smile." He tried twice to get leave to come visit me, but finally gave up.

My new unit, the 1st Cavalry, was a front-line division. They guarded the west half of the Demilitarized Zone, the DMZ. The big, yellow Cavalry patch was the symbol of the "hardship tour." Most of the troops in other parts of Korea were comfortable, except that they missed their families. The Cavalry lived in the most difficult area, and I was proud to wear their patch. The units were so close together we gave six programs a day instead of three or four. I had to learn to pace myself to keep that schedule. The soldiers were tense. Stories circulated that someone had stepped on a land mine or someone had shot an infiltrator. People expected the Chinese to invade the country. The worst enemies were boredom and loneliness. Men would watch television and leave before the program ended, to join another distraction. Away from home for the first time, they struggled with culture shock. To see an American girl reminded them of home.

One day I went alone with a driver north of the "Spoonbill," an isolated area above the Imjin River close to the DMZ. The driver was supposed to carry a rifle and live ammunition. I asked him if he knew what to do. He said, "Yes. If we're attacked, I'm supposed to shoot you."

I exclaimed, "No! You're supposed to defend me. Try to get that straight." This was a relatively safe area, but every once in a while, something unexpected could occur, especially that close to the DMZ. We were always watchful.

Koreans crowded the 1ˢᵗ Cav area in crushing poverty. Once on a train, I sat in a seat for two. Soon there were six sitting there, plus chickens and children. One woman carried a bundle of rice on her head tied up in a cloth. She set it on the floor. It got bumped and some rice spilled out. The people nearby helped her pick it up. They didn't touch the rice, they pointed out the grains on the floor so she could pick them up one by one, like coins. When she left I tried to hand the bundle to her. It was so heavy I couldn't lift it. The more I saw, the more grateful I was to be born in America.

A girl in my unit was sent home because it looked like she had been alone with a man. I don't think she had been. I believe headquarters didn't think she cared enough about how she appeared. They gave her one warning. She was so new, that when she had to check out before she left, she didn't know how. I was assigned to escort her to the various offices where she had to report.

One spring day, all six Cavalry DDs took a trip to Pan Mun Jom ("Pan moon jom") site of the talks between North and South Korea. We saw the Bridge of No Return, where prisoners were exchanged, and we watched the peace negotiations. A long table sat exactly on the 38ᵗʰ parallel. A miniature North Korean flag stood on one end of the table, and an identical United Nations flag stood on the other. The interpreter explained that the North Koreans had complained that our flag was higher than their flag. The Americans replied that the flags had been measured, and there was no difference. The two sides argued for a few minutes, and then negotiations ended for the day. Talks had continued this way in 1965 ever since the Cease Fire in 1952. I decided that the peace activists had been wrong. They said, "It takes *two* to make war. If we refuse to fight, we will have peace." At Pan Mun Jom I saw that it takes *one* to make war; it takes *two* to make peace. What has happened since 1952? Nothing.[15]

By this time, Seoul Red Cross Area Headquarters had finally left me in one place for more than three months, enough time to attract a man. I still wasn't looking for one, but he materialized, nonetheless. My 1st Cav boyfriend was a burly, Private First Class (PFC) Military Policeman. One day I thought it would be fun to try some judo with him. I ended up dangling from his outstretched arm while he laughed at me.

On Thursday, July 1, 1965, the 1st Cavalry went to Fort Benning, Georgia, and we were redesignated as the 2nd Infantry Division. Their symbol was the profile of an Indian in a war bonnet. I wrote home, "The Indians will replace the Cavalry. . . . We went in the gate of a First Cavalry Division unit. When we came out an hour later the sign said Second Infantry Division."

Some men talked about the Division as if it were a person who wanted to go home the same as they did. "It's good that the Division got to go home." We all went to a grand change-of-colors ceremony where Chinook helicopters flew a few feet off the ground the length of the football field. I thought, *Remember this. We're making history.*

My tour was supposed to end on August 1. I requested to extend, and Seoul approved for two more months. In September the now-named 1st Cavalry Division (Airmobile) shipped from Georgia to Vietnam. Suddenly we knew why they went to Fort Benning. A chill spread through the troops like an unexpected frost. Everyone went on alert, wore battle gear, and moved into defensive positions. We girls received combat gear and instructions for evacuation. Soon after we came off alert, I left Korea on October 1.

I went to Korea because I wanted to see the world. When I got overseas I found that the men were so grateful for even the smallest things I did, I had to go back. As a college student, my ambition had been to make a difference. In Korea I saw how much I could do, that I could realize my dream. I imagined how much more I could do in Vietnam, where the men were in danger fighting for our country. I wanted to go.

Maybe this was how I could help make the world better. I didn't learn until years later that I would make a much more far-reaching difference than I had ever imagined. I didn't know that the Red Cross girls were pioneers. We were the first women officially allowed in a combat zone. In 1966, military women were confined to a narrow range of non-combat jobs, which excluded them from promotions and career advancement. The Red Cross girls' success opened up opportunities for military women. It was also an impetus for the great strides in equality that civilian women enjoy today.

Some would disagree. It could be argued that expansion of women's military roles after Vietnam was not because of the work done by Donut Dollies or other women. Women's roles expanded in the all-volunteer army because of necessity. The military simply would not have had enough soldiers if it hadn't expanded roles for women. I argue that we should recall that during World War II, women did a wide range of both military and civilian jobs, due to high demand for manpower. However, when the war was over, all those women were sent home. Their contributions did not develop into advancement of opportunity. On the other hand, when the Vietnam War was over, women were not forced to go home. They were allowed to remain, and many have achieved careers as a result.

Ever since I could remember, I knew that someone in my father's family had fought in the Civil War. My grandmother told me that her sister was a nurse in France in World War I. I learned later that "The first victims of King Philip's War in Massachusetts were the wife and son of Matthias Puffer, killed by Indians at Mendon July 10 or 14, 1675,"[16] more than 100 years before we were a country. Matthias was the grandson of the first Puffer in America.

"Lieut. John Puffer . . . was a soldier in the French and Indian War . . . May 3, 1757,"[17] still 20 years before the birth of our nation. That war began with the struggle of the British against the French and their

Indian allies for the upper Ohio valley and ultimately for North America.[18] John Puffer, fighting on the side of the British, likely fought in the battles for Pittsburgh, Montreal, and Quebec, places I had seen while in school. Other Puffers followed in every generation. My father's generation had fought in WW II. All those people were heroes. I was grateful for the sacrifice they had made for the freedoms I enjoyed. I wanted to help the people who continued that battle. Vietnam was the war of my time. I wanted to be part of the fight for our values, our freedoms.

In Vietnam people asked me, "Why did you come here?"

I answered, "To make it easier for the people who have to be here." Every day, both in Korea and in Vietnam, I helped to make the world better.

In Vietnam people showed their gratitude by worrying about us. "It's raining, it's dangerous, it's hot," they would say. I thought, *How unimportant. Here, I have a unique opportunity to make a difference, for thousands of American warriors.*

After I left Korea, I returned to the United States and became a substitute teacher. After six months I was rested and ready for another tour of duty. I contacted the Red Cross and volunteered for the new Clubmobile program in Vietnam. Among the paperwork was one document that queried, "What would your parents say if you asked them for permission to go to Vietnam?" I wrote, "They would say no." I don't think anyone asked my parents for permission. I figured the Red Cross knew what they were doing. SRAO was a small function. The women in charge had come up through the ranks. They had lived the life of a Donut Dolly, and they had paid attention. They knew what worked, and why. Everything I saw told me they made the right decisions. By April the Red Cross issued my orders, and I traveled to Washington, D.C. for more training.

My mother and father went to the airport to see me leave. Just before we reached the steps to the plane, Dad said to me, "They'll probably waste my tax money to ship the body back." He must have been hurting inside. I learned years later, that he bought a cemetery plot for me. I thought, *I'm not doing anything dangerous. I'm a non-combatant. It's my job to stay out of danger.* Dad knew that wars come and people have to go. You risk losing them when they do.

For Vietnam I was in a training class of one. At headquarters they gave me a desk and a stack of papers to read. They checked my shots and replaced the uniforms that were worn out.

When I arrived in Vietnam, my sister met me and showed me around Saigon (pronounced "Sigh gahn") for the weekend. I had a day of briefings at the Red Cross office, and went on my way up country. I received the same military orders for travel as the men. To go to Vietnam, after 14 months of service in Korea, my travel orders gave my rank as equivalent to a captain. Ironically, a year and another promotion later, I would leave Vietnam with travel orders giving my rank as equivalent to a lieutenant, one rank lower. I figured, *The Army doesn't know what my rank is any more than I do.*

Part I:
Arrival and
An Khe

✦ CHAPTER 2 ✦

A Blacked-Out Runway

Friday, May 6, 1966, Tan Son Nhut Air Base, South Vietnam

Mini-skirts came in. Detroit rolled out the Ford Mustang. Martin Luther King Jr. led a march from Selma to Montgomery, Alabama; and *pot* was still something to cook in. I was leaving that world and entering another.

The 707 descended, and just before its wheels touched the runway, I refreshed my makeup. I was there to bring the soldiers reminders of home. Some of them hadn't seen an American girl since they arrived in Vietnam. The sun had long set. Out the window I saw flashes of artillery fire on the horizon all around the sparse lights of Saigon. America's involvement in the war had just begun, and within six months, my old unit, the 1st Cavalry, would mark its one-year anniversary. Soldiers had started to rotate home. My introduction to real war began.

I was the only girl on board a chartered passenger jet filled with identical crew cuts and khaki, pressed uniforms. We had crossed the International Date Line, and I couldn't figure out what day it was. I didn't know whether we had lost a day or gained a day. We stopped for 20 minutes in Honolulu and for a short time at Clark Air Force Base, in the Philippines. A few other women had boarded at San Francisco, but when we left Clark they were gone. At the start of the flight all the men were angry at the Viet Cong. They were going to war, and they wanted to kill some Charlies (Viet Cong, VC, Victor Charlie). Patriotism permeated America. Staff Sergeant Barry Sadler's "Ballad of the Green Berets" had been number one on the Billboard charts for five weeks.[1] I watched those enthusiastic recruits become more and more scared as we neared Saigon. A sergeant strolled down the aisle and stopped to talk. He tried to cover up his tension with swagger.

Everyone watched the artillery flashes, like frequent lightning. We knew it wasn't practice. I thought, *Men are being killed. Some of the men around me will be killed within a few months—maybe the sergeant who is talking to me now.* The war was real. Below, the airfield was dark. Our landing lights came on, stayed on for only a short time, and then went off. They came on again just before we touched down, but went off quickly. There were no lights on the airfield. We had traveled for 23 hours and landed on a blacked-out runway at Tan Son Nhut (pronounced "Ton son noot") Air Base outside Saigon. A soldier came on board and bellowed the landing order. We began to unload. Waiting to exit, stories flew. Hostesses and soldiers had been cut down by machine gun fire as they stepped out the door. I wasn't sure if it was true, but I thought others believed it.

Finally at the entrance, tropical air hit my hair and makeup like a steam bath. Armed guards flanked the bottom of the steps. The only light came from a circling Military Police jeep, mounted with a spotlight and a machine gun. We walked briskly, single file into the darkness toward the invisible terminal. I struggled against fear and took strength from the men, who couldn't show weakness. A single soldier marked our path with a flashlight, as the long, dark column moved across the open space. I felt the fresh mascara become a rivulet down my face.

I thought, *This is not right. A Donut Dolly is supposed to be a fresh-faced girl next door, someone's sister. We are one of the reasons why these young boys are here to fight for our country's values, God, motherhood, and apple pie. I'm supposed to be a sexless, yet provocative reason for them to defend their country.* The dripping mascara must have made me look almost clown-like in that swelter. Certainly not appealing. I had been there no more than a few minutes, and had already lost my first battle. We reached the terminal. Another defeat: no air conditioning. There wouldn't be any for the next year. The dim, stifling building marked the break between the bright, air-conditioned interior of the stateside jet and the grimness of Vietnam. Apprehensive faces of tired, aching men surrounded me. I wanted a cold drink, a shower, anything cooling.

The heat was only half of it—the rest was fear, not of anything in particular, but the dread of the unknown. I began to feel faint, as the men wilted. Their outward show was no longer crisp and military. The surroundings forced everyone to become sober, tense, and human. The men's shoulders sagged, their gaze moved around the terminal, searching for where they were supposed to go.

A sergeant pulled the officers and civilians to one side and lined up the enlisted men, restoring order and calming the uncertainty. The men returned to their crisp, military bearing; their shoulders straightened. "Don't drink the water. Don't let the Vietnamese carry your bags. . . ." The rest of us waited. I had never known anything like the oppressive heat and strength-sapping humidity of Vietnam, and it was the middle of the night. I thought, *What must the day be like?* Throughout my year in Vietnam, the heat weighed on everyone as a constant reminder that we were in a foreign and threatening place. In college, I had read Ernest Hemingway's "The Short Happy Life of Francis Macomber" and concluded that if you're not scared, you're not brave. In order to be brave, you have to be scared, but you do what you have to do. As I stood alone under the half-light, in the middle of the crowded terminal, the voice in my head contradicted what I had read. *I'm scared, but I don't feel brave. I'm scared, and I keep waiting for the brave part to kick in.*

* * *

It didn't take me long to figure out that we Donut Dollies were military targets. Our light blue uniforms blasted their contrast to the drab country around us. Red Cross trainers had hinted that our jobs could be dangerous. Everyone knew that the Viet Cong wanted to kill us. We were civilian, American women, and our purpose was to improve morale of the soldiers in the combat zone. Nurses wore combat fatigues to blend in. We didn't. As each of us realized this, a dimension of fear crept into our lives.

Then my sister, Phyllis, and a Red Cross man arrived at the airport. His reunion with the ARC man who had sat beside me on the plane softened my apprehensions. Phyllis, a WAC, had worked for Army Intelligence in Saigon for six months. I would stay with her for the weekend and report to the Red Cross office on Monday. She lived at the McCarthy, a Vietnamese hotel that the Army had leased for officers. The Red Cross had put a cot in her room for me. We had an enjoyable visit full of activity despite Saigon's being congested, filthy, and sweltering.

The mix-up of days and nights kept me in a fog. Saigon time 3:00 in the afternoon felt like 3:00 in the morning, body time. I was restless all night, but couldn't stay awake past noon. On Saturday Phyllis took me swimming in a local pool. I waited for the water to cool me down, but it never did, as if it wanted to start something, but couldn't finish. That evening, we went to a piano concert. Phyllis apologized for the music. She told me that the heat and humidity had warped the piano so badly that the pianist couldn't keep it in tune. I was so groggy, I couldn't hear anything wrong, and I didn't care. At midnight I got my second wind, just when it was time to go to bed.

On Monday, I met Imogene "Gene" Huffman, the assistant area director, in front of the hotel. She would take me to the Red Cross office to complete my paperwork. We flagged a taxi. The traffic was saner than in Korea, although maybe I had gotten used to crazed drivers. At the Red Cross office, a barrier of sand barrels blocked the front of the building. An MP and a Vietnamese guarded a metal gate, weapon butts on their knees. They were the first alert, wide-awake guards I had ever seen. Gene told me no vehicles could stop in front of the building, so the driver dropped us off a few yards away.

The ground floor was empty. Sandbags covered the walls from floor to ceiling, a defense against grenades. Gene took me to the office on the roof. I filled out forms and had a round of briefings along with half a dozen others who had come in over the weekend. I was the 45th Red Cross girl to arrive in Vietnam. Another girl from the recreation service had stopped in to the office, and Gene took us to lunch at an officer's mess. We rode through the city in a military bus. Heavy wire screens covered the windows to keep out grenades. After lunch, a driver took the two of us around the city where clerks issued identification cards. Then we returned to Red Cross headquarters for more briefings. My body time was now in the early hours of the morning. I could barely see. Later, as I took a cab back to the hotel, I saw bicycle-taxis. I remembered a warning from weeks earlier: *Do not ride with them. The driver could be Viet Cong and might put a bayonet in your back.* I learned later that many Americans used them.

At the hotel I tried to make sense of the papers I had collected. I had I.D. cards to eat in mess halls and shop in Post Exchanges (PX), military stores. One puzzled me. It said I was a civilian non-combatant; I should be treated as an officer. I thought, *OK, that's right.* Then, at the bottom it said, "Give this card to the enemy if you are captured." I thought, *Nobody ever said anything about being captured. I never thought about it. I don't think such a little card would be much protection. Besides, it's in English; I don't think the VC could read it. Most of them are illiterate. They probably couldn't read it in Vietnamese.* I put it in my wallet and quickly forgot it was there.

Tuesday, May 10, Saigon

The next morning, shortly before 7:00, I went to the lobby to meet Imogene and clear my expense voucher. She wasn't there. The sergeant at the desk said, "She just went outside." I stepped to the entrance and suddenly sirens ripped the air. A truck full of Military Police bristling with rifles raced through the rush-hour traffic only a few feet away. An ambulance sped after it, and then a second. Imogene stood across the street on the taxi corner with another Red Cross woman. I caught her as pedestrians and more MPs dashed after the ambulances through the melee.

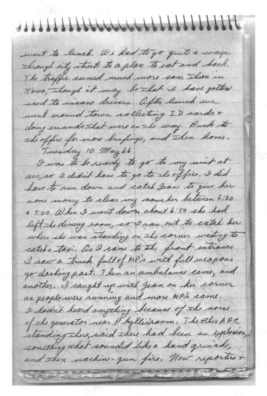

A page from Joann's diary telling about the explosions in the street in Saigon.

The other Red Cross woman exclaimed, "There was an explosion, something that sounded like a hand grenade, and then machine-gun fire!" I hadn't heard anything because of the generator near my sister's room. Several people stood on the corner, nervous and wide eyed, while American reporters with cameras and more MPs rushed to the scene two blocks away, around the bend. I couldn't hear any firing. The people on the corner looked scared, but I wasn't because I didn't know what was going on.

I went back and told Phyllis. In the past, she always acted as unconcerned as if she were at home. She had told me, "The secret service men aren't worried, so why should the rest of us be?" Now she stopped what she was doing. She became tense and her eyes darted around the room. She mumbled, "Maybe I should put my helmet by my bed the way I'm supposed to. It probably wouldn't fit over my curlers, anyway."

A few hours later, I said my goodbyes and caught a cab. My taxi took me off towards the airport and my flight to An Khe. Adventure was about to begin.

Tuesday May 10, An Khe

My first assignment was with the 1st Cavalry Division (Airmobile) at An Khe, 290 miles north in the Central Highlands. I flew on a C-130 Air Force cargo plane with 150 soldiers, their combat gear, and weapons, going to Pleiku ("Play Koo"). We lost an engine during the flight, and at Pleiku the mechanics tried to fix it. That gave me a chance to walk around. A man in jungle camouflage stood out from the sea of green.

"You look colorful," I said.

"It was all I had clean." He smiled and squinted against the bright sun. I learned he was a reporter and former combat marine who had served in Korea. He wore a camera around his neck and a pistol just below it in a holster at his left front.

I asked, "When do you think the war will end?"

"I don't know. Maybe ten years." That sounded impossible. Ten years is half your living memory when you're 25 years old. That was

May 10, 1966. The war would officially end on April 30, 1975.[2] He was off by less than a year.

I overheard an aviation man say, "The airstrip at An Khe is daylight landing only." The mechanics couldn't fix the engine in time, so about 15 of the soldiers and I boarded an Army Caribou, a light, twin-engine, cargo plane. From the large, open cargo door at the back, the lush, green countryside passed below. The rice fields in Vietnam could feed millions of people. I could see why the Chinese wanted the land.

We finally came in over An Khe. Several hundred helicopters sat on the huge field. Liz, a friend from Korea, waited for me with a jeep and driver. I felt at home again. "Welcome to 'the Golf Course,'" she smiled, "the nicest base in Vietnam."

Camp Radcliff, 22,000 people, eight miles across, contained a flat, oval airfield with helicopters and small fixed-wing aircraft parked neatly around the runway. The 1st Cavalry Division spread out around the airfield in an open, flat area on one side and low, wooded hills on the other three. I had no idea how old the strategy of that location was. Years later I learned that Sun Tzu says: "In dry, level country, take up an easily accessible position with rising ground to your right and on your rear, so that danger may be in front, and safety lie behind."[3] Sun Tzu is a widely influential Chinese military strategist who lived in c. 500 BC.[4]

From almost everywhere on the base at An Khe, I could see the 1st Cavalry patch, the big yellow horse blanket, on the side of the hill, Hon Cong, that dominated the area. It said, "This is who we are!" I thought, *I'm back with the Cavalry again, my old friends.* The jeep drove straight to my new home, a general purpose tent across the street from the hospital, directly under the Cav patch. Instead of poles and ropes, like the other tents, ours rested on a wooden frame of two-by-fours. The sides were mosquito netting with a flap extended to each side for shade and privacy.

Inside the front door, the tent had a sitting area large enough for four aluminum lawn chairs. Wooden shipping pallets formed the floor.

The tent at An Khe. Sandra, Joann, and a friend compare the tan on their arms.

A big poster on the wall read, "Welcome to An Khe." Sandra, one of the girls, had drawn caricatures of Liz, Nancy, and herself. They introduced themselves. We sat together in the suffocating heat. Nancy handed me a can of Coke. The tent didn't have a refrigerator and the pop was warm. It left me vaguely unsatisfied. After a brief rest, Liz showed me to my room. Reed mats on two-by-fours partitioned the tent into cubicles. We each had a space of our own with an Army cot, a blanket, and mosquito netting. The doorways were hung with yellow or pink plastic ribbons about two inches wide, like the oriental bead doors in the movies. I loved it.

A five-gallon, olive drab can held water. A soldier brought it in fresh daily, to drink, brush teeth, wash hands, and do laundry. In time, I learned to pour a glass of water out of the awkward container. A generator roared outside the back door. You could have a conversation or play a radio and the person in the next cube couldn't hear you. Light bulbs hung along the center of the roof.

The outhouse was up the street. Under each hole sat an oil barrel cut in half. To clean it, once a week a soldier lifted a trap door in the back and pulled out the drums. He replaced them with empties and took the full ones to a burn area. He poured gasoline onto the contents and set them on fire. Our back yard was a ravine. We could walk through it on a path. The men cautioned us, "Watch for wait-a-minute snakes. If you get bitten, just wait a minute, and you're dead."

The temperature and humidity were so high I was constantly drenched with sweat. Heavy vehicle traffic on the gravel roads kicked up volumes of dust that clung to my skin. I was so hot and dirty I could have showered several times a day and still not felt clean. I missed the water on the first day, because I arrived near evening, but on my second day I learned that the hospital had a bath house across the street. The nurses all showered at 4:00 in the afternoon and the doctors at 4:30. If the women took too much water, the tank would run dry and leave the men covered with soap. This would be uncomfortable for the men, and later the doctors would make it uncomfortable for the women. Some were deviously clever. The serious head nurse, Major Frost, kept the peace between the two factions.

Someone turned on the water at precisely 4:00. Liz told me to drop everything, grab a clean uniform, soap, shampoo, a towel, and hurry. Later, I learned that if you got there at 4:05, the major would meet you at the door with a scowl and demand, "Where have *you* been?" A water pipe stood in the center of the room. Four showerheads shot in all directions. Two could shut off, two could not. Eight nurses and four Red Cross girls took turns. You got wet and then stepped away to suds down. With your eyes soaped shut, you stuck out your hand. Someone would put it under the water. I didn't find out until later that this was the only hot water I would see in Vietnam. We probably got it because the hospital needed it. Major Frost stood to one side, lathered up, and barked orders like a traffic cop. Her rank showed whether she had clothes on or not. "There are only two people under this shower. You people in the back can shut off those showers and come up front." We were out of there in record time with minimum water. One day I got there 15 minutes late. Everyone was gone, and the water was off.

The gang shower was a shock and embarrassment at first. The young nurses took their clothes off, talked, lathered, rinsed, and toweled as if they were reading a book or eating dinner. Water glistened on a dozen naked bodies.

Growing up I was used to the locker room at a swimming pool. Girls didn't pay much attention to each other's bodies. Girl Scout camp brought modesty, sometimes embarrassment, in front of each other. Through high school and college we had semi-private rooms and showers. It took a few days for the shock of my Vietnam gang shower to wear off.

On that first day I realized that the nurses were attractive, including Major Frost. She was a few years older and a few pounds heavier, but she carried her authority with attractive grace. All the nurses were shapely except one. Naked, she was perfect, the most perfect woman I had ever seen.[5] I was enthralled and jealous. I wished I looked even a bit like her. I wanted to hunch over and cover myself, but I held my head high, stuck out my chest, and took off my uniform.

The next time I ate with the perfect nurse, Lieutenant Allen, in the mess hall, I discovered that she was married. Her husband, a male nurse, sat beside her. They were the same size. Their name tags and insignia were identical. I figured they could wear each other's clothes. Pointing to a little permanent building at the end of the row of tents and smiling with pride, her husband explained, "That's our house. I built it myself out of scraps from other buildings. We just moved in."

Major Frost invited me on a tour of the modern surgical hospital. An invitation from a major is not optional and I went the next day. She guided me through a series of interconnected Quonset huts and explained each area. A nurse sat at a desk where several fever thermometers stood in a small pencil holder. They all read 103 degrees. I realized they showed the temperature in the room. Finally, Major Frost brought me to a trophy case of weapons surgically removed from wounded soldiers. Describing all the gory details, she enjoyed knowing she could make me sick. She just didn't know how long it would take.

The worst-looking souvenirs were punji sticks. "They're made of sharpened bamboo. The Viet Cong smear them with dung." She watched me out of the corner of her eye. "Then they put them in traps so soldiers will fall on them." The sticks varied from a few inches long to over a foot. Some were thin; others were an inch wide. Several had blood on them for six inches or more. Major Frost pointed, "Look closer. You can see the blood on this one." Until then I had kept a straight face and a steady gaze, but finally, I had to look away. The thought turned my stomach. Her words had penetrated my jet lag. Major Frost stretched out her description. "The puncture wound heals very slowly, and the dung produces a life-threatening infection." I must have turned white, but I wouldn't let her make me faint. I knew I couldn't win a duel of fortitude with a seasoned Army nurse major. The best I could hope for was a draw.

The following day, the Red Cross field director took me on a tour of An Khe village. He drove us in a jeep across the compound. Just outside the gate, entertainment waited for the soldiers: large, windowless buildings with names like "Miami Beach" and "Kiss Me Bar." A man could get a drink, have something to eat, and meet a willing girl. I thought, *A good, stiff wind could blow these buildings away.* In the eight months that the 1st Cavalry had been there, a number of businesses had sprung up. Women washed soldiers' uniforms in a fountain. A couple dozen tin roofed, lean-to shacks provided almost everything a soldier could need, including a tailor and a shoe repair. Every shop employed at least one prostitute, who was usually the dominant source of income.

The sight of a school shocked me. The school at An Khe was one room with three walls. The street side of the building was missing. The children's elbows were no more than two feet from speeding military trucks. It looked like they had to exit directly into the traffic. Each row of children sat squeezed against each other on one continuous bench with one continuous plank for a desk: the girls in the front two rows; the boys in the back three. Perhaps ten in each row, 50 children sat in a room barely 12 feet by 12 feet. More urchins[6] crowded around me in the street than sat in the school. An open sewer ran along the road. Three soldiers manned a gun overlooking the bridge nearby.

The school in An Khe village. The children sit next to the traffic.

We made our first Clubmobile visits from the recreation center. An early trip was to a field hospital, a general-purpose tent with canvas cots. Patients wore fatigues, not blue pajamas as in the hospital. A few slept; some were awake, but didn't move. Others were naked. For the Red Cross girls to visit, someone had placed a cloth over their middle. They lay on waterproof sheets in pools of liquid, shivering. A hand-made sign said F U O. I asked, "What does that mean?"

Children crowd around Joann in the street in An Khe.

No nurses here, the corpsman answered, "Fever of Unknown Origin. They have a dangerously high fever. We strip them down and have
them lie in alcohol to chill them and reduce the fever. It doesn't matter
what caused the fever, we have to get it down. Some of them just didn't
take their malaria pills." Over my objections, the corpsman woke the
sleeping patients. He explained, "They would be disappointed if they
missed your visit. Besides, we want them awake during the day so they
will sleep better at night."

We talked to everyone. Those who were alert enjoyed telling us stories. I heard from several, "War is 80 minutes of boredom and ten minutes of hell."

In Vietnam in the evenings men of all ranks came to visit us. They
were always well behaved. We kept soft drinks and beer to offer them.
Everyone knew we had no refrigerator. Some officers had access to a
telephone and would call before they came, but enlisted men usually
didn't. They would visit us to arrange a future get-together. As part of

Joann with three soldiers manning a gun on a bridge at An Khe.

our job, we tried to accept all the invitations we could. Also, it was grati-
fying to see the men enjoy themselves.

We didn't want to stay in our quarters all the time, because that
would become boring. The combat zone had few places to go on a date,
and we were mindful of our reputation. We deliberately stayed in public
areas where people could see what we were doing. One place we could
go was to church. We would also shop in the villages during the daytime, sit and talk in our living room, or go in groups to parties at service clubs. The men treated us like celebrities, all of them gracious and
determined to impress us. Red Cross trainers in Washington warned us
that we would be the center of attention because we were rare, whereas
in the States we would be one of the crowd. We knew friendships would
be casual, but that made them more precious. We reminded ourselves
that the men weren't interested in us in particular. They were interested
in an American girl.

We were aware that some of the men could be married, including enlisted men in their late teens, so we treated everyone equally. We knew that our purpose was to act as *a sister or the girl next door*. I didn't learn until later that it was not unusual for officers to visit us when they had lost a lot of men and needed someone to talk to. You've heard about a friend in need? That was one of our roles that was most rewarding.

If any of us stumbled into romance, the combat zone encouraged us to stumble out of it. There was no chance to be alone. Vietnam teemed with eager watchers, some we could see and some we couldn't, hungry to get a glimpse of an American girl. The soldiers, Red Cross hierarchy, and our own conscience hovered over us day and night. The only place private enough to show affection, was our living room.

One day when I was in Korea, I was sitting in a mess hall with several officers. One was a pilot wearing captain's bars and a wedding ring. I talked with everyone. A few days later I was at a table with the same captain. Soon I began to look for him at that mess. Sometimes he looked for me. He was more relaxed, more interesting, and easier to talk to than most men. We had developed a friendship, but I respected that he was married and remembered the warnings in training about being friends with married men.

The pilot became a company commander and left *to fly a desk*. I missed him. When he came back for a visit, he had changed. No longer relaxed and pleasant, he was now aggressive and bossy. I concluded he had to act that way to gain the respect he needed to command a company. I had lost a friend, but had avoided falling in love with a married man. I vowed to avoid married men, except in the course of my work.

It was a vow that was difficult to keep; married men were everywhere. But I held the vow in my mind. I was more aware of what could happen. Some men did not wear wedding rings. We could ask a man's commander if he was married, but there were so many men that it wasn't practical. We learned to treat every new acquaintance as if he were married. The rules of engagement applied to every man I met until I learned that he was not married.

May 1966

I had been at An Khe for a few days, when Nancy came to my cube. "Our escorts are here." I followed her to the sitting room.

Liz was with two newly scrubbed and shaven officers. Their hair was so unaccustomed to being combed, it didn't stay in place. Their smiles were shy, but eager. "This is Captain Myron Diduryk, ["Did rick"] and this is 1st Lieutenant Jim Brigham, from the 2/7th Cavalry," Liz said. They came to take us to the party at the new officer's club. Seeing the tall, lean men frightened me. In their faded fatigues, their presence filled the living room. Faded? The lieutenant's bushy mustache startled me. In Korea and Vietnam, every man I saw was clean shaven. At the University of Michigan it was fashionable to look unkempt. I had learned that the most disgusting-looking person could be the class president or an honors graduate. I gave them the benefit of the doubt. I knew their unit from Korea. It was General George Custer's regiment. He was from Michigan, my home state.

The mustachioed Lieutenant Brigham ducked his head as he went out of the tent. Brigham drove the jeep while Diduryk rode in the front, the place for the highest-ranking person in a vehicle. Nancy, Liz, and I sat in the back in our party clothes. We rode a short distance. The officers had designed the club to be surrounded by trees, about 40 feet from the perimeter road. We left the jeep and walked across a grassy area. Just before we reached the club we came to a shallow ditch spanned by a log about 10 feet long.

Diduryk led. "Be careful. Here, let me take your hand." *Nice ploy*, I thought. *He pretends we can't walk across a ten-foot log, so he gets to hold our hand.* I stepped onto the log in my high heels and, predictably, started to lose my balance. I grabbed for air and gratefully found Brigham's outstretched hand. Once across, the men politely released our hands. The club, built from scraps, had two levels and Brigham and Diduryk took us to the bar in the top level. A crowd of noisy Cavalry officers greeted us with warmth and courtesy. We enjoyed a dinner of steaks and beer, the soldier's universal favorite, and then gathered for drinks. The most senior officers crowded around us. Then Diduryk brought us over to a group of lieutenants. One of them, Larry Gwin, a striking blond, said, "We didn't think we'd get to meet you now, with all this brass."[7]

Nancy whispered, "I think they screen only handsome guys for Vietnam." Lieutenant Rick Rescorla[8] invited everyone to gather around to sing.[9] First Lieutenant Jim Lawrence brought out a guitar and Rick passed around song sheets. One was "The Caisson Song" and "The Mountain Battery Song," two rousing Artillery pieces that I had loved in Korea. I didn't know the third one, "Sergeant Flynn." It turned out to be a great ballad about Custer's Last Stand.

> Here you men stand fast and rally
> Make a last stand in this valley
> For the Seventh Regiment and Garry Owen

Lieutenant Brigham nodded toward the man organizing the group. "Rick Rescorla wrote the words to that song, just for 2/7th." Rick started everyone singing; they sang with enthusiasm. Brigham queried, "How does it feel to join a bunch of drunks singing 'Garry Owen,' led by Rick Rescorla, an Englishman?" Because of the noise, I could only answer with a big smile. I joined the chorus with unaccustomed exuberance. I especially liked "Sergeant Flynn."

> There are better days to be
> For the 7th Cavalry,
> When we charge again for dear old Garry Owen.

368 E. Philadelphia

Flint 5, Michigan

May 11, 1966

[Part of a long letter from my family in the States. It took about 5 days for this letter to reach me.]

> Dear Joan,
>
> Yesterday morning, I got a telegram that you had arrived safely in Vietnam, and when we got home at night, headlines told about their shooting up the main street of Saigon. As much as you like excitement, I hope that you didn't miss seeing the fireworks. I am glad I was not the one who ordered the clearing of the street by machine gun fire, and have to live the rest of my life with those deaths to my credit.
>
> Love, Dad

The explosion in the street in Saigon made the evening news at home. I had seen the reporters. I wondered, did the people at home get an accurate picture of what happened? Was the explosion that big, or was it a slow news day? Was anyone killed, as Dad thought? He was worried about me. I believed I would never learn the answers to my questions, but eventually read that "Viet Cong terrorists exploded a mine in the heart of Saigon. . . . Five [Vietnamese] persons were killed. . . . Eight Americans and at least 21 Vietnamese civilians were reported wounded. . . . A US Army spokesman said there was no evidence of Viet Cong fire in the half-hour fusillade that followed the mine explosion. He told a news conference that an American military policeman opened fire and that other MPs thought they were being fired on and began spraying the streets with 'machine' guns and automatic weapons. Crowds of Vietnamese on their way to work ran in terror or fell under the hail of bullets."[10]

Within days after my tour of the village, the whole base went on alert.[11] The fight had spilled into the area around An Khe. The village went off limits, and the clubs closed. The first siren woke us at 4:00 A.M. We grabbed our combat gear and ran to the bunker in our night clothes. We carried our helmets because they wouldn't fit over our curlers. We waited together in the dark. I was tense, but not scared. Nothing seemed to be happening, more like a fire drill at school. We didn't have our fatigues to protect our bare arms and legs, so we slapped mosquitoes for two hours until the all-clear sounded. The sun had come up by the time we walked back to the tent. Soldiers sat six to eight feet apart in the drainage ditches beside the road in front of our tent and around the hospital. The men watched us in silence as we hurried back to our tent, red faced, in baby doll pajamas, curlers, flak jackets and combat boots. The next two nights, we slept in our fatigues.

In the days that followed, activity in the area stepped up. At dusk over 450 helicopters took off and dispersed to avoid mortar attacks. Throughout the night, artillery fired random patterns around the perimeter to keep intruders at bay. Flares lit up the horizon, several at a time making their slow descent, their light like sunbursts, turning night into day. In the morning, things quieted for a few moments, until the helicopters started to bring in the dead and wounded. Hueys flowed in like water almost on top of each other and didn't stop. Then the lumbering Chinooks began to arrive. Crewmen and ambulance drivers loaded stretchers and drove past us to the hospital. Everybody available helped those who could walk. I felt sad to see so many people wounded, but I was gratified that almost all of them would survive. The dead arrived in black body bags. Crewmen loaded them into covered 2½-ton trucks, called "deuce and a halfs," that drove off, away from the hospital. The stream of dead and wounded continued for almost two days.

Casualties poured into the hospital at An Khe all during May of 1966. The Viet Cong continued to maneuver around the compound, while

Helicopters bring in the dead and wounded.

major battles were erupting five miles away, the doctors said. The enemy attacked several times each night. It was my second week at An Khe, and I hadn't slept a full night through. During the day, things on base relaxed. We weren't able to set up a mobile program so we spent most of the day at the recreation center, welcoming an estimated 270 visitors a day.[12] When soldiers came in from the field, we served food in the mess halls. It never failed; the men couldn't believe their eyes. All we had to do was smile while we handed them some dessert or gave them some bread. The trick was to pick something cold. If we served something hot, the steam would destroy our hair and makeup. One day I chose to serve the salad. It was pretty, and I thought people should eat it because it's healthy. As each man came to me I smiled and asked, "Would you like some salad?"

I was pleased that nearly all of them smiled back and said, "Yes, thank you."

Only a few soldiers were still in line, when I heard one cook say to another, "Most of the men took salad today. They don't usually do that."

The rule in Army mess halls was "Take all you want, but eat all you take." As I filled another soldier's plate with salad, I knew that he might not want it, but he would eat it.

My arrival brought the An Khe unit to four girls. We could make Clubmobile visits with recreation programs. In Korea, each program had taken about six weeks to write. We made sure that a new one came out every week. We designed the activities to be flexible and humorous. We tried to get everyone to participate, and encouraged them to think of home. The programs allowed the soldiers to see and talk to an American girl.

Vietnam a year later would be different from Korea. We would set up everything for the first time, we wouldn't have six weeks to write a program, we would rarely have a mess hall or coffee, and we never had donuts. I was eager for the experience.

Shortly after we went on alert and the clubs closed, the Baptist chaplain came early one morning and got Nancy. He needed her to come to the emergency room to hand out Red Cross gift bags. Volunteers made them at Red Cross chapters to be given out to soldiers and sailors. Gift bags contained personal items such as combs, sewing kits, shoelaces, shaving cream, and razors. Nancy came back later in the day, her face white. "It was very difficult for me. I recognized some. Lieutenant Gwin and others we met at the 2/7th party. One of the sergeants had his leg blown off, and they are still in their fatigues.[13] June Collier, the new nurse, looked shocked. Dr. Fitzgerald told me to go around and feed them gum . . . no water. I did." The atmosphere was so emotionally charged, she had trouble talking. "Because of triage, there were so many wounded that it took two days for Lieutenant Gwin to be treated." Nancy visited the hospital every day and talked with Gwin and others. "He improved and stayed with his unit. The rest were evacuated. Gwin's men came to the hospital to visit. They were loyal to their leaders. Others came also, Myron, Jim Kelly, and other officers. Then, they went back out into the field."

May 19, Ho Chi Minh's birthday.[14]

Ho Chi Minh was 76 years old. The men told us that Hanoi Hanna, the Tokyo Rose radio voice of the war, said the VC were going to give 1st Cavalry to "Uncle Ho" as a gift. Everyone expected a big mortar attack. As the time got closer, everyone became more and more nervous. Evening came and the division went on stand-by alert. The men put on field gear and the guards went out. We girls were scared. The stand-by order said that a full alert would probably be called at midnight, so we began to assemble our field gear and put on our fatigues. The alert meant the center was closed, so I couldn't go to work. I swept and cleaned my room. I took my dirty sheets off the bed and went to linen supply to exchange them for what was "clean" by military standards. On the way back I passed a guard already out, posted on the road. He wore full field gear, steel helmet, armored vest, and held his weapon in a rest position. I said hello, as we did to everyone. He saw my fatigues and his face fell. Disappointment in his voice, he asked, "Are you girls going to be wearing fatigues from now on?"

"Oh, no. I'll put a dress back on as soon as we come off alert." He brightened. I asked about several plumes of black smoke coming from a small, empty area a short distance away.

"Those are the containers of waste from the latrines being burned." He added, "Some of the local people have a rumor that the smoke is from burning babies that we have killed."

"What?"

"They say we kill babies and then burn them. That's what the smoke is." I barely believed him. It sounded ridiculous, but I didn't dismiss it.

A few days later I sat on an ammunition box in the stifling office tent, because we were short of chairs. I struggled to finish a project between interruptions. As soon as I started, a man would poke his head in and ask something. I could answer a few questions without getting up. At other times I would have to leave my work and go into the center to find one thing or another. If most people really had questions, it would have been one thing, but these lonely soldiers dreamed up whatever pretense they could in order to talk to an American girl. After all, it was my job; it was what I was there for. But I thought, *I have to get this done. I wish I could have some peace, so I could do it.* I began to smile less and less at each man, when a young sergeant came in and stood around. He didn't have a question or anything to say. I was losing patience. He stammered around for a minute and then looked hurt. "Don't you remember me? I talked to you on the airplane."

He was the sergeant who had been nervous and had tried to cover it up with swagger. I was glad to see him. I thought, *It's good to know that he hasn't become a casualty.* I believed the war movies I had seen. I thought most soldiers would end up dead, as the media had led us to believe.

Years later I learned that in Vietnam about 2 percent of our soldiers were killed.[15] That number is logical when we consider what Col. Chester B. McCoid II, a combat unit division commander, complained in a letter to his wife: "Only about one man in three in this brigade kills the foe. The average for the theater is perhaps one man in eight. All the rest are sock counters and paper pushers, pill rollers and legal clerks."[16]

That real soldier in the office at An Khe said to me, "I only have a minute. I have been assigned to 2nd Battalion, 7th Cavalry, and we're about to leave for the field." My heart gave a thump. I thought, *That's the "hard luck" unit of the whole Division.* Not many men who started out in that unit were still on active duty after eight months. Most of them had been killed or wounded. The sergeant went on, "If it's all right with you, I'll stop in again and say hello the next time we're in base camp."

"Please, do that. I would be glad to see you." I thought to myself, *That way I'll know you're still alive.* I believe he stopped in to see me one more time. Then I was transferred and lost track of him. I never found out if he lasted his year.

May 23

I had been at An Khe for two weeks, and already my shoes needed repair. Major Hayne insisted on taking them with him to the village to get them re-stitched. He was on his way to the 2nd Battalion 8th Cavalry headquarters in the field. He explained, "Since I'm second in command, I normally stay in the rear while the battalion commander directs the operation forward. That's in case the forward headquarters is over-run. The executive officer is safe and can pick right up." Major Hayne was supposed to visit the forward headquarters and be back that night.

When he left, I awkwardly tried to ask him, "Is there much chance you will get shot?"

He answered simply, "You always assume that you won't. I'll see you when we get back." Shortly after he left, one of the soldiers told me, perhaps it was a rumor, that 2/8th forward headquarters had been over-run. I was worried. Major Hayne didn't come back that night and I didn't see him for a long time. When I finally saw him again, I told him how worried I had been. He brushed it off and didn't tell me what had happened. The forward headquarters had not been over-run, but the division had "backed into (Operation) Crazy Horse," a major development that lasted almost two weeks, until June 5.[17]

With 22,000 men and four girls on base, the odds of a man seeing a Red Cross girl were slim, even though our blue uniforms stood out. It was the same everywhere in Vietnam. Our job was to be friendly, approachable, and, above all, professional. Wherever we went, we watched for soldiers. No matter whom we saw or where we were, we smiled and waved. We never tired. Everyone waved back as if to say, "Wow! Am I glad to see you!" Their warmth flowed over the heat. Even when we were dragging, the men's response renewed our energy. You can get tired of smiling if you don't mean it. Your face can hurt, but you still mean it. I was sure every American military man in Vietnam knew there were

*Sandra, Joann, and Nancy pose for GIs to take their picture after a USO
show. The guys paid as much attention to them as to the show.*

Red Cross girls in the country because when they saw us they knew
who we were, and they always responded to us like long-time friends.

One day I walked down the road past the hospital. I saw a man a
short distance away, and waved to him. He returned it. When he came
closer I recognized him, and gave him a "Hello, Friend" greeting. When
we met on the road he said, "At first you gave me a Red Cross wave." It
had acquired a name. Months later, two of us girls were riding across
a field of rice paddies in a jeep, when we met a truck full of soldiers. It
pulled to the side and stopped to let us get by on the narrow road. We
waved at the men, and they erupted in a wild cheer and wave as we
passed. As we drove on, I looked back. The men wore helmets and carried weapons; they dismounted and moved into the rice paddy. They
were going out to fight the war, enthusiastically. I was gratified to be
able to make people feel good. This was why I came to Vietnam, to
make a difference.

✚ CHAPTER 3 ✚

A Disguise to Fool a Sniper

May 1966, An Khe, South Vietnam

During my assignment at An Khe the war became personal. Our recreation center sat next to the hospital, so we saw many patients. One man was proud of his face. "My scars are better than all of my buddies." One anticipated his recovery, "The muscle in this arm was so messed up, the doctors took it out. Now the muscle underneath will build up and take its place. I'll be as good as new." Another was amazed, "The dentist put my teeth back together." Still another showed me how he could light a cigarette with one hand while the other was in a sling. All of them bragged about what great medical care they were getting.

A doctor in the mess explained, "If the Medevacs can get a wounded man to the hospital, he has a 98 percent chance of survival. We don't count head wounds." What a relief I felt to conclude that Hollywood was wrong; all the soldiers don't die. Some live to continue being heroes.

We usually scheduled two girls in the recreation center, a short distance from our living quarters, while the other two visited troops around the division. Men came and went at the center all day and evening. We tried to have coffee and some kind of juice available; sometimes we had food. One day Sandra arrived with two fresh loaves of bread. "I talked the guys at the bakery into giving us these." Her slicing job was primitive, but nobody noticed. Another time, she showed off a canned ham: "Look what I got." Her slicing skills improved, and the ham disappeared in ten minutes. We also had games, cards, and books, but most of the soldiers just wanted to laugh or talk.

One day I moved from table to table and talked with each soldier. I saw a man who sat alone. He was bent over, concentrating on a newspaper, a pen in his hand. It wasn't a newspaper page the size of a daily. It was smaller. He had it folded, so he could hold it in one hand while he marked it with the other.[1] I asked, "What are you reading?"

He included me. "They have the casualty list here, from the last operation. I marked the guys I knew, that were killed." He had penned a dash next to a dozen names. Only four or five were not marked. I was shocked, but struggled to conceal it. His eyes didn't show pain; I saw sadness, but also pride. His friends were heroes. "Here are two more," he added, as if he saw his buddies again. It hurt me to look at the list, but it didn't hurt him. He missed his friends, and to mark their names was a way for him to be with them one last time and to honor them. He chose our center for that last reunion because it was a safe, cheerful place where everyone understood how he felt.

When the day ended, the other two girls returned. We walked home and changed into civilian clothes. As usual, we each ate in a different mess hall so we could see more men. After dinner Sandra sat on her cot reading a new PX catalog. We had no stores, so Captain Porter, who was in charge of the Post Exchange, gave us catalogs. We could mail order anything we wanted, at a discount. Sandra had transferred directly from hospital recreation at the US Naval Hospital in Guam. After more than a year and a half away from the States, she was running out of civilian clothes. Excited, she shopped for a new dress. I tried to repair my broken fingernails. In Korea, I had had perfect nails, but in Vietnam it was a lost cause, although I still tried. My mother had sent me a package with a year's supply of nylons and a spectacular nail file. It was covered with crushed diamonds and it had a lifetime guarantee. I learned later that it had much more meaning than it would have had at home. In fact, to the men, it meant "Home." Liz and Nancy sat at the front of the tent with a major, a captain, and a bottle of Scotch.

Suddenly, heavy artillery started to fire, and then mortars. The VC often probed our perimeter. Liz and Nancy dashed to their cubicles. We all reached under our cots, slapped on our steel helmets and combat gear, and grabbed our boots. We burst out of the tent right behind our guests, raced down the hill, crossed the road, and dove into the bunker. Seconds later, two lieutenants piled in after us. The bunker was an 8-foot by 10-foot shipping container covered with sandbags. There wasn't room or light enough to move around, so everyone stayed where they fell, sprawled on the steel floor. I couldn't see the person next to me, even after my eyes got used to the dark. We didn't dare open the door for light or air. No one spoke.

The urgency of the first moments wore off and the men began to relax, but we girls couldn't. The men had been there for six months or more, while we were still new. Every time a gun boomed, we jumped. The sandbags offered some protection, but a direct hit would kill us. We expected every shell to be our last.

The men could tell how scared we were. The major explained, "Notice that every time an artillery piece fires, it's followed by a swish. The swish is the shell flying overhead. Listen. Do you hear it?"

I listened. I heard a swish sound, right above my head. "I hear it."

"Now listen again. Right after the boom, you hear the swish." *Boom! Swish!*

"I hear it."

"Right," the major continued. "That means it's our gun firing. The shell is going out. There's nothing to worry about."

A lieutenant added impishly, "Unless the shell falls short."

The major ignored him. "The target is so far away we can't hear the final explosion." *Boom! Swish!* "On the other hand, if you hear the swish first, then the boom, it's incoming. Then we might get hit."

The lieutenant tried to redeem himself. "They say, 'You never hear the one that gets you.' It won't do any good to worry, as long as we can hear booms and swishes."

We girls worried anyway. Now when we heard a boom, we tensed, then waited for the swish. Eventually, we relaxed somewhat and started to make conversation to take our minds off the danger. We kept track of the noises all the same.

We heard other sounds. *Bang! Ssssss! Bang!* That was a mortar. It is a steel tube, fired from a pit lined with sandbags. The soldier drops a 15-inch round down the tube. The round flies out. It's for targets within about a mile away. You can hear the final bang when it explodes. *Bang! Ssssss! Pop!* That was an illumination round from a mortar. Instead of a shell, the round carries a flare that pops open and floats down on a small parachute. It lights up the area so that the soldiers can see their target. It is good for moonless nights, the VC's favorite time to attack.

We knew we had to get accustomed to a dangerous workplace. The only way to survive was to adapt to its demands, or leave it. Since we all had a strong sense of duty, we learned that booms, fizzes, bangs, hisses, and pops meant specific problems. We accepted their warnings and went on with our job.

The lieutenant next to me in the bunker was eager to talk. "I'm due to rotate home in the morning." I could hear his anticipation, but couldn't see him. Everyone's greatest fear was to be killed during the last 30 days of his tour. The lieutenant had to get his mind off his fear, and so he started to talk about anything he could think of. "When I get home I'm going to celebrate. I'm going to my favorite bar with my mother. She has been my drinking buddy for a long time. I have a bar stool reserved next to hers for day-after-tomorrow night." But first, he had to get through this night. I imagined how he must feel.

Suddenly, close by, we heard a *swish*, but no *boom*. We all caught our breath and froze. Fear gripped me. I thought, *You never hear the one that gets you.* We waited fruitlessly for the explosion and the urgency of the first moments returned. When we were able to speak again, no one dared talk about what had happened to the *boom*. We couldn't calm down again until the *boom swish* finally stopped after a long time. We continued the conversations until the siren called the all clear, then everyone dispersed. It felt like an eternity inside the bunker while I knew I might die, but it had lasted only about two hours. That night, I learned that a conversation could divert attention from the possibility of death at any moment. When you face death, it's better not to pay too much attention.

"An Khe is off limits again this afternoon because the Buddhists are marching."

I turned around. "What?" The young soldier was wide eyed. In mid afternoon in the recreation center I poured a can of pineapple juice into our drained punch bowl. Three soldiers had just crowded into the tent.

The second man continued, "They're out in force, marching down the street with their arms folded, and half the town of An Khe is with them."

The third one reached for a paper cup. "The Military Police are madly racing up and down the streets chasing down the GIs and telling them to get themselves back to camp."

Two men overheard the news. Anxious, they looked at each other. I asked the question for them. "An Khe has been off limits for more than two weeks. This morning was the first time we have been allowed to go downtown. Now it's off limits again?" The line forming at the punch bowl began to buzz. The three friends became the center of attention as I headed for the office to tell the other girls. I remembered the explosion and commotion in the street in Saigon less than a month ago, when sirens screamed and people ran. I had heard on the news in the States that Buddhist monks had set themselves on fire in public places. It was wise to be cautious.

In the office Sandra's face fell. "Nancy and I wanted to go downtown to buy some things we need for the center. I'll call the MPs and see if things have quieted down."

As she lifted the phone a fellow stuck his head into the office. "Do you have any writing paper?" I left the office to help him. I didn't see Sandra or Nancy again until 5:00 and time to go for supper. I asked Sandra what the MPs had said.

She laughed. "I asked them about the big Buddhist demonstration. The MP thought a minute and said, 'Well, there was a Catholic funeral in the village this morning.'" False alarm.

The pressures of An Khe were heavy: the danger, the guns, the heat and bugs, the interrupted sleep. Everyone, the girls and the men, faced it. We had to find ways to cope. The Army worked seven days a week. I only knew what day it was part of the time, but keeping busy helped reduce the stress. Having someone new around also renewed our energy. We shared our excitement when a stream of visitors came to An Khe. The Viet Cong continued military pressure, and we experienced one alert after another. Gene Huffman came from Saigon at about 5:00 P.M. on Thursday, June 2. Half an hour later the siren went off and we sat in the bunker for two hours. I figured we gave her the VIP treatment by providing enemy fire for her arrival. When we came off alert and walked back to the tent, instead of the usual single armed guard who patrolled the hospital area, a large number of soldiers had been posted in the drainage ditches around the hospital.

The men's response to stress was to trade rumors and war stories, heroic, scary, or humorous. Some fabrications grew like bar room bragging. Most rumors were harmless, but occasionally one could grow into something big or damaging. A person who sat in a bunker or a ditch couldn't know what else was happening. Each man added his own scrap of information and made the story better. Nothing was exempt. We girls fought our own battle with the rumors. What the men didn't know about us, they sometimes imagined. We knew that people would make up rumors about us, no matter how careful we were, and tolerated the rumors all the while I served.

One rumor changed for several days. People told us that the Viet Cong hit Company A, 15th Medical Battalion with a mortar attack on Thursday, June 2, in the early morning; one person was hurt. I had slept through it, although the 15th Medical Battalion was within walking distance of us. That was the same day Gene Huffman came from Saigon. Some stories said it was friendly mortar rounds; a few said it was VC. Two days later, people said it was two rounds; one was a dud, the other injured one person. The VC had fired the rounds from the hospital area in downtown An Khe because they knew we wouldn't fire back. After two more days the mortar attack was merely a short round from one of our own guns, a round that fell short of its target. Everyone loved rumors. They were born of stress and they relieved it.

One day I saw an enlisted man in the officer's mess. This was rare. A high-ranking sergeant sat with Lieutenant Colonel McKusker, the white-haired chief nurse. Somebody told me, "He's her husband. He's visiting from somewhere in-country." I checked his name tag. It matched. I thought, *I wonder what his job is. It must be hard for them to be separated. I wonder if they're ever stationed where they can be together. It must be difficult, one being an officer and the other enlisted. How did they ever meet and get married, when officers aren't supposed to fraternize with enlisted men?* I was so shocked, I didn't think to ask.

Monday, 6/6/66

Yesterday, three days after the rumor about the mortar round finally died, it was Sunday, another regular workday. 2nd Battalion 8th Cavalry came in from the field. As soon as we came off alert Liz and I served supper, snacked, and circulated at a few barbecues. Then we ate at their officer's club. Afterwards, I left to help Sandra at the recreation center. We had a good crowd. The regulars played cards near the food table. Two men were engrossed in a game of checkers at the other end of the tent. Several men looked at the bulletin board. They had to duck their heads where the tent liner hung down next to the outside wall.

Boom swish, artillery fired intermittently to keep the pressure on the VC. I spoke a few words to each visitor, made sure everyone had what he needed, and watched a card game for a while. Suddenly, at 8:45, *swish boom, swish boom.* Shells started coming in instead of going out, a lot of them. *Swish swish, boom boom.* Sandra called from the office, "Something's going on; we'd better close up."

I told the men, "Pack up your games. Hurry." Most of them were already out the door.

Someone hollered, fear in the voice, "Get those lights out across the road there." Sandra threw the switch, and I got really scared. I tripped

Joann watches a card game in the recreation center tent at An Khe.

over a chair, and crashed my knee against a table trying to stumble out of the tent in the dark. We ran for the bunker. Flares lit the area like daylight. Guns fired, one after another. *Boom swish, boom swish.* The lights were already out in the hospital. Dark shapes ran between the shadows. We scrambled into the bunker. Fear surrounded us. The female nurses arrived. They had their helmets, flak vests, fatigues, and combat boots. Sandra and I wore short sleeve dresses and loafers. Later, Lieutenant Colonel McKusker, the chief nurse, her husband from Saigon, and the chaplain burst in. He still had on his Sunday uniform, short sleeve khaki shirt and slacks, helmet and pistol belt. Ironically, the chaplain's pistol was the only weapon in the bunker.

We listened to the *boom swish* of artillery going out. We strained to hear any *swish booms,* of incoming. Suddenly we heard, almost on our doorstep, *swish, swish, boom, boom.* We all jumped, and froze in terror. Then we realized mortars were shooting flares. The VC didn't shoot flares. I had landed where I could see out the door, open so 13 people could breathe. The searchlight from Hon Cong Mountain came on. That was the steep hill behind the hospital with the radio equipment at the top, and the Cavalry patch on the side. I saw smoke and muzzle blasts in the searchlight's beam. Were the VC attacking Hon Cong again? People had told me that happened the previous December. It was more than just a skirmish. If the Viet Cong took Hon Cong Mountain, they could drop mortars anywhere. Our air superiority would wipe them out, but they wouldn't need to hold the hill long to do damage.

The action died down, and the searchlight went out. The fear wore off, somewhat. We began to settle down. Liz and Jody, a visiting Red Cross girl, came in, and we relaxed enough to talk quietly. It got stuffy and hot in the bunker, but hot was relative in Vietnam. Two hours later, everything was quiet. A messenger told us we could sit outside, but be ready to pile back in a hurry. From part way up the hill, we could see the airstrip. The 400-plus helicopters began to take off five at a time.

One made three circles of our area. Others went behind Hon Cong. The mosquitoes found our bare arms and legs. Malaria mosquitoes don't annoy you by buzzing. They just bite you and leave. Their abdomens stick straight up into the air, not parallel to your skin as the abdomens of most mosquitoes do. I made a mental note *Always take my malaria pill every week, as sick as it makes me.*[2]

By the end of the third hour, about 11:45, everybody began to fall asleep from boredom. The messenger brought word that we could return to our tent, but we couldn't all go to sleep. We must be able to move out immediately. We got into our fatigues, made sure we could reach our combat gear in a hurry, and set up watches for every two hours. Liz took the first one, and I had the second, but we got an all-clear at about 12:30. Liz had bad dreams all night. She yelled, "Help, help" two or three times and woke me up. Near morning I had bad dreams, too.

Next morning the rumors started. One GI said, "About 30 rounds dropped into the 2nd Brigade area. 2nd Brigade wasn't home."

Another said, "Two rounds dropped." I thought, *probably two VC kept 22,000 people up all night. Just harassment to amuse themselves.*

Another GI said, "A guard tower took a direct hit and killed a medic." I wondered, *What was a medic doing in a guard tower?*

Later in the day two of us walked the perimeter with juice for the guards. We encountered the division operations officer, Lt. Col. Jim Mapp, still in full combat gear. He told us, "Nine rounds landed. The only casualties were a skinned knee, a couple of fellows who dove into a bunker with a couple of scorpions and got bitten, and a few minor wounds that are good for easy Purple Hearts. It was a good practice."

Years later, on the internet I was surprised and delighted to meet a man who was eye witness to that perimeter trip, Bud Alley. He followed the officer's duty to think first about taking care of his men. He reminisced in an email in August 2009.

If my foggy memory recalls correctly, the previous night or so you ladies had been over at our club dancing and having deep intellectual discussions solving the world problems when I asked if you ladies had ever been to the "perimeter?"

The negative answer provoked me to see if you would be willing to correct that situation if I could drive you up there . . . I am not sure if it was the Jack Daniels or Budweiser that said, "Hell yes you all would go." So I got the lemonade done up at the mess hall and the cookies came from where I have no idea, but the next afternoon, my driver and I picked you all up and off we went to the 2/7 part of the perimeter. As we pulled up on a position, you ladies would hop off and serve the lads . . . they were incredulous and couldn't believe round eyed women were actually speaking to them as they were in their foxholes . . . pretty much you all had been heard about but never seen . . . but our trip went off without a hitch and you were safely returned to your quarters . . . I am sure there are photos of the adventure somewhere . . . I am pretty sure A Company was on line at the time along with our Charlie Company. Most of the positions by then were 4–8 man "dugouts" that were fairly well fortified . . . Anyway, it seemed like a fun thing to do at the time . . . seems I ran the notion by Major Henry, our XO and at the time he thought it was pretty harmless . . . By then, I was a first Lt and had been around since the USS Rose Cruise line[3] and more than likely, since I was the Commo [Communications] Officer[4] and the only person with jeeps in the battalion, . . . it is the kind of thing that the 2nd Bn 7th Cav would think was a great idea . . . We all had a good time, no one was really "exposed" to imminent danger it seemed pretty much a lark!

I am not sure that you really believed it would happen for real . . . but it did.

Garry Owen!

Bud[5]

Later, I asked Bud if a medic would have been in a guard tower during a mortar attack. He answered,

On the Green Line [perimeter] in An Khe in 1966, a medic would have only been in the tower if he was off duty. . . . we never had any major casualties on the Green Line, especially after we got the towers built. . . . A medic should have been very close to his direct superior who could have been a squad leader, or platoon leader or even a company commander . . . but make no mistake, Medics were combatants . . . the 2/7 lost 22 of them KIA [killed in action] in that one year I was there, and I cannot begin to tell you the number of WIA [wounded in action] . . . It would have been probable that one or more medics were alert during the evening as part of their duty, but certainly not on guard duty [in a tower]. . . . I hope [your readers] begin to appreciate you ladies as much as us GI's did . . . you were the only "round eyes" we saw that year . . .

Garry Owen.

Bud

Bud Alley is in Galloway and Moore's book, *We Were Soldiers Once and Young,* in both photo and narrative.

The photo is on the next to last page of photos, and the story of John Howard's and my Escape and Evade is told in Chapter 21, page 269–276.

. . . your book is about you girls . . . as young ladies going to a foreign land at a time when polite society said ladies were secretaries or housewives . . . you girls were the ground breakers. . . . Your soldiers are so proud of you and honored to have had you share that time.[6]

Bud Alley has a fist full of medals. He apologized, "I have way too much recognition for what I did." He spends more time telling me about other people's accomplishments than about his own. ". . . we knew that America had called and it was our turn to answer . . . same as others have done since the American Revolution." That modesty was typical, of all veterans.

Their reluctance to talk about the war is not always Post Traumatic Stress Disorder (PTSD). Soldiers told a Donut Dolly stories they wouldn't tell anyone else, because they felt a kinship. Alley says he and those around him made a decision to "write a blank check payable by and up to their life to the people of USA." To offer your life for another: that is a profound sacrifice.

Saturday, June 11

Becky Fey came up from Bien Hoa ("Ben Wah") for the weekend. I knew her from Korea. She went with me to a party at 2nd Battalion 8th Cavalry. Every time the girls had gone there, an alert had broken it up. Two other girls, visiting from Cam Ranh ("Kam Ron") Bay, went with Liz to dinner at the finance mess and a party later at 8th Engineers. Nancy came to the 2/8th party from work, and Liz and the other two girls arrived later.

Lt. Kerry King said, "It's not as bad [in Vietnam] as I thought it would be. It's different than you would expect. I didn't expect the living and the food to be as good. When you do work, you're working hard. In the States you have to keep telling the men to clean their weapons. You never have to here. And, there is a constant concern for your men."

Then, something unusual happened. The animated crowd of 30 or more friends pushed a fresh-faced, pale-haired lieutenant with a broad Danish face unsteadily to the front. The guitar player strummed a familiar chord, the old hymn, "Rock of Ages." Lt. John Weist began his solo with enthusiasm. The officers of the 2nd Battalion 8th Cavalry stood, drinks in hand, in anticipation.

> Victor Charlie at Plei Me ("play mee"),
> Threw a hand grenade at me.
> So I caught it in my palm,
> Threw it back, but he was gone.
> Victor Charlie at Plei Me,
> Thanks a lot, you SOB.

When Weist finished, the men applauded and cheered. I wondered about the song. Several things were unusual about it. For example, I had never heard a drinking song sung as a solo. On that Saturday evening in June of 1966, I had been in Vietnam one month. The Viet Cong surrounded our 15-mile perimeter. Six of the Red Cross girls were there in response to an invitation from the executive officer, Major Paul "Woody" Hayne. It was a dinner party, but it was also work. Now and then, high-ranking commanders requested that we visit their officers. They knew that they would benefit from our visits, too.

After dinner everyone had a few drinks and began to sing. I enjoyed these rare parties. The songs were the best part. They often expressed group fear. At that officer's club at An Khe, after several drinks, someone had asked the lieutenant to sing the solo anthem. They had timed it carefully. Lieutenant Weist was drunk enough to comply. The song was simple. Everyone knew the words. It had only one verse. I guessed that

Weist had written it, so everyone let him have the credit. It expressed the sentiments of these soldiers. It helped them cope with real danger. They walked up to fear and defied it. The song was in the first person, as if it were a story told to a friend.

The ballad referred to a fierce fight not long ago and not far away. These people would have participated in it, and the story probably chronicled an actual event. I learned later that in the previous fall, the 1st Air Cavalry had been in Vietnam just over a month.[7] Two thousand North Vietnamese Regulars attacked the Special Forces camp at Plei Me in the Central Highlands. Their plan was to cut Vietnam in two and seize the entire country. The 1st Air Cavalry flew over the enemy roadblocks, went to the relief of Plei Me, and broke the siege.[8] The 2nd Battalion of the 8th Cavalry made first contact.[9]

Lieutenant Weist, himself, might have actually caught the hand grenade, an unusual, but possible feat. The admiration everyone showed might have been not only for the act, but also for him who had performed it. They probably couldn't get him to tell the story when he was sober, because that would be bragging. But, they could celebrate his heroism and tell the story to their visitors through the song, when he was drunk.

Why was the song set to the tune of the old hymn, "Rock of Ages"?

> Rock of ages, cleft for me,
> Let me hide myself in Thee. . . .

"Rock of Ages" is a hymn that asks for protection. Weist's song not only celebrated a heroic act, but was a prayer of thanks for that man's survival. Most soldiers had or got religion, once in Vietnam. They sought comfort in God to protect them in battle and embrace them when their work was done. To quote an old saying, *there are no atheists in foxholes.*

That irreverent song, at a lively party, was a prayer.

We continued to sing and drink. Suddenly, two loud explosions rocked the building. Everyone froze. We strained to hear the alert siren—nothing. We warily went back to singing. Then the phone rang. Everyone groaned. Major Hayne took the call, then announced, "Three rounds have landed where they shouldn't have. They couldn't be ours, but no one knows for sure. This isn't an alert, but I think we should get the girls home." Every visitor to our unit so far had been in on some excitement. The record had not been broken.

Two weeks later, June 26, 1966, was believed to be the 90th anniversary of Custer's last stand, in 1876.[10] Everybody in 1/7th and 2/7th Cavalry, Custer's regiment, was jittery. They went out on an operation again, hoping history wouldn't repeat itself.

On that same day our chapel quartet sang on Hon Cong Mountain at a church service. If we didn't want a half-day hike to the church, the only way to get up there was by helicopter. Our transportation was a medical evacuation chopper, and our pilot was an unusually tall, thin black man. He was only the second black pilot I had ever seen. From his collar insignia I saw that he was Medical Service Corps (MSC), a medic.

I expressed my surprise to him, "I've never seen an MSC pilot before, but I guess it's logical to have one in medical evacuation."

His kind reply, "Yes, it is. The advantage is that I can make decisions on which medical facility to take a wounded man to, depending on what his wounds are, what care he needs, and how far we should try to transport him." I decided, *I would want that corpsman to be my pilot if I were wounded.*

The helicopter's doors were off, and the passengers rode back-to-back facing out. We had about a foot of floor room, and then an unobstructed drop to the ground. We squeezed in around the gun and buckled in. I thought, *Medevacs are armed?*

After church, a soldier gave me a tour of the perimeter. We stood next to the barbed wire on the top of the hill and looked out over the

base camp. The man mentioned that he knew someone who had received a medal for bravery on that spot.

I asked, "What do you think made him do that?"

He answered without hesitation, "You never know how you're going
to react. There's a fine line between being a hero and being crazy. If you
survive, you're a hero. If you get killed, you were crazy."

Monday, June 27

If people liked rumors, they adored war stories. Sometimes I could
spot a flaw in the story that told me it was a myth. Sometimes I couldn't.
The next day, I had dinner[11] with the two First Sergeants of 15th Med,[12]
the current one and his replacement. The seasoned, highest-ranking
medic in the division told me, "A while ago one of our units took over
an area vacated by the VC. They found a pilot hanging by his feet. He
was skinned from his ankles to his head. There was no sign of other
injuries." I wondered, *If he had no uniform on, how could they tell he
was a pilot?* The story may have been a rumor, but everyone believed it.
I thought, *Little wonder some of our troops tell me they are reluctant to
take prisoners.*

I asked my friend, Gerald Burns of counterintelligence, "Did the
VC skin pilots?"

Burns replied, "Not sure if they picked on pilots, but I did find one
of our guys hanging in a tree and when we found him we were not sure
he was a human. Had been skinned."

"Did our troops fail to take prisoners?"

"If they could get by with it, they killed a lot rather than taking
them. I never saw it, but as an Intel. guy, I heard about outfits not taking
prisoners. . . . We need to be savage when it comes to fighting wars. We
were savage in WW II, and those soldiers are called the Greatest Generation. Now we want to feed them tea and crumpets. B.S." Like bar-
room bragging, stories made the rounds. No one tried to separate fact

from fiction. That was not the purpose of songs and stories. They eased the soldiers' boredom, drew up their courage, and fought their fear. For someone who hasn't experienced war, in the safety these soldiers protected, to question the meaning of these stories is an empty exercise.

Joann with her sister, Phyllis, just promoted to captain. She made a two-hour visit to An Khe on the 4ᵗʰ of July. Army Public Information Office photograph.

Monday, The 4ᵗʰ of July, 1966

Phyllis came to see me at An Khe. She stayed for less than two hours while her plane was unloaded and loaded, and then she returned to Saigon. It was great to see her. She beamed with excitement. "I've just been promoted to captain. I'm wearing my silver captain's bars because I haven't had time to sew the new rank on my fatigues." We had a quick lunch at the hospital mess. With pride I showed her my new surroundings. With equal pride I showed her off to everyone. My sister, the Army intelligence captain. Just as I expected, everybody was astonished and impressed to meet someone's sister. The Public Information Office (PIO) people took our picture, and she was gone. I thought the picture would be in the An Khe paper. Later it surprised me to learn that the photo made it all the way home to the *Flint Journal*.

Some time before July 9th

I was on a Clubmobile run making conversation with some of the guys while we packed up our props. One man boasted, "The VC are really scared of us. When we kill a VC we cut off an ear for a souvenir. Then we leave an ace of spades on the body. The others know it was us, and they get really scared."

We had playing cards at the center, but we only had three or four packs. They were hard to get. I wondered, *Where would anyone find extra aces of spades?* I responded, "You must use a lot of packs of cards."

The man looked surprised, then sheepish. He mumbled, almost under his breath, "Yeah, we do," then backed away and hurried out of the mess tent. I thought I had exploded a myth, but I felt sorry I had embarrassed the young soldier.

Years later I found the part about the ace of spades was true. The practice started in January 1966 near Pleiku, a short distance from An Khe. One company of the 25th Division[13] began leaving an ace of spades as a calling card at the entrances and exits to villages they cleared of VC. The Tropic Lightning soldiers posted the cards along trails and left them on VC bodies. When the company returned some weeks later, there had been little or no VC activity there.

Four lieutenants had hatched the plan.[14] They capitalized on the Viet Cong superstition that the ace of spades was a bad-luck symbol. Lieutenant Charles Brown wrote to the United States Playing Card Company in Cincinnati, Ohio, requesting 1,000 extra aces. The president of the company, Mr. Allison F. Stanley, had lost a son in World War II. He pulled 1,000 aces from the production line and shipped them at no cost. United Press International picked up the story, and requests for aces of spades flooded the company. Whether it worked, nobody knows, but it was great for the American troops' morale.[15]

We visited the hospital as often as we could. Two of us talked to everybody and passed out writing paper and anything we might have to give away. Wounded men took nothing with them when they were evacuated. The Army tried to get their mail and pay to them, but they had little else. One man's polite question surprised me. "Do you have any writing paper without the Red Cross on it?"

"I think so, why?" as I sorted through to look for it.

He apologized, "My mom gets scared when she sees the Red Cross on the envelope. She's afraid I've been wounded." That stopped me. I thought, *You <u>have</u> been wounded.* He continued, "I want to be able to tell her I'm all right before I tell her what happened." I knew he wasn't going to tell his mom anything that happened. We learned to carry plain writing paper.

The patients always wanted cigarettes. The Red Cross could not give out cigarettes any more, because the Surgeon General had just issued a ruling that smoking was dangerous to your health. We also had to be extremely careful not to give the appearance that we asked the soldiers to pay for anything we gave them. We told the men, "We're going to the PX. If you want to give us money to buy something for you, we'd be happy to put it on our list."

One man said, "I want some cigarettes, but I don't have any money."

The man in the next bed offered, "I'd be glad to let you have some of mine. You can pay me back."

"Thanks, Buddy."

At the PX tent we waited in the rain in a long line of soldiers. Everybody watched everything we did, and we were on duty everywhere we went. We talked to as many men as we could. "What are you guys going to buy today?"

"I don't know. We had a chance to come, so we thought we'd see if there's anything we can use."

"Are you girls on a shopping trip?"

"We have a whole long list of things to buy for the guys in the hospital."

"I'm looking for a toothbrush. I only have one left in my footlocker."

The line snaked into the tent and up and down every aisle. The light bulbs in the ceiling hardly gave enough light for us to see what we bought. The homemade, wooden shelves held whatever had arrived on whatever transport had landed recently. As we shopped, we watched for anything that we might need for ourselves or for the center in the foreseeable future, such as toothpaste, shampoo, a comb, maybe writing paper for our next trip to the hospital. Sometimes the PX had candy. Nobody complained that we held up everyone to check out for a couple dozen wounded soldiers.

At the hospital we passed out all the purchases. The soldiers showed their gratitude. One man stumbled around for words until he finally managed, "Gee, thanks."

Another confessed, "I really needed that. I didn't know how I was going to get it."

And, from one man who didn't buy anything, "It was really nice to see you."

It brought tears to my eyes that these men were so grateful for such a simple thing we did.

July 16

For the last three days I have seen jets in the morning. They were intimidating, but strangely attractive. They climbed into the clouds and disappeared, then suddenly one dropped from the sky like a hawk. One would dive, and then another, while the third hid in the clouds to give cover. A single-engine L-19 spotter plane circled low with an aerial observer, one of the most dangerous jobs in Vietnam.

The fighters continued for 20 to 30 minutes, then like distant poison darts, they disappeared for a moment. Suddenly they thundered overhead, low, in formation. They streaked toward home with all the rockets gone from under their wings. They wagged a salute and disappeared.

A few days later, one of the girls told us she knew some of the pilots. "They're from Bien Hoa Air Base. When they come over on their way north, watch them." They tipped their wings to say hello. What a thrill. I felt like I had just gotten a greeting from someone important.

Two days ago we watched a night operation from the road in front of our tent. We saw flares, six at a time. Then a helicopter came. It fired two rockets, white streaks in the night, at a target on the ground, and then quickly climbed into the sky. Another came after it and fired two bursts, with red tracers from a machine gun. Then it sped away. I heard another helicopter, invisible without lights, circling above. It was so close I heard the *hiss* of rockets and *one-note clatter* of the machine gun. The helicopters made three passes, and then went away. Something must have been in the area, because for the following three mornings the jets came back.

On another night the helicopters returned. One flew higher than the rest when he made a firing run. I wondered, *How could he hit anything from way up there?* As I walked along the road with two officers, one of them looked up and indicated the higher helicopter. "Those are the [cautious] married guys."

This morning as the jets came in over the camp, a GI looked up and said, "Go get 'em!"

✳ ✳ ✳

I realized that Major Stout was too eager because he had a crush on me. He was commander of a helicopter company. He came calling a time or two at our tent. A little over weight, nice, though not my type. Like many soldiers, he drank too much. I was sure he was married. He invited me to go swimming at Qui Nhon ("Kwee Non"). I always loved to swim, but I knew we would be on a remote beach all day. That was against the Red Cross rules, not to mention my own rules. As my father had explained in second grade, I told Stout, "We have to take another girl with us." When I went off to college my father told me to date in groups. I told Major Stout, "And we have to fill the helicopter." I thought, *That's a nice trip. Anybody who wants to go should be able to.* I reasoned, with another girl along and several other people, the major wouldn't try anything that my Korean judo training and I couldn't handle. We will go on the trip tomorrow.

Sunday July 17, Qui Nhon

Miriam, the newly arrived, physical education major from South Carolina, came with me. Major Stout brought three captains in a UH-1D Huey helicopter to pick us up. They were some of his pilots, all lower rank than he. He had to be on his best behavior in front of them, and they in front of him—two more elements of restraint in my favor. I could relax and have a good time. I stayed alert, anyway.

Miriam and I made sure to act like sisters. There isn't much that will spike an unwanted advance as effectively: Keep your distance. Back away if he gets too close. Duck if he reaches or grabs for you. Don't let him catch your eye. Don't look at him. Pay for his lunch, ouch, you might as well throw a bucket of cold water on him. I always tried to be subtle and not hurt a man's feelings. He's just showing that he's attracted to you.

We flew low level for the first fifteen minutes of the half-hour trip. It was like being on an elevated super-highway. I felt like I was let out of a cage. With all the VC activity, this was the first time I had been allowed off the compound since being at An Khe village when I first arrived.

Neither Miriam nor I had seen the countryside around the base. We flew with the doors wide open, following Highway 19 east to the South China Sea. Whenever we passed any Vietnamese people, the gunners trained their sights on them, ready to fire. Children waved at us and some of the adults, too. Miriam and I waved back. It was exciting. When we came to An Khe pass, the edge of our plateau, the helicopter climbed well up out of range of small arms fire. Ahead lay a coastal plain, wild and lonely VC country.

At Qui Nhon a large building stood on a cliff overlooking the beach. As the helicopter descended, a nun came running across the sand, her gray and white habit flying. We landed at the base of the cliff long enough for Major Stout to jump out with a covered food container. Then the helicopter moved a short way along the beach and shut down. Major Stout soon rejoined us. "That is a leprosarium. An order of French nuns takes care of a leper colony there. I wanted to pay our respects, and I brought them some steaks, excess from the mess hall." He continued, "I didn't want everybody to get out, because the nuns would insist that we stay for a seven-course French dinner. With six of us, they couldn't afford it."

That day we swam, and splashed, and played on Army air mattresses in the South China Sea. The men observed every courtesy. We sat on the white sand, Major Stout played a ukulele, and we ate steaks and baked potatoes the men cooked on the beach. There was no alcohol.

At the end of the afternoon, the gunners came back. Miriam and I walked down the beach with Major Stout to thank the nuns. We followed a path up the cliff to the leprosarium to a large, high-ceilinged hallway. Airy, sparkling clean, and filled with sun, the hallway had windows on one side and rooms on the other. We sat on a well-worn wooden bench. The French Mother Superior and one of her thinner, younger nuns sat properly on two small, matching side chairs drawn up to the bench. They served us cakes and Cokes, and we chatted for half an hour, mostly in French.

As we prepared to take off from the beach, Major Stout took the controls. I overheard him ask the gunner, "Do you want to get off a few rounds?" We flew over some hills around the water's edge, in VC territory. Major Stout picked a tiny, hidden beach nestled at the foot of a hill. I was sure he was showing me the beach where he had planned our tryst, a perfect hideaway. The helicopter made a pass, and the gunner on the left fired several bursts at the hill. We made another pass and the gunner on my side kicked up a trail of waterspouts on the sea below. Stout explained, "I flew over this peaceful beach before when on the other side of that hill, there was fighting."

As we neared An Khe pass, a thunderstorm covered the plateau, blocking our way. Lightning streaked down in front of us, black clouds piled on top of a wall of fog. If we couldn't find a way through the storm we would have to turn back and spend the night in Qui Nhon. All of us would be Absent Without Leave (AWOL). We eased up to the storm and peered ahead. There were trees. We could see.

We flew only feet above the winding road, swinging this way and that. Occasional Vietnamese people, in US Army ponchos and straw hats, padded below us, barefoot, in the gloomy, cold rain, a contrast to the hot, sunny beach we had just left. The gunners pulled the doors shut. We ate dinner with our hosts at their mess when we got back.

On Monday, the day after we went swimming, Staff Sergeant White, manager of the 2nd Battalion 12th Cavalry Enlisted Men's (EM) Club invited us to come that evening. He was a rare black sergeant, a little overweight, earnest, a little rumpled, and looked tired. "The battalion is coming in today. They've been in the field for 83 days, and they'll go back out tomorrow." Troop movements were *Classified*, only revealed to people with a *need to know*. Our *Confidential* clearance allowed us knowledge of troop movements, strength, and officers' names. One day was just enough for the men to get a shower, get good and drunk, sleep in a bed, and then go out again—wonders for morale. Sergeant White was tired because he had just about as much notice as we did to get everything ready.

Miriam and I were the only ones available to go, even for this high priority. We should arrive early and leave early because an EM Club could get rowdy. At the end of the day we saw the guys at the rock quarry and took some juice, not cold, but welcome on the scorching rock pile. The guys laughed and talked as we walked around to their work areas. We cut the visit short, reluctantly, and made a dash for the 4:00 shower. Sergeant White arrived at 4:30. His EM club was the only large, permanent building on the base. There was no parking lot; the barracks tents were nearby, and everybody walked. When we pulled up outside the club we could hear a loud party. I was skeptical, "How long have they been drinking?"

"Since 2:00." I gasped. "Don't worry, there won't be any trouble. There *will not* be any trouble." I got out of the jeep slowly. Sergeant White took us to his office. He telephoned the mess hall and had them send food over. Soon a tall, black soldier arrived with two paper plates covered with wax paper. He wore a white jacket trimmed in blue; his arms stuck way out of the sleeves. His face glowed with a shy, proud, anxious smile; I wondered how he had won the privilege of bringing the dinner to the Red Cross girls. We made sure to chat with him and thank him.

"Look at that. Our dinner is here. It looks wonderful. Thank you. I hope you didn't have to walk too far with your hands so full."

"Oh, no, ma'am. It's not heavy. The mess hall is just a little way."

"You're sure? I hope it wasn't too much trouble."

"Oh, no, ma'am. It was no trouble at all."

"Well, thank you. And please tell the cooks thank you for us."

"I will. Have a good supper."

"Thank you."

We ate on Sergeant White's desk. The food was good, but on the trip from the mess hall it had picked up a lot of sand. I needed a cup of coffee, but there wasn't any. The sergeant gave me a warm Pepsi. I don't think Sergeant White ate. He took us in to the party. The club was one huge room, fairly well lit, filled with four-man tables. It was packed with 600 to 800 men, probably the whole battalion. Four to six men sat at each table drinking beer. Others stood or moved around. Sergeant White chose a table at one end of the room, evicted the men who sat there, scooped off the beer cans, and sat us down. Miriam and I were the only women in the club. The soldiers all stopped and stared. A couple of them came up to us, none too steady. One held a can of beer, his shirt badly tucked in. Trying to get his fogged brain to comprehend what he saw, he asked, "Are you human?"

Sergeant White made good on his promise, there *would not* be any trouble. He announced that we were there and made everybody take off their hats. Most of the men were tousle-headed and needed a hair cut, but they were all clean, though wrinkled. People pressed in nearer and nearer, almost on top of us. Sergeant White moved them back. The division dance band came in and set up. I knew the Army had marching bands, but I didn't know the Cavalry had a dance band, who wore combat fatigues. Our table was next to the band, the best table in the house, to see and be seen.

The band started with a slow number; one brave soldier asked me to dance. I got up, and the whole room buzzed. Everybody melted back to make room, then stood in silent awe as we danced. With the next song, the soldiers' courage grew. One asked Miriam to dance, and four or five people cut in on each of us. The room stirred again. The band played one more slow number, and then picked up the tempo; the party got livelier. Even more people cut in, one after another. Sometimes we danced with two soldiers at once. Everybody laughed and cheered.

Then, the band played a fast number. Fellows started to dance with each other. They were outstanding dancers. They did spins and slides and tossed each other around. Their arms and legs flew in every direction. The hundreds of men roared with laughter.

Sergeant White stayed less than ten feet away. He prevented several fights, keeping absolute control. Between dances he asked, "Would one of you girls be willing to sing with the band?"

I apologized, "I think I could make it through one verse of 'Hello Dolly,' " the only song I knew. I looked at Miriam, hoping she could do better.

"That's more than I could do."

The bandleader had me stand up with the band. A big man, with a kind smile, his collar was crooked. He leaned over me, "Sing a few bars so we can find your key." I thought, *He must be a professional musician.* He gave me a microphone. Sergeant White announced the song. Everybody went wild. The band played an introduction, the leader nodded. I gave it my best.

> Hello, Dolly.
> Well, Hello, Dolly.
> It's so nice to see you back where you belong . . .

One verse wasn't much, but the band played a few bars of interlude, and I sang it again. This time, everybody sang with me. What a chorus! I couldn't imagine feeling more appreciated than when I offered that song for that 600-plus crowd of homesick, hardly sober GIs. Miriam and I left shortly after that, because the group got harder and harder to control. We had been there about an hour.

The next morning, Sergeant White, still rumpled, still earnest, still tired, came to our tent and brought two cases of mixed soft drinks, and he gave me $20. I told him, "We aren't allowed to accept money for anything."

He insisted, "Use it to buy something for the unit." So I thanked him. I decided to pay for part of a refrigerator. The other girls were glad to donate the balance. I was transferred before the refrigerator came.

Wednesday, July 20

Two days ago I got word that I'm being transferred to Dong Ba Thin. Sandra said, "I think it's a Vietnamese cuss word." Ann, here temporarily from Phan Rang, told us, "It's between Nha Trang and Cam Ranh. The group is small, 10th Aviation."

Friday, July 22, Buon Blech

Red Cross girls had to be ready to face the same danger as the men. Our charge was to see the troops any way we could, to bring them reminders of home. At base camp, we had mess tents, we could give recreation programs, and men could visit our recreation center. Sometimes, when there was a lull in the fighting, we went to the front line foxholes.

On the Saturday after we visited the EM club, Sandra and I planned to go forward to some artillery positions, south to Buon Blech. Instead of our usual light blue dress, we wore the men's combat gear: green fatigues, combat boots, dog tags, flak vest, and steel helmet. We prepared small items to give out. At 11:00 our escort, Warrant Officer McDonald, arrived. When we got to the command post in the forward base camp we learned that Buon Blech was socked in because of the monsoon. We finally got clearance to take off at noon.

Sandra and I climbed aboard the ship. Surprise, a lieutenant colonel greeted us. He was the battalion commander who had invited us to visit his men. We would ride in his personal helicopter, a Huey with additional radios and other specialized equipment, the best of the unit's fleet—VIP treatment. We usually hitchhiked in whatever chopper wasn't full. Everyone wore flak jackets and steel helmets. Before we started, the colonel ordered, like an uncle, "Roll down your sleeves, for two reasons.

First, the light skin is easy to spot from the ground. Second, if we have a fire, your arms will be protected." I rolled down my sleeves in the July, noontide, Vietnam swelter. My arms started to sweat. I thought, *What fire?* Then I knew, *If we crash and burn, if we're shot down.* Pilots didn't say, "crash," they said, "crash-and-burn."

We took off. An escort ship carrying six armed men in combat gear took off with us. *Extra guards. I never saw so much security.* At that time, some of greatest Viet Cong strength was right where we were, in the Central Highlands. We refueled, and headed south to Cheo Rio, then turned a little west for Buon Blech, toward Cambodia. We flew with the doors open. Since the chopper doors weren't armored anyway, to leave them open made an easier exit. Until then I had flown with the doors on or off depending on the weather, not the danger. We flew high, out of range of ground fire, and fast, more protection. I sat on the right, in the outside seat. The other ship hung in the air next to us, a little ahead. I felt as though I could reach out and touch them. I waved. They smiled and waved back. I had touched them.

We sailed over an abandoned Special Forces camp in VC territory. I took a moment to fix a broken fingernail with the diamond nail file my mother had sent me. The crew chief behind me sat casually, one arm draped across his machine gun, and watched me. He didn't try to conceal his smile. "Wow. That's something. Here you are filing your nails, and the jungle is down below." Suddenly, I realized that my nail file was special to him. I had discovered something more I could do to remind the soldiers of home.

As soon as we turned west at Cheo Rio we entered some hills. The pilot climbed higher; the trees came up almost under our feet. Several large gray birds skimmed the treetops. We overtook three small green parrots that flew below us. We traveled with them for a few minutes, and then left them behind. When I was a kid in Michigan, and read about far-away places, I never dreamed that some day I would fly with wild parrots through a jungle.

Fog and rain shrouded the hills. We had to get down next to the ground to see where we were: altitude maybe 50 feet. The pilot found an asphalt road. He followed its black trail through the forest, dodging the trees. It felt as if we were riding in a ball like a suspended Christmas ornament. We careened and slipped above the winding road through the misty rain. The crew chief and gunner, on a break while we were out of range of ground fire, went back on duty. They squared off behind their weapons, sighting every potential target. I had the uncomfortable feeling that a VC could hit us with a rock at that altitude. Body tense, fear just below the surface, my eyes scoured the trees and bushes. I tried to guess where a VC might hide.

Suddenly, blind in the fog, we burst atop a village of thatch-roofed houses on stilts: Montagnards, the original inhabitants of this part of the world. We had traveled back in time. A bigger village materialized, and beyond it, a complex of tents and a flock of helicopters parked in rows. We landed, safe among them. I thought, *An hour flight. These troops are a long way from base*. Most trips were 10 or 20 minutes.

On the ground, two American girls created a sensation. Most of the soldiers stared and eased closer, afraid to believe their eyes. Sandra and I split up. Escorts took us to two field messes, a tent kitchen and serving line with no tables. Mr. McDonald and a pilot followed me. The kitchen always open, mounds of hot food waited: fried ham, hash brown potatoes fixed with bacon. I snacked while we stood and waited for what would happen next. I thought, *Delicious, better than anything at base camp. Hard to leave it alone*. I ate a plateful before I realized it.

A few tentative men approached. "Would you like a cookie?" I chatted with them. With scared enthusiasm, they took what I offered and thanked me under their breath. Some hastily melted back into the drizzle. I recognized one lieutenant, greeted him, and shook his hand. Back at the club he was loud and fun with plenty to say and full of enthusiasm. I was surprised that here, he was withdrawn.

I asked, "Where are the rest of the men?"

A major watching from the edge of the group of about 30 soldiers answered, "Most of the men are on the perimeter."

I asked, "Can we go out there?"

The major tried to be stern, but didn't succeed, "Yes, if your escort, Mr. McDonald, wants to assume the risk of exposing you to sniper fire." He looked at McDonald, a towering man standing behind me like a brother. I couldn't see his reaction. *The major's teasing me. Everybody loves it.* The major took a helmet liner from one of the men, "Here, you'd better put this on."

I thought, *My helmet's in the helicopter. I didn't think I'd need it on the ground.* "I'll wear a helmet when Mr. McDonald wears one," playing to the crowd. Translation: *Aren't you being overprotective?*

McDonald offered, "Wear it to keep the rain off." Translation: *Always obey a major.*

My hair, a wet mess. I worried about how I looked, not about speculative danger, and put the helmet liner on. Mr. McDonald and I started out of the mess area; our pilot came along for entertainment. A soldier guided us. He wore no unit patch or rank, but people called him Bell. Young and slim, a twinkle in his eye betrayed him. Another soldier followed us. His black, not green, baseball cap told me he was a Pathfinder, a specially trained paratrooper. They dropped in small teams into hostile territory to find sites for aircraft to land, to clear trees, brush and booby traps to bring in troops. They knew the jungle.[16] The pathfinder stood an inch or so taller than Bell, with the same build. He looked unflappable. A handful of other soldiers tagged along. Everyone carried their M-16 rifles casually, as combat soldiers who never went anywhere without their weapons. Mr. McDonald and the pilot wore the officers' .45 pistol.

Terrible weather. Cold rain, unrelenting. Gray, depressing haze hung in the air. The camp sat on a hilltop stripped of vegetation, a sea of yellow, chunky, mud that tried to suck your boots off. We slopped a few yards to the perimeter, where the men were bundled in warm clothes with waterproof ponchos. They had been out in the rain for days, and were wet in spite of everything. Their feet had to be cold, soaked through. I didn't know the temperature, probably 70 degrees, but felt cold to us, who were accustomed to over 100. I could understand why the commander had invited us to this awful place, isolated, bleak, lonely, everything soggy. The men had been there for weeks, would be there for weeks more. It was dangerous: like bait, they waited for Charlie to hit and run. Great food was the only thing this place had going for it. Yet no one complained.

For an hour I walked along the outermost rim of the fire support base, smiled and laughed and greeted everyone. I wasn't worried about danger; if anything, I thought everyone overdid the protection. These people may have seen a Red Cross girl at An Khe, maybe months ago, but they never dreamed they would see us at Buon Blech. I knew I looked as if I had crawled out of a swamp, but nobody cared.

Each two-man foxhole was deep enough for a man to stand and fire his rifle. Logs stacked with layers of sandbags protected each fighting position. Behind it, a poncho formed a tent for two air mattresses. The men had been alert all night. Bell approached each tent with care. If he startled a dozing combat soldier, he might be shot. They would know his voice. "Anyone awake in there?"

From inside, a sleepy mumble, "Hey, man, what's happening?"

Bell gave me an impish grin, "There's a lady here to see you."

"Aw, go on, will you?"

I smiled at Bell. "I have some cookies for you." Stunned silence. The man's hand fumbled at the flap, and his head came out. He rolled his face up and blinked, shook his head, and looked again. His eyes locked on me, he crawled out and stood up. *So young. Looks like a high school kid.* I smiled and handed him a cookie. His buddy crawled out the other end, but couldn't speak. He stared and wiped the mud off his hand before he took the cookie. They thanked me gratefully and politely. I asked, "Could you use some cards or writing paper?"

The first soldier replied, "Yes, ma'am. I would like to have some playing cards."

The other spoke in a Carolina drawl. "I sure could use some writin' paper." Carolina stuck the paper under his poncho. I asked some questions about their foxhole and about Charlie. The men were modest, but proud of their work. They expressed genuine thanks again for the gifts as we moved on.

At another position I asked, "How does this set-up work?"

The proud answer, "The foxhole is to jump in, in case Charlie tries to come."

"Did you ever have to jump in it?"

"Well, I did once so the colonel could see how it looked."

"Do you stay in it at night?"

His tent-mate put in, "He does. I generally sit on top." His buddy shot him a sideways glance.

Each foxhole crouched within sight of those on the left and right, 30 or 40 yards away, depending on the slope of the land. If one pair of men was under fire and in trouble, the others on both sides could help. They had interlocking fields of fire. I looked outside the perimeter down the hill, and shuddered to imagine what it would be like to see a real enemy burst out of the woods and try to shoot me. Those soldiers lived with that every day and every night. I admired their courage.

I asked a couple of other fellows, "Is your shelter dry?" They looked like twins in their identical ponchos.

Twin One[17] said, "Not really. We also have ants and bugs. At least we used to."

Twin Two said, "Yeah. We put down a poncho liner."

The twins finished each other's sentences. "But the ants ate through that. Now we use . . ."

". . . a piece of cardboard."

"That seems to work . . ."

". . . better."

I started to get dizzy. The Twins had formed a mental connection. Men said that happened in combat. We continued from one foxhole to the next. Soldiers came along to laugh at their neighbors. Eight or ten of us sloshed along the perimeter, boots covered with mud, spattered up to our knees, handing out gifts, chatting, and laughing. It rained all day; visibility was poor. Just as we were ready to leave Buon Blech the weather closed in and grounded us again. When the helicopter finally lifted off, badly behind schedule, it rushed out of there as fast as it could carry us.

Later, I thought about the men who wore no rank. I described the visit to Lt. Jim Brigham, Headquarters Company, 2/7th Cavalry, a remnant of the Battle of Ia Drang.

I learned later that Ia Drang, November 14–16, 1965, was the first major engagement of the war. After the siege of Plei Me, the North Vietnamese Army (NVA)[18] regrouped in the Ia Drang Valley, combining the 700 survivors of the siege with 2,000 troops in neutral Cambodia. The 1/7th Cavalry, 430 men, made a helicopter assault on Landing Zone (LZ) X-Ray, and the NVA attacked. The 2/7th Cavalry arrived on the second day, the 2/5th Cavalry on the third day. Massive artillery and air support, including B-52 bombers, routed the North Vietnamese. Some fled back into Cambodia and others eastward into the jungles of the Ia Drang Valley. On the fourth day the NVA attacked the 2/7th Cavalry at LZ Albany, north of X-Ray, with 93 percent casualties. Total casualties were US 234 killed, 242 wounded, NVA 2,200.[19]

I asked Lieutenant Brigham, who had survived that battle, "What is the real reason the men in the field don't wear any rank insignia or unit patches on their uniforms?"

He knew. "Early, with the first contacts we learned that anyone with stuff on the collars or stripes on arms along with those carrying radios were prime targets. So, patches started coming off. The officers used magic markers to make indication on collars. The same reason officers were normally referred to with nicknames when on operation. Later on in the war the subdued insignia came in. Some wore it, but that was mostly REMF ["Rear Echelon M--- F---"] troops." Brigham made a sour face.

"Another reason is after the first year a supply of clean uniforms would be sent out to the operation. Guys would take off the dirty and pick up clean. This cut down on the amount of weight the troops had to carry."

"What was a Pathfinder doing there?"

"After the Landing Zone was established they controlled all air traffic in the area. Normally a Pathfinder team of two or more was attached to direct traffic," a note of thanks in his voice for their help.

"What about the handful of other men who went along?"

"Most likely headquarters types and had no specific location on the defense line."

"Who was Bell? I just assumed he was a sergeant."

"He was probably a platoon leader, would have been a lieutenant." *Brigham's counterpart.*

"No one saluted him. No one called him 'Sir.' He carried an M-16 like the enlisted men."

"Normally when they had been with the unit for a while they looked like normal grunts."

I assume that's good. "Did the major order Bell to guide us on the perimeter?"

Brigham nodded. "Yes, for sure."

"Now I wonder if the major also sent the handful of five or six other men who surrounded me. They all carried weapons and they all stayed with me for the whole trip. If the major wanted me to wear a helmet liner, would he also want me to have bodyguards?"

"Yes. You had bodyguards. Besides the VC, there was the danger of attack by some grunt." Brigham's eyes narrowed in disapproval. He brightened, "Besides, the bodyguards got to watch you walk in a short skirt and you probably smelled good." A smile of appreciation danced around the corners of his mouth. "Visits to the operations area by Western girls are rare."

I burst out laughing and couldn't stop. "You are absolutely wild. Too bad for the bodyguards. I was wearing fatigues and combat boots, but you can be sure I was wearing French perfume."

Years later I thought again about the bond I had seen between Twin One and Twin Two and the ways wars affect individuals. I saw that bond a number of times over the years. I wondered if, when two men face the enemy together, they know they must depend on each other and trust each other and they create a bond for survival. What forms in combat is so strong, it lasts a lifetime. It will be there the next time there is a threat. This happens whenever men fight an enemy together. I think it also happens when men might fight together in the future, anticipating the need to protect each other.

These same men might never be friends at home. Without the survival threat, the bond does not form. I see this survival mechanism developing in the evolution of man-animals in tribal hunting and warfare. Those who developed it survived. Those who did not, became extinct. I asked a Marine combat veteran what he thought.

He responded, "You are absolutely correct . . . that men and women in combat have a trust and bond that transcends differences . . . This deep foundation becomes the essence of survival."[20]

I did not see this bond developing between me and any of the girls. I did not experience combat and the threat to survival as the men did.

Back at An Khe that evening after I walked the foxholes, the commanding general was giving a farewell cocktail party for Sandra and me. We were both being transferred in two weeks. The party was to begin at 4:30, but the weather had kept us over so long in Buon Blech that it was 4:45 by the time our escorts got us back to our tent. It was a tall order: be ready for a cocktail party in our honor, as fast as possible. The general and his guests were waiting for us. We had missed the daily shower, so that put us ahead several minutes. We traded our combat boots for high heels and our grimy fatigues and armored vests for frilly cocktail dresses. We shaped and coaxed our wet hair into place, with no time for a hair dryer. In 20 minutes, Sandra and I started out of the tent. There, we met the head nurse, Major Frost, who noted, "I went to your party." We made apologies and hurried on. Out of sight, we winced.

A jeep sped us a short distance. The parking lot overflowed with identical vehicles, most with bumper codes ending in 6, the highest-ranking officer of the unit. Inside, a sea of green fatigues greeted us. Maj. Gen. John Norton's farewell party crammed itself into a small officer's club. There wasn't room for so many people. All the division's majors and colonels had come, and a few lower ranking officers, a rare gathering. Only one or two of these field-grade officers would usually attend a farewell for Red Cross girls. I was exhausted beyond what I thought I could handle.

The celebration was planned, timed, and executed with military precision. The room was as crowded as a New York subway. No one was offended that we were late. They understood what it meant to be weathered in and had learned long ago to be flexible. The moment we arrived, an aide asked what we wanted to drink and returned with it promptly. There was no ice and no *hors d'oeuvres*. The general believed the cooks should take care of the troops, not the officers. Sandra and I split up, moved around the overcrowded room and greeted and talked with everyone.

Major Flint said, "Sorry you're leaving. It's been great having you in the chapel quartet."

The man standing next to him said, "Yes, everybody loves it when the chaplain starts his sermon with, 'Gentlemen, and Beloved Lady.'"

Miriam and Mary had arrived at An Khe to replace Sandra and me. Mary had made trips to a number of units to see if we could visit them. She told me, "Some of the crusty old sergeants think the combat zone is no place for a girl."

I barely saw the other girls. All except Liz disappeared in the crush of tall men. Major Sutton remarked, "The soldier in Vietnam is the best product the American people have ever fielded." Those nearby murmured assent. These field-grade officers were restrained, courteous, and warm—looser than in front of their men.

Executive Officer Maj. Woody Hayne of the 2/8th Cavalry appeared. We shook hands. He thanked me for visiting his troops so many times and then he reminded me, "Every time you girls came to our club, we had an alert."

I had met almost all of these commanders when we visited their units. They were friends in the way that combat brought people together. I spoke to everyone, and they all expressed their thanks for what the Red Cross had done for their men. A lieutenant colonel reminded me, "When you first got here, you were so pale."

Maj. Gary D. Collier, commander of 191st Military Intelligence Detachment, recalled our visit. He had sent an invitation in the shape of a clever spoof of a military memo. I laughed, "I expected item number six to be, 'All participants are hereby ordered to have a good time.'" It was like a big family.

These officers only had time for one or two drinks. At the right moment, Major General Norton stepped onto a small platform, compelling, with two black stars on each side of his collar. Everyone fell silent. "Gentlemen and ladies," his eyes traveled to each of us around the room. As we stood in place, he gave a short, military, kindly speech. "We are privileged to have the Red Cross girls here at the 1st Cavalry Division (Airmobile). They have been tireless, visiting our troops and raising morale everywhere in the division." The officers in the room nodded and gave us approving glances. "In fact, Sandra and Joann have just returned from spending the day at Buon Blech." Eyebrows went up. A few people murmured. The general went on to tell the gathering that the two of us were being transferred. The mood moderated. "We wish them well in their new assignments." Then came a surprise. "To thank them and to show our appreciation we are making them Honorary Sky Troopers." The officers broke into applause. Nobody expected that. Commanders didn't give certificates at farewell parties. That was the only one I ever saw in Korea or Vietnam. People moved apart and helped Sandra and me squeeze our way to the platform. As the general handed us the certificates, he said to us, "This is the same award we gave to Bob Hope when he visited us."

This two-star general, who commanded 22,000 troops, took the time in the middle of a war to do that for us. As a civilian, I wasn't eligible for medals, but felt as though he had given me one, anyway. General Norton had presented each of us with a handmade certificate. There weren't any printers at An Khe. I traced my fingers along the black letters, the raised seal, and the yellow Cavalry patch—the work was perfect. Everyone admired the certificate, and few people had ever seen one. I treasured it. Soon after the speech, all said goodbye and returned to preside over their own mess halls and their own duties to their men.

The next day, one of the pilots told Miriam that he flew out of Buon Blech right after us. He traveled fast at low level, as we did. His ship took five hits from small arms fire out of the trees. I felt a thump in the center of my chest. *Wow! That's why the excessive security.* I thought everybody was over protective. Wrong. That area must have been loaded with VC.

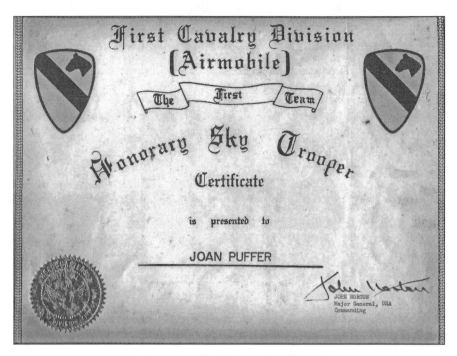

The Honorary Sky Trooper Certificate that
Maj. Gen. John Norton presented to Joann.

When our two ships went in to Buon Blech at about 1:00, every Charlie in the area saw us. When we came out, we flew so low and so fast they couldn't take aim at us. When the next ship came through, they sprang the ambush. Most ships would take one or two hits, not five. The men explained that the Viet Cong hadn't learned to lead their target. To hit a fast-moving aircraft you have to aim in front of it or by the time the bullet gets there, the helicopter is gone. You might not even hear the shots. Five hits!

That's why the foxholes were manned 24 hours a day: to prevent attack. The major wasn't kidding about sniper fire. That's why he told me to wear the helmet liner. Even a steel helmet wouldn't withstand a direct hit, and snipers targeted the head. But a soldier once showed me his helmet with a bullet hole in one side and out. He was still alive because the helmet sat on the helmet liner, an inch away from his head, and not flat on his head.

No number of armed men would protect me from a sniper as I walked on the perimeter. Once a sniper realized I was a woman, all he had to do was wait for a clear headshot. The major, the warrant officer, and all the men knew that the only way to protect me was to disguise me as another soldier. Suddenly, I realized how close I had been to the enemy and why the officers at the general's party were so surprised that Sandra and I had been to Buon Blech. Then, I got scared.

July 24

Yesterday one of the doctors, Captain Halpern, told me, "One of my best friends went down in a Medevac chopper. Four choppers have gone down in four days. That one crashed in flames, killing all four crewmembers." Captain Halpern needed to talk, "My friend was an MSC pilot. We were going to go on vacation together next month. Only last week we were talking about it. The bodies were so mangled and burned they couldn't identify him. All they knew was that he had been on the aircraft. Last week he showed me pictures of his family, his wife and children."

I got a bad feeling. "Was he a Black fellow?"

"Yes"

"A long, tall one?"

"Yes"

I had a lump in my throat. I struggled to speak, "I remember him. He flew me once up to Hon Cong Mountain when our quartet sang at church." It really hits you when a thing like that happens.

Captain Halpern tried to sooth both of us, "You can't always tell why the ships go down. They could have taken a round from one of the villages and you would never hear it."

I wondered, *Could that be why we lost an engine when I came up to An Khe from Saigon?*

+ CHAPTER 4 +

Hot Landing Zone

Monday July 25, 1966, An Khe, South Vietnam

About two weeks before I transferred from An Khe to Dong Ba Thin, Sandra and I were working in the office. Opening the mail, she mumbled to herself, "Here's a letter from the division commander. I wonder what he has to say." She opened the letter. She startled. "It's an invitation to dinner at the general's mess. This is big." She glanced at the calendar, and then reached for the phone. "We'll have to clear a couple of things from the schedule. I'd better call them back right away and let them know we're coming." At that dinner we would meet the general's aides, the brightest bachelor officers.

Wherever we went, we were quickly surrounded by attractive, intelligent men. But we never knew which ones were married. This general had certified his aides to be single.

In training, the Red Cross director had warned, "Some men will not tell you that they are married. If you want to know if a man is married, ask his commander. He will know, and tell you."

Thursday, July 28

An officer from the 1/9th Cavalry, air reconnaissance, telephoned. "We're celebrating our 100th Anniversary. We want to invite the Red

Cross girls and the nurses." The men usually invited the women when they had a party. "It will start in three hours. I'm sorry. We didn't find out about it until a day and a half ago."

We usually had more than three hours to get ready for a party, but for a 100th Anniversary, we could do it. On time, a tall captain wearing an old-fashioned black Cavalry hat with a gold band stood in the door of our tent to escort us. I thought, *Wow. Does he look sharp. A Cavalry hat, right out of history.* The captain drove the bouncing jeep with all four of us clinging to it. "We threw everything together. Nobody knew it was our 100th Anniversary until we got a note from our counterpart, the Vietnamese 9th Cavalry, to congratulate us." I thought, *They've been busy fighting the war.* "We went scrambling to our records, and, sure enough, it's our 100th Anniversary.[1] We started to work on it on the double. We pulled all the men in from the field, set up the banquet, and a day and a half later, here we are. We appreciate you girls coming on such short notice."

The evening had begun with the banquet of wine and steak. We arrived late, so by the time we ate, the party was well underway. Our dinner completed, all the Red Cross girls left the table for the ballroom. As I walked through the double doors, a captain put his arm around me. "Would you like a drink?" Military and Red Cross protocol dictated that nobody touched us. Putting an arm around us was unheard of. It annoyed me. But these men had been in the jungle and could be excused some things. I smiled, ignored the question, and walked on. People were singing accompanied by a guitar, and then a band arrived. Dancing was fast and energetic. The party got louder. By now it was on the verge of a fight. The 9th Cavalry was known for its bad behavior. I figured, *That's what you have to be for reconnaissance.*

I was having a good time, except for the groping captain. Every time I got near him he put his arm around me, frustrating my attempt to stay away from him. He was the burdock seeds that used to cling to my socks when I was a kid. I went outside where it was warm and humid and was talking to a group of people when someone came up behind me, put his arm around my waist, and pulled me away to another group. I thought, *Keep your hands off me.* It was the captain, drunk by now. "I want you to meet some people." I let him introduce me to three or four officers and then excused myself. I was gone about a minute, when that arm went around me again. He knew, when it came to the Red Cross girls, the rule was: don't touch.

I became angry. I took a judo position and gave a short yell, "Hhaa. Get away!" I hoped he would get the hint. All officers had learned judo in basic training. He understood, but he didn't believe me. I calculated, *He's tall, so I'll have to use the leg throw, even if it's easier to defend against. He's strong.* I took him by the collar and sleeve. "Are you ready? I'm going to throw you."

He said, "OK, I'm ready." *I think he's enjoying this. Not for long.* I rehearsed the move as I executed it. I didn't want to hurt him. I pulled him toward me, stepped behind and kicked his legs out from under him. *He didn't defend against me.* I pulled up on his arm to keep him from landing on his face, and let go. I should not have let him go. I should have continued to pull up on his arm, to make sure he landed on his back so he wouldn't be hurt. But I was angry. He flew into the air, bouncing off two people, then off a wall. I saw him lying on his back stretched out on the ground. Two dozen people stood there, drinks in their hands, staring at him.

Our escort instantly appeared. He picked up my watch and handed it to me, ordering me to "Come this way." He steered me through the crowd to the jeep and steadied me while I climbed in. I was wobbly because one of my shoe heels had broken off. Another officer guided the other girls. The jeep headed for home. Our escort said guardedly, "Did you see the green tabs on his epaulets?" My eyes fell on our escort's shoulder—a green tab. "He's a combat leader."[2] I thought, *He could have killed me.* "He must have been humiliated to have you throw him like that." *In front of all those officers. Some reported directly to him.* I admired his restraint. *He had a great deal of self control to let me do that.* It was true that the military trained men to be officers and gentlemen, even when they were drunk.

Our escort laughed, "That was a good party. The only fight we had was yours."

Sunday, July 31

In Vietnam I learned to adapt to everything. Falling in love was not part of my survival training. One week after we received the invitation to the general's mess, six of us got ready to go to the year's social event. In the half-light of the electric bulbs we couldn't see each other over the six-foot partitions. We couldn't see to put on makeup, either, but nobody complained.

Sandra's voice came over the screen, "I'm going to wear my yellow dress." It had just arrived through the PX catalog. "There's a single captain at the general's mess. I saw him. He's handsome."

"Well, I'm breaking out my special perfume," Nancy rang back. She had bought real French perfume during her assignment in Korea.

I joined the chorus. "OK, everybody. I'm going into the competition. I'm wearing my red patent leather high-heeled shoes." I had raised the stakes. Nobody could answer.

The escort came on time. Sandra whispered, "That's him. That's the captain." I thought, *She's right. But he's even more than attractive.* He had military-cut brown hair, sharp blue eyes, and a strong jaw. He was medium height with an athletic build. We walked in the dark a few yards. The captain, unusually attentive, shined a flashlight at our feet to catch every step on the dirt footpath.

Outside the mess tent, General Norton introduced an enlisted man. Young, tall, and spare, his nervous eyes reflected his shyness. He wore stiff, new fatigues and new boots. General Norton explained, "He did a fine job for us in the field. We brought him up here to show our appreciation." The military doesn't wear medals on fatigues. He must have received an important one because the general was giving him the highest reward he could. He had brought the private out of the field to be recognized by command officers and staff, and to provide a break from combat. Each of us greeted the hero.

General Norton stood a bit taller than most men, with dark hair, sharp features, and a few worry lines. Hollywood handsome, his confidence revealed his strength. His fatigues were clean and pressed. He wore two black stars on his shirt collar. He didn't wear a nametag, a custom of the highest-ranking officer.

When I was in Korea at Camp St. Barbara, I ate at the general's mess for three months. On that night in Vietnam I knew that, as a visitor, I might find myself seated next to the general with the top officers. All of them were charming, but in their 40's and 50's. I would rather make conversation with people my own age. However, where you found generals, you found generals' aides, the sharpest men in the Army.

A tent like our living quarters housed the general's mess at An Khe. The general led us inside. A special water resistant wax or oil kept out rain, but not insects and animals like lizards, mosquitoes, and other annoyances. A table long enough for 20 people was at the center of the tent. The aides would be at the end farthest from the general. That's where I had to be when the staff announced dinner. I needed good timing. Etiquette said that I should be introduced to everyone for mandatory conversation before dinner.

General Norton introduced each of us by name. He called me "Ms Puffer" in his Virginia drawl. He had learned our names from reports, because we wore civilian clothes with no nametags. Even with uniforms, our nametags gave only our first names. He had done his homework.

In the moments before dinner I met important people, including two other generals. I looked for their aides and spotted two lieutenants

in the crowd of officers. Lieutenants Brennan and Burton, as their nametags read, stood at a distance and watched their bosses, alert for any
sign they needed anything. General Norton introduced a man in civilian clothes, "This is General Marshall. He's visiting us." No more information than that. General Marshall was stocky and well built, with a
graying brush cut. He wore a short sleeve shirt and slacks. I assumed he
was an active-duty general, but he wore no insignia and had no aides.

I didn't know at the time, that "General Marshall" was the prolific
S. L. A. Marshall, chief US Army combat historian during World War II
and the Korean War. He authored some 30 books about warfare, including *Pork Chop Hill: The American Fighting Man in Action,* which was
made into a film of the same name.[3]

General Norton introduced his chief of staff, a colonel; the commanders of his staff functions, personnel, intelligence, and operations,
three lieutenant colonels; and the command sergeant major, the highest
enlisted rank. The operations officer, Lt. Col. Jim Mapp actually conducted the war. We had met him on the perimeter after the mortar attack in early June, which he had called "a good practice." The other staff
officers, and the thousands of people who reported to them, supported
the operations function. Those men would see combat at a distance.

I hurried to the aide's place ahead of the other girls. Each of us chose
a different portion of the table, so we could sit with as many people as
possible. It was pleasant work. When a cook announced dinner, I took
my seat, pleased with my tactics. Next to me were two warrant officers
and a lieutenant colonel. I had chosen the right place, but I forgot to
notice who would sit there. Older men surrounded me. I wasn't sorry
for my mistake, though. They were pleasant but they were not part of
my strategy. The two chairs across from me were empty, however, and
farther down the table sat a captain and lieutenant. The warrant officer
on my right remarked, "The only two bachelors in the mess, and they're
sitting alone. Come here and sit with us, Sirs." They both got up and

moved toward us, smiling. I was not surprised that all the higher officers, even the aides, were married. The Army preferred married men. They felt they were more responsible than single men. They weren't as likely to do something outside of the play book and risk getting killed.

The warrant officer introduced me to the bachelors. We shook hands across the table. Captain Windsor was the officer who had escorted us to the mess. He stood when the warrant officer introduced us, showing precise manners and the lieutenant followed his lead. Captain Windsor appeared military stiff with a correct smile. His warmth hid just beneath the surface. I asked the captain, "What did the general mean when he introduced the PFC and said, 'He did a fine job for us in the field'?"

Captain Windsor answered, "I don't think I was present for that introduction. Maybe I was distracted and didn't hear it."

I persisted, "I took it to mean that the man was a hero, and his reward was a safe job in the rear."

Captain Windsor replied as if on the record, "I was not included in the decision to bring him to serve on the division staff. That was probably something that was arranged by the division sergeant major, Westerfeldt." *Translation: Likely.*

I asked, "Do they do that often?"

The captain answered, "General Norton is a compassionate man. He constantly looks for chances to reward the actions of his command, officers and enlisted men, that are beyond the call of duty." *Translation: yes.*

I guessed that the PFC had received the Medal of Honor. Otherwise, why did the aide use the phrase "beyond the call of duty"? I asked, "Do you know the man?"

"No, unfortunately not." I could see that I would never find out.

During dinner Captain Windsor's etiquette was impeccable. His conversation was polite, and he listened to everything I said. My year teaching in Alabama had shown me that most Army men follow the

military tradition of the South. Captain Windsor was a Southern gentleman. Yet, I couldn't hear a Southern accent.

General Norton's cooks didn't serve special food. In Vietnam, the
best supplies went to the people in the field. All the mess halls in the
division that evening, including the general's, served the same menu.
The tradition is: If the food is good, the army should do well.

The base camp at An Khe got ordinary food. But, the soldiers in the
field got better provisions. I used to think that the baked beans tasted
like sand. But Army cooks didn't get enough credit. It took effort to
make the food taste passable. The kitchen staff worked under difficult
conditions. They fed thousands of men with food that came halfway
around the world. In Vietnam they even had to bake their own bread. If
the beans tasted like sand, they probably were part sand.

The intoxicating conversation made up for the meal. I felt sorry for
our new unit director. Protocol said her seat was at the head of the table
with the gray-haired General Marshall. But I was having a great time.
Captain Windsor charmed us, me in particular, as he entertained everyone with his stories.

We had just had heavy rains and cool weather. We girls had been
lucky, though. Our tent had remained dry and sturdy.

The captain portrayed his experience with the storm. "My [two-
man] tent is sturdier than most others. It's on a metal frame instead of
wooden poles. The morning after the winds and rains I crawled out and
the other tents around me were flattened. I was lucky." Listeners winced.

"Later that day someone called me and suggested that I should go
home. My tent had blown over. It was raining hard at the time. The wind
had picked up the tent, frame and all, and turned it over. The weather
had destroyed everything that was left. The telephone was hanging a
dozen feet up in a tree." We laughed. Living was rough at An Khe.

Late in the dinner I noticed Lieutenant Colonel Mapp, the operations officer, sitting by himself. He had coffee but no food. He talked

on the telephone non-stop. We always tried to include everyone in our conversations. I asked him, "Are you going to eat?"

He said, "No. Too busy. For the past two days, it's been cigarettes and phone calls." The phone rang again. I watched him. This was the first time I had seen him up close without his helmet on. He was a striking man, tall, with chiseled features and streaks of gray in his hair. Eye catching, but married. I wasn't about to fall into a trap.

When everyone had finished dessert, Norton stood and invited us to see a movie in an adjoining tent. As the guests rose and moved toward the door, General Norton approached me and asked, "Will you join me?" As the host, he set the agenda.

As my mother had taught me, I had been watching him for cues. I was able to give the right response, "Thank you. I'd love to." Inside the tent I saw a movie screen at one end and rows of folding chairs like a theater. War maps decorated the walls. The general escorted me to the place of honor on his right. All those days when I ate at the general's tables in Korea had paid off. I was comfortable. I was with a man who was responsible for the welfare of tens of thousands of people. He honored me.

Into the movie, several explosions shook the tent. The audience of high-ranking men had all been in combat. They had been subjected to "in-coming rounds" and hostile acts before. They were cool. It was another day at the office. It was as if someone had said, "Your 2:00 appointment is here." They looked at each other to see what their reactions were. We listened and focused on the sounds. We didn't hear any nearby tents or buildings crash, or more explosions. Without speaking, these commanders formed a consensus. They should find cover and wait. Mortar attacks on An Khe base had become routine. The camera operator stopped the movie. A phone rang. General Norton took the call, listened for a minute, and then hung up. As the commanding general he was responsible for the welfare of his people. The general announced, "I have decided to return the guests to their quarters." Hastily, everyone thanked the general for the evening. Captain Windsor escorted the six of us back along the uneven dirt footpath to our tent.

I thought back to college. After a party, we girls would stay up half the night to talk about everything that happened, reliving the big moments. We would discuss what every move and conversation meant. That didn't happen after parties in Korea or Vietnam. In Vietnam everybody worked seven days a week. Tomorrow was just another day, and the Army rose early.

With no intrigue to discuss, we went to bed. It was a dinner with all married men. I had sat with the only prospects. We had given the officers a memory of home, a chance to have dinner with the girl next door. We did our jobs well as the Red Cross expected us to do. The general had introduced us to his staff, and we had shown him we could help morale.

During the dinner, my end of the table was different, however. The warrant officer had set us up. He invited us to take an interest when he said, "The captain is a bachelor." The captain and I secretly romanced each other. The others couldn't help but feel the low-voltage electricity.

I learned that the day after the general's mess, the 1st Air Cavalry Division started Operation Paul Revere II.[4] The general and his staff went to Pleiku. He had timed our visit to his mess as a last minute boost for his staff just before a month-long battle, ". . . the whopper of the summer."[5]

Tuesday, August 2

Two days after we went to the general's mess, I packed to leave An Khe. Late in the afternoon, the phone rang. "Red Cross, Joann."

"Hello, I love you. I want to come and see you before you leave."

I figured, *It must be one of the gang, but I don't recognize the voice.* "Oh? That's fine, who is this?" I thought, *I can't fake it. I have to ask.*

He said, "Bob." We knew that many people, including VC, could listen on the line. Names of officers were classified and not spoken over the phone. We used first names or call signs. An enlisted man would have told me his last name. I thought *OK, that means he's an officer.* Now I began to wonder, *Could this be Captain Windsor? What <u>was</u> his first name?*

I asked, "Bob who?" I winced. *This is not the way to make a good impression.*

"The one you came to see last night." I thought *He's talking about our having dinner at the general's mess on Sunday. It <u>is</u> Captain Windsor.*

I asked, "Where are you?"

"Pleiku."

"What are you doing there?"

"My boss is here, so I have to be here." *He's referring to the general.* "But I really want to come and see you before you leave."

Thursday, August 4

Few of the military flew at night; no one flew through thunderstorms, but Captain Windsor did. Two days later, at 7:00 at night, he flew through a thunderstorm from Pleiku to be with me for an hour and a half. The captain had called to tell me he was coming, but I was busy in the back of the tent and I didn't get his call. I was in my work uniform when he arrived. Liz, who was sharing a beer with a sergeant in our sitting room, came to get me. Embarrassed, I went to the front to welcome Bob. I was thrilled to see him. We smiled at each another. The men never minded if they had to wait for us to change. It was special for them to see us in civilian clothes. I asked, "Would you mind waiting while I put on some regular clothes?"

He surprised me, insisting, "I came to see you. I want you here." I thought, *This is unusual. This man wants to see <u>me</u>. He's looking past the uniform and sees me. I'm not just another American girl.*

After I invited him to sit down, Bob explained, "I asked the general for permission to leave when he was busy. Distracted, he said, 'Yes, go, go.' I took his helicopter and flew down. I justified the trip by setting the staff to getting all kinds of reports and papers for the general." Bob had decided to fly through a thunderstorm in a "rustled" helicopter to see *me*. If the ship had gone down, he wouldn't have lived through the crash. I shuddered. The excitement had begun to build.

We sat side by side on lawn chairs in the front of the tent and drank warm soda in the piercing heat. People walked in and out of the room and shared our conversation. Everyone understood no one had much privacy. He asked me the question that everyone seemed to want answered, "Why did you join the Red Cross?"

I explained how I made the decision, "I came to Vietnam to make it easier for the people who have to be here."

He confirmed I had made a difference. "Your visit to the general's mess created quite a stir for the staff. It was a highlight for everyone."

I was flattered. "What did they do?"

He smiled, "Word spread in the headquarters that the Donut Dollies were coming to dinner. We all tried to hide our excitement. But our hearts were thumping to a quick time beat."

"What is quick time?"

"Regular march cadence is 120 beats per minute, quick time is 180." We both laughed. I thought, *This man is really military.* He said in a low voice, "I was attracted by your red shoes. I was taken with them when I first saw them. When I was escorting you girls to the general's mess I kept the flashlight on those shoes the whole way. I couldn't get my eyes off them." *I thought he was just being overly careful to show us the way. My red shoes didn't let me down.* I admired his candor. He continued, "I was struck by your fingernails when we shook hands across the table. I wanted to kiss them." He saw the surprise in my smile. "I didn't want to let you go." *I had no idea. He hides his feelings well. My diamond nail file worked its magic, and he wanted to kiss my hand.* My heart melted. I hoped he wouldn't notice my blush.

Liz and her sergeant stood up. They said good night to us and to each other, and he left. She went into the back of the tent.

I asked Bob, "At dinner, who was General Marshall?"

He answered with respect, "That was Brigadier General S. L. A. Marshall, the military historian. He's known world-wide for his accurate war stories. He's here to gather material for a book.[6] It will be published after his visit."

I thought, *Talk about foolish. I passed up a chance to have dinner with a famous man. Bob is a close second, though. On second thought, I made the right choice.* "Who did General Marshall sit with during the movie?"

Bob sat erect in his chair, "Sorry. You may have detected my attention was in your direction." *What? No, I hadn't "detected." Go ahead and shock me.* My face felt flaming and I was glad the light was so poor. My heart pounded. I couldn't speak and looked away. I thought, *I have got to get him off this subject before I make a fool of myself and kiss him.* We both knew people would start rumors. My value to the military and to the Red Cross would be gone, and I'd be sent home.

I tried not to choke on my words, "Who were the two one-star generals, Becker and Wright?"

Composed, the captain answered, "Those are General Norton's two assistant division commanders. Becker is support, administration and logistics, and Wright is maneuver, overview of operations." My fogged brain knew that "operations" meant carrying out the war. A twinkle in his eye told me he had heard the waver in my voice. *He knows he caught me off guard. He's clever.* Miriam came home and I recovered. After introducing herself, she told my guest that she was from South Carolina. He said he was from Georgia. They chatted about the people they knew, and then she went into the back. I felt more composed. *I've got to watch out for him.* He continued from the conversation with Miriam, "I went to a military school in north Georgia."

"But you don't have a Southern accent."

"I knew people would notice the accent instead of me. I worked at losing it." *I was right. He's part of the Southern military tradition.* He continued to tell me about himself. "I graduated with the rank of lieutenant colonel." I didn't know what that meant. "That's the second highest rank. The only rank higher is the brigade commander, the colonel. Only one man held that rank." I had no idea what he was talking about. The only graduation rank I knew about was based on academic grades. *He's trying to help me get to know him in one visit, because I have to leave An Khe.* "In my first job in Vietnam I was a scout. I arrived in April as a replacement for H-13 scout pilots who were lost in the Ia Drang conflict." An H-13 was the two-seater helicopter with a plastic bubble cockpit, which I had ridden in in Korea. I had heard about the fierce battle of Ia Drang. I thought, *That must have been encouraging.* "We need you to do this job. Everybody who tries to do it gets killed." I gasped.

The captain continued, "I was initially assigned to A Troop 1st Squadron 9th Cavalry, under Lt. Col. Jim Smith." *That's the unit that had the 100th Anniversary celebration last week.* "My job was to look for the enemy." Bob continued, "I flew around until someone shot at me, then I called in the Cavalry."

That would be a good way to get killed. "Wasn't that dangerous?"

"It was. There was limited capability to shoot back. The aircraft was armed with machine guns. They were unreliable. Or, we had rockets. But, they weren't accurate because the helicopter was too light. You hoped the VC didn't hit you." *You're looking for someone to shoot at you, and you can't shoot back?* The captain elaborated, "It took both hands and both feet to fly an H-13. It was a challenge to shoot at anything." *It was a suicide flight.*

I responded, "I know that most officers wear a .45 sidearm, but that was designed for self-defense. I fired a .45 once. It had a terrific kick. You have to use both hands to cock it. You hold it in one hand and slide the barrel toward you with the other, right?" I had to change our conversation to something that wouldn't embarrass me.

Bob took out his .45. He held it in one hand and used his other to grab the top of the barrel. "You're almost right. You take hold of the slide which is over the barrel and bring that back toward you." He passed his hand over the slide to show how it would move. He pointed at the weapon and explained, "It has safeties on the slide and on the grip and trigger."[7] He re-holstered the pistol.

"A .45 wouldn't be much good in an H-13, when you need both hands to fly," I concluded. I was managing to redirect the conversation more to my comfort.

He continued, "The 45-caliber semiautomatic pistol, M1911A1, developed in 1911, is the largest caliber handgun in the US Army inventory. There are many stories about it. They say a 2nd Lieutenant in a combat zone was asked why he carried a .45. He answered, 'Because they don't make a .46.'"

"I understand a .45 is accurate up close. Could you hit a target from an H-13?" I was sustaining the harmless conversation.

"Not likely. We don't fly that low." The captain added, "Pilots are issued a .38 caliber revolver which is easier to fire." The .38 was ineffective under most circumstances.

"Now I'm in the general's office." I could hear him sigh. His relief conflicted with his hopes to rise through the officers' ranks. The best way to get promoted was as a combat officer. I remembered the shy hero in the general's office. He was there because "He had done a fine job in the field." Captain Windsor must have "done a fine job in the field," too, if General Norton had promoted him. I wondered what medal he had received.

I asked the captain, "Why did General Norton invite me to sit with him during the movie after dinner? Because I'm being transferred?"

Nothing betrayed what he thought. "I gave him credit for being a smart man." A twinkle appeared in his eye. I laughed. He had shocked me again. *That may be the best compliment I have ever received.* I think my face was hotter than the steaming tent.

It was time for my visitor to go. Miriam and a major sat talking in the other chairs. Bob took a few steps toward the tent door. Miriam and her guest averted their eyes. I thought, *I am going to get a great kiss.* I wanted to kiss him back. Instead, he shook my hand. I was disappointed, but then I realized he was an old-fashioned man who didn't kiss on the first date. He gave me a warm look and departed for his jeep outside the tent. I stood in the doorway and waved as he drove away. My heart hurt. The bumper markings said "DIV HQ 6," Division Headquarters Commander. He probably used the general's jeep whenever he needed to, but it impressed me.

A few minutes later, I heard a roar and saw a chopper take off from the general's helicopter pad, a roar like none I had ever heard. The jet engine seemed to express his hidden excitement. He flew low, landing lights still on, until he was almost overhead. I ran outside and waved, and he hovered even lower, close to blowing down our tent. I thought, *He thinks he loves me.* If I didn't love him, I was still sorry to see him go.

Two days later I transferred to Dong Ba Thin. A win or a loss?

Saturday, August 6, Landing Zone Oasis, Pleiku

That afternoon I traveled from An Khe to my assignment at Dong Ba Thin. I had an escort wherever I went. That day I had no escort.

I raced out to the An Khe airfield at 1:30 to catch the 2:00 flight to Cam Ranh Bay. The Army dispatcher at flight operations told me, "That flight is full, but you can get on the regular 3:00 run." No need to hurry. I unloaded my luggage from the jeep.

For the next two hours the dispatcher bumped me off one flight and onto another. Finally he said. "I can schedule you on a flight that will come in at 4:00. It's a Caribou from Dong Ba Thin that's working for the Cavalry. It is taking troops to Oasis." That was a landing zone west of

Pleiku near the Cambodian border. "When it's finished, it will go back to Dong Ba Thin, empty."

Later, the dispatcher made still another change. "We've discovered that there are so many troops going to Oasis that the Caribou will have to make an extra trip. You can ride with the last load of troops. The plane can go to Dong Ba Thin from there, instead of coming back to An Khe to pick you up."

Operation Paul Revere II was five days old. That explained why so many planes were flying to Pleiku. The dispatcher had worked hard to get me on a flight; he had scheduled a plane to make a special trip to pick me up. It wasn't the first time someone had done something like that for the Red Cross girls and I suspected that it happened more than we knew. When I got to the runway, about 30 soldiers were already waiting. They didn't move around on the blazing-hot, empty runway. Standing near them, I overheard the movement control officer say to a mechanic, "One of our ships got hit at Oasis and isn't flyable."

The mechanic answered, "So that's why we keep getting behind. That landing zone must be hot."

The officer answered, "Must be. Help me with these bags." I thought, *Oasis is a hot landing zone?* When the dispatcher put me on the transport he told me it would make a stop at Oasis, and then go to Dong Ba Thin. "Hot" meant there was a war. I would fly into the war. I couldn't tell how many of the troops also heard the conversation. I thought, *That must be part of the back-up that has bumped me all afternoon. One of the ships has been shot down.* That made me apprehensive, but there was nothing I could do. Besides, lots of ships had come and gone all day. Only one had been shot down. The odds looked good.

My plane came in a half hour late loaded with cargo. I watched to see what would come back from Oasis. First, the ground crew pulled off boxes of cigarettes. When troops were in the field the Army gave them free cigarettes. In base camp, soldiers had to buy them. Next, the workers unloaded duffel bags. That surprised me since soldiers usually carried their own duffels. Rain and mud had soaked the bags. Instead of Army green, they were red-chocolate brown. The wet bags contrasted with the crisp boxes of cigarettes. The tired crew inside the plane dragged the bags to the cargo door and heaved them to the edge of the runway, as if they were indestructible.

I remembered I had heard that a company of the 5th Cavalry had been wiped out the day before. Probably a rumor. The company more likely had been in a fight, but had not actually been wiped out. I wondered if these bags were the personal belongings of the men who had been killed. Some of the bags fell open. One spilled out some pieces of paper. Probably they were pages from a letter. A crewman scooped the pages up, stuffed them back into the bag, yanked the top shut, and gave it a heave. One page blew away.

A bag full of baseball bats came off the plane. The fresh troops looked on in their clean fatigues and new helmet covers, though no one had spit-shined his boots. The men had packs on their backs; hand grenades hung around their bodies; mosquito repellent and gun oil stuck in helmet bands. Each man seemed to have glued his rifle to himself. The men stood, some with weapons slung by the strap over one shoulder. Others held their M-16s by the handle with one hand, down at their sides, or with the butt resting on the ground. They moved little, didn't talk, and their crisp posture had faded. They had been standing and waiting for some time in that heat.

I looked at the soldiers and then at the sad duffels that flew through the air. Did each bag represent someone who had stood here a day or two before? Had that man watched the bags come off another plane? Would some of these men follow him and would their possessions be heaved off a plane tomorrow without care? I thought of the Chinook that had landed near the hospital last month. A covered truck backed up to it and men unloaded black body bags. It was hard to find dignity in death when there was so much of it. If we mourn the dead or think about them too much, we would be frozen. We had to harden ourselves, otherwise we would break. Crewmen continued to heave the bags like sacks. The bags landed side by side, with military precision, in neat rows. At first it had looked like the crewmen threw the bags with disregard but after awhile I saw it was with care and precision.

I looked at the faces of the soldiers who waited, and wondered which ones would come back. I stopped myself, remembering what Major Hayne had told me: "You assume you will come back. You have to."

I stood on the airstrip now. My thoughts shifted to watch men getting off another plane that had just landed. The soldiers looked like the duffel bags. From helmet to boot, mud had soaked them through. Even their faces and hands were brown. They looked tired. I was relieved.

These were the men who belonged with the bags I had seen earlier. To make it easier on the combat-worn soldiers, the Army had transported their bags on a different plane. The men sagged with a fatigue that comes when adrenalin is drained. They were safe. I felt myself quietly smile at how filthy they were. They were a contrast to my fresh memories of shined and buffed soldiers in the States and Korea. The difference between the exhausted and fresh soldiers was remarkable— these were two faces of warriors.

The crew finished unloading the plane and we scrambled aboard. Thirty of us sat against the sides facing center, and from the front, I could see everyone. Every man on board lit up a cigarette as if on cue when the loaded Caribou took off. Every one was smoking, even though I knew that not everybody smoked regularly. They were nervous. Had some of them overheard the mechanic say that LZ Oasis was hot? They were young. Once again I wondered which ones wouldn't return and stopped myself. No good to think. That flight was the same as the bunker when I sat and listened to the shells fly overhead. I needed something to occupy my mind. In the bunker, it was a conversation. To these men, in an airplane too noisy to talk, it was a cigarette. Maybe the Army knew what it was doing, issuing cigarettes to men in combat.

The first thing I always did with a group of soldiers was smile. That was all it usually took to lighten them up. I smiled. They didn't smile back. In training we had been taught how to catch a man's eye and smile. I tried that. One man gave me a half-hearted smile. No one else responded. They were stressed. That wasn't going to work.

I got out my diamond nail file and filed my nails, the feminine gesture that had delighted the door gunner on the way to Buon Blech. The magic failed. I put on some fresh lipstick, another gesture that men found endearing. Still no one responded. Nothing worked. Instead of smiling I realized that it would be better just to look pleasant. I settled back and tried to relax. They knew I appreciated how they felt.

The plane engines were too noisy for anyone to talk, but one man asked me where I was from. It was a question everyone asked each other. I was tired of it, but this time it didn't bother me. I gave him the answer that always got a laugh. Since so many men were from the South, I would answer, "I'm from the South, southern Michigan." He appreciated my joke.

Well into the flight, one of the more bold soldiers asked the crew chief, "The area we're going to. Is it hot?" I thought, *Yes, they know.*

The crew chief shook his head. "Naw, there's nothing much going on."

The boy couldn't believe his ears. "Nothing going on? Really?" It was too noisy to frame the obvious question, *Then, why send all of us up there in such a rush?* The answer was the crew chief had lied. Oasis itself may have been quiet—only one plane had been hit—but near there, where the troops would go, the Viet Cong were waging a fierce battle. The weathered crew chief knew it was best to ease the tension. It seemed to work a little. Nobody needed to confirm that the troops had waited so long for a ride because their plane was shot down, at LZ Oasis.

One man asked me, "Are *you* going the same place *we're* going?" I gave him a pleasant smile and said, "No, I'm going on."

About half an hour into the flight, the crew chief sat down and strapped himself in. The drone of the engines changed to a deep growl, and the wing flaps whined to maximum drag. The nose of the aircraft dropped; we went into a steep dive. The plane shook. Gravity pulled me forward out of my seat as we plunged toward the earth. The landing gear ground open and thumped into place. The pilot couldn't abort and try a second time if he came in wrong. He had to be right the first time, with a load of troops and their gear. He knew the VC were watching.

Finally we leveled off, then landed, fast and hard. The engines revved up to a scream, straining to stop the loaded Caribou on a short runway. We had made a combat approach to a hot zone. Cruising at altitude, we were safe and on the ground, no hostile fire in the zone threatened us. The danger lay when we descended into the range of fire from the ground. If the VC had shot at us, we hadn't heard it. If they had hit us, as long as we could still fly, the mechanics would only count the bullet holes.

If this had been a helicopter drop with enemy fire, the aircraft would have stayed on the ground for a few seconds. Everyone would have had to dive out shooting and running for cover. When we landed at LZ Oasis in our Caribou, however, no one hurried to get out of the aircraft. I spoke to the men as they got off after some of the noise had stopped. "When you get back, come over to our recreation center. It's right next to 2nd Surgical Hospital, under the big yellow Cavalry patch." It was the right thing to say. Major Hayne's words helped several of them visibly relax and smile.

A handful of men commented, "I may do that." "I'll have to do that." I had assumed that they would come back. Major Hayne had told me never to lose my optimism. These boy-soldiers needed all the encouragement they could get. I didn't know if it lasted until they got out of the plane, but for a moment they smiled. I hoped that the soldiers knew what I was trying to do for them. I had learned from the doctors in the mess hall that if a wounded man could get to the hospital, he had a 98 percent chance of survival. These men would be all right. Out of 30, a few might be wounded, but they would all make it back home.

But the doctor had said, "we don't count head wounds." What did he mean by that? That head wounds were fatal more often? It's better not to think.

The Caribou now empty, the pilot suggested, "Would you like to ride in the cockpit?" Pilots did that for Red Cross girls, even when the aircraft was full. I was sure the pilots kept me with the soldiers on the inbound flight because they knew the men would benefit. Take off repeated the hot landing in reverse: a short, fast sprint down the runway, a leap into the sky, a climb, engines racing, the plane straining, and then we leveled off and relaxed into the familiar cruise drone. Safe at altitude again, the pilot invited me to fly the plane. I was eager to try. I loved it. Those moments in the cockpit too, were part of my work. They gave the pilots reminders of home, as we cruised toward our base.

Part II:
Dong Ba Thin

✚ CHAPTER 5 ✚

Poison Booth at the Carnival

Saturday, August 6, 1966, Dong Ba Thin, South Vietnam

Some secrets are meant to be shared, some to be hidden. Dong Ba Thin was a self-contained civilization, a small unit with Susie, Gini, and me. My new home was a green Quonset hut. It sat in the middle of an open area away from other buildings. There was a perfect palm tree in the front yard. No guards, no barbed wire, and no bunker. Inside, the hut had the same configuration as our tent at An Khe: a sitting room in the front and small bedrooms partitioned off in the back. You could hear everything in the house. A small patio with a privacy fence on two sides adjoined the house. We could lie outside and sunbathe.

Every morning my clock radio woke me up to Adrian Cronauer's morning show. He was on Armed Forces Radio in Cam Ranh Bay. Robin Williams made Cronauer famous in 1987 in the movie, *Good Morning, Vietnam*.[1] I hadn't heard him at An Khe. He was as good as any radio personality in the States, and he had a unique signature program opening. He greeted every new day with a hearty and elongated "GooOD MORning, Vietnam!" It was impossible to sleep through his signature line. He reminded everyone where they were. We all groaned

117

Dong Ba Thin girls in the recreation center. Left to right: Susie, Joann, and Gini.

at the sound of his wake-up call. He repeated his loud greeting through-out his show.

Every evening Captain Windsor called me. Maybe he did love me.

Wednesday, August 10, Tuy Hoa

On this day, four days after I arrived at Dong Ba Thin, I had been in Vietnam for three months. Susie and I went to Tuy Hoa (pronounced "Too ee Wah"), a forward base camp. Susie was short with a round face and quick smile. All this, and she was easy going. She tied her long, brown hair in a twist. Until Tuy Hoa, the worst place I had ever been was the foxholes at Buon Blech in the Cambodian border hills. It was cold, rainy, and gloomy. Ground fire and snipers threatened every mile and every mud-slogging step.

Tuy Hoa defined the opposite. It sat about 120 miles north of Dong Ba Thin on the coast of the South China Sea. From our helicopter it looked like any other forward camp: row after row of tents. Tuy Hoa stretched like a beach without water, nothing in sight but sand in every direction. When we landed we jumped out and waved our "Thanks for the ride," to the pilots. They waved back, waited for us to get clear of the rotors, and then took off. The blast from the helicopter created a sandstorm. The tents strained against their stakes, their flaps snapped in the wind. We headed for shelter. The gale drove sand into my eyes. I put on sunglasses, but sand still blew into my eyes. Nonetheless we stumbled into an office.

Susie, who knew the clerk, introduced us. We checked the schedule with him and verified our plans. I was able to get the grains of sand out of my eyes, but they burned for the rest of the day because the sand was salty. When I could see again, we left the office. It was understandable why a now-anonymous commander had chosen this place. The Viet Cong wouldn't want to be there any more then we did. The sun blinded us, and its oven-like heat pounded us. The wind whipped through the camp the entire day. Helicopters came and went on one business or another. I learned that this wasn't just an isolated, bad day. It was the same for the two months I stayed at Dong Ba Thin. Sand blew into everything, our hair, our clothes, our food. My discomfort was short-term. Some of these men lived with this every day for months.

It was so hard to see that I never figured out where I was. All I saw were glimpses a few yards ahead, blasts of sand to the eyes, and then the inside of a tent. With each step, our shoes sank deep into the sand. It was perfect for a beach, but almost impossible to walk in. We took our loafers off frequently and poured the sand out like water. *How can these men stand to live here?* We Red Cross girls were eager to visit the worst places, because that was where the men needed us most. Tuy Hoa was so bad we took turns *not* wanting to visit. These men endured. They never even talked about the misery. The men at Buon Blech, another Hell, only talked about their discomfort when I asked them, but I didn't ask the soldiers at Tuy Hoa and they never volunteered their opinion. I think they were grateful nobody was shooting at them. Years later I met a veteran who had been stationed at Tuy Hoa and commented that it was a miserable place. He said he didn't think it was so bad. I thought, *I can't believe we're talking about the same camp.*

Susie and I walked around through the morning with armfuls of used paperbacks. In one mess hall after another, sheltered from the wind, we set the piles of books on a table and invited the men to take whatever they wanted, while we chatted and laughed with everyone. One fellow found a book with a picture of an attractive girl in a sheer nightgown on the cover. He saw me watching him and put it down. A moment later he turned the book over, picked it up, and said, "I like these science fiction books."

I said, "Good, I do, too."

At lunchtime, Susie and I split up and went to two different mess tents to serve a meal. I ate with the officers, so we could see them too. She ate in another mess hall. After lunch I made conversation with some of the men who worked there. I complained, "This wind is terrible. It makes my hair look awful."

A cook spoke up. "Frenchie, here, was a hairdresser in the States. Would you like him to cut your hair?"

I felt better. "Yes. Anything would help."

The deal was struck. Frenchie offered, "Let's go over to the medic tent. I can borrow a razor from them."

I sat with a towel around my neck. Medics and others who were in the area joked and teased. News spread everywhere that two ARC girls were in camp. Everyone was watching where we were and what we did. One medic queried, "Are you sure you want Frenchie to cut your hair?"

Another, "You believed him when he told you he knew how to cut hair?"

Still another, "You should see the last haircut he gave. It took months to grow out. You should see what he's doing to *your* hair."

I wasn't worried. I was pretty sure my hairdresser-cook knew what he was doing. A simple haircut had become a morale booster. I realized that most of these young men had never witnessed the mysteries of a girl getting her hair styled.

An angular, open-faced boy came into the tent. He asked me, "Were you in Korea?"

I looked at him hard and read his nametag. It was difficult to tell the color of his hair, it was so full of sand. Then I recognized him. "You were the recruit who sat beside me on the plane on the way to Korea." We shook hands as old friends. I remembered, "That was over two years ago." I had seen him twice after that in Korea, but only for a few minutes. "What are you doing here?"

He smiled, pleased that I had recognized him. "I spent a year there. Then I went to flight school. Now I'm a chopper pilot." I looked at his rank. He was a W-1, a warrant officer, with pilot wings. He had turned up in desolate Tuy Hoa. Small world.

The ARC recreation center at Dong Ba Thin was a permanent building with bright lights—one big room with an office walled off in a corner. A stream of men flowed through the center. Many sat together at four-man tables on hard, folding chairs. Some relaxed on aluminum lawn chairs. Others played cards, read magazines, worked the same wilted puzzles over and over, and played board games. They listened to a handful of 45 rpm records on our scratchy player until they wore it out.

After a few weeks we acquired two ping-pong tables. The men set them up and then never left them. The soldiers who came to the center didn't talk about their work. They came to get away. They didn't know much about what was happening around them and didn't want to. I circulated among them and played every game with them. As we played, we always talked about the games, never about their jobs. I didn't hear gossip or rumors as I had at An Khe.

One day we received a shipment of furniture from the Philippines. It was a major event. I asked the guys, "Would anyone like to help me unpack this furniture?" A dozen men attacked the boxes.

One man waved papers in his hand. "Here are the instructions. They're in a foreign language. Does anybody know how to read this?"

The men hesitated. A couple of them looked at it. "We don't need instructions." The shipment was a couple of couches and several easy chairs made of bamboo, fully assembled. They had loose cushions with a green and yellow bamboo-leaf design.

One man said, "I can hardly wait to sit on a soft chair."

Another said, "Yeah, it's been six months since I sat on a couch."

Another declared, "These are the only soft chairs anywhere around here." As soon as one piece was open, somebody sat on it.

I said, "Let's put this couch over there." The men who sprawled on it bounced out, lifted it like a toy, smacked it down close to where I indicated, then bounced back down before anybody could grab their place. I thought, *These men hardly know their own strength. What positive attitudes they have. I'm glad we can do something that makes them happy.*

August 1966

At Dong Ba Thin most of the activity revolved around the recreation center. It was open every day from 1:00 to 10:00 P.M. On Wednesday two of us took our weekly trip to Tuy Hoa. The third girl ran the center. Each day we had some unique activity, ranging from write-a-letter-home day to ping-pong and pinochle tournaments. Every week we planned a major event, such as a carnival, an art contest, or a pancake supper, on a different evening, when all three of us were there. The biggest successes we had were activities that gave the men memories of home.

The Red Cross Operation Helpmate, in Minneapolis-St. Paul, sent us packages every month full of games, puzzles, books, and pens. They also sent a weekly package of the latest hit records. The men played them non-stop. To a lonely, scared soldier in Vietnam, letters and packages from home, even from strangers, eased homesickness and took his mind off the heat. They helped him forget the war, his meager tent, and flavorless food. When a man received a letter, he reached for it with anticipation. As soon as he saw the handwriting, he felt the writer's presence; when he read the letter, he could hear the person's voice and see them and for a few minutes, he was home. As he read, he concentrated so hard that nothing disturbed him, his body bent over the letter to absorb its contents. He smiled with temporary contentment. When he finished, he looked around for someone to share the news. Sometimes, they received letters from schoolchildren they didn't know and talked about them for days.

The men had a sense that life in Vietnam was surreal. They needed to know that home was still there, just like when they left. The letters they got helped to get back perspective. They wanted to know what Aunt Jane and Uncle Joe and the neighbors were doing "back in the world." They wanted to know what the weather was like at home and what the temperature was. Those men who received pictures in their letters were the happiest. On the other hand, they didn't want anyone to ask them about the war, or to worry about them, especially those who were in combat.

In Korea and Vietnam, when a man opened a package from home, he touched America. When he bit into a cookie, he saw his Mom in her kitchen wearing an apron. He knew that people at home cared. When a soldier shared the treats, it was as if friends had for a moment joined his intimate family. Once when I was at An Khe, a lady's church group sent a large quantity of cookies in decorated coffee cans. I helped the chaplain give them out in the hospital.

Wide-eyed warriors reached for the gifts: "Is this real? Hey, don't forget me. You mean they really sent these to us? Hey, Miss, we sure do thank you." And the highest compliment of all, "Gosh, it's just like being home."

Every Red Cross unit held a planning meeting once a week. These meetings were all business, but relaxed and enthusiastic. Everybody contributed to taking care of administrative problems. Nobody wasted time. At one Susie said, "The needle on the record player doesn't work. Does anybody know how we can get it fixed?"

Gini responded. She had beautiful naturally white-blonde hair. "I'll ask an officer I met last week. He knows the shops in the village. Maybe someone can repair it."

And we wrote the recreation activities. I said, "For the art contest we are getting lots of entries, and we need an outside judge. Does anybody know who might want to do it?"

Susie answered, "Ask the clerk at Admin Company. He is an artist." We volunteered for assignments, and we decided everything by consensus. Everyone contributed ideas, and if anyone needed help, we all pitched in. One week Gini was going to use a quiz as an activity. We brainstormed questions and answers for her game. We always kept in mind that in training, the staff had told us, "The men will stand on their heads if you ask them to. Be careful not to make them look foolish."

At Dong Ba Thin, everything focused on the recreation center, and I felt a little out of place. I wasn't good at thinking up games for the carnival. I made a bigger contribution when I ran contests. I wanted to get back to combat units in the field and asked Saigon for a transfer.

Monday August 15

Today we held a carnival. We created a number of diversions. The unit already had a ring-toss and a throw-a-baseball game. With just three of us to man all the activities, we had to invent some that ran themselves. Some could be outdoors. The land adjacent to the center became a midway. We strung light bulbs across its length and breadth, creating a ceiling of lights as bright as daylight above the sand. Carnival attractions lined the wall of the building. Susie designed a fortune-telling booth. She fashioned a showy scarf around her head, put on some big hoop earrings and wrapped herself in a flowered shawl. She rigged up a crystal ball, and sat in the booth with a smile framed by red lipstick. Her sign said, "Fortune Teller." Anyone could see her from across the street.

The noise and lights brought men from everywhere. Groups of soldiers in combat boots crowded around the games. A murmur of conversation grew louder as the crowd swelled. Sporadically, shouts or groans went up from one of the games, as someone succeeded or failed in a ring toss or other sport. More men came as the noise increased. They crowded the center and the midway and tried all the games—except Susie's fortune-telling booth. The combat veterans left a wide open space around her, as if she were poison. Any other time, the men would have flocked to talk and laugh with Susie, but not then. Why? Had we touched a nerve? We had to solve the mystery.

How could Susie have been a flop? She was one of the five girls who started the original unit in Vietnam. When she rotated home in less than a month, she would be the first girl to complete a full tour. Her imagination produced some of our most successful ideas. If anybody could predict how the men would react, she could. We discussed it in our planning meeting afterwards.

I said, "This activity had all the elements of a winner. Susie could give each man attention. Lots of men could participate. There would be variety and spontaneity. What was wrong?"

Gini said, "Everybody likes to have their fortune told. The memory stays with people. It gives them something to talk about while they wait for the prediction to come true or not. We want the men to remember the good times they have at the center."

Susie wasn't used to failure. She leaned forward, her elbows on the table. She listened to the discussion. Suddenly her eyes lit up. She sat back in her chair, a satisfied smile on her face. "These are combat soldiers," she said slowly. "They don't want to know their future. Everything that makes this a good activity, makes it a bad activity for them."

These men's fear of their future was buried deeper than anyone knew. It was a secret they could not share. That was the first time any of us Red Cross girls had seen it. How much power did that fear have? None of us could guess, but I would glimpse it again several months later.

Many years later I related the story to a Marine who had known Susie at Danang. He responded, "I can appreciate how the troops felt about the fortune teller booth. Poor Susie, she must have been terribly puzzled. Through my travels in and around South East Asia I picked up on so many taboos, omens, signs, myths, legends, etc., I should have kept a journal. That subject alone would have made for some interesting reading."[2] This made me think of baseball players, who are notorious for their superstitions. Control of their situation is out of their hands. Though their situation is not as life-threatening as a soldier's, both seek help from a power stronger than themselves, be it magic or religious faith.

August 21

Captain Windsor has called me every day since I came to Dong Ba Thin. It's unbelievable. No one has ever paid this much attention to me. He confided that he loved me. He told me that General Norton writes a letter home to his wife every night. The general has told his staff that he believed that for a balanced life, everyone needed their work, their God, and a spouse. The captain expressed his hopes and dreams. He likes travel, card games, and sports cars, and he wants "to have one little girl to spoil." I wonder if this is love. His tenderness is winning me. The telephones are manually controlled, which makes for amusing times with the operators. They listen when they know an American girl is talking, but you can't tell if the switches are open unless someone speaks. At one point I asked, "I wonder how many operators are listening?"

A voice cut in, "Two at Typhoon switch."

Another said, "About 13, I'd say." Soon they were all chiming in. Last night when Bob and I said "goodnight" at least four operators wished us good evening. I think they have discovered that he is a captain, and they don't joke with us any more. They just listen quietly.

What does this lack of privacy do to courtship? We nurtured what we had and shared our hopes. Forming a powerful but impossible connection, like the twins I saw at Buon Blech, we anticipated what the other was thinking. Because we couldn't touch, our friendship deepened with our daily phone calls.

Why were we so attracted to each other when we didn't know each other well at all? There are many ways to bond or pursue a relationship. Some fall in love at first sight; for others it may take years. In training, the Red Cross cautioned us to be wary of our feelings. Separated from home and family, men quickly formed lasting bonds with other men, and this could also happen with women. The shared danger, the pressures of uncertainty, compelled both men and women to draw together for comfort and strength. In addition, a man might be attracted to an American girl because of her rarity. She represented home, the life he missed, when in the States he might not even notice her in a crowd. There are many complex facets to relationships between men and women and not all of them are sexual.

The girls never had enough Red Cross pins for their uniforms. Everybody wanted them as trophies. At Di An ("Zee on"), I ordered the supplies. Saigon allowed me to make a requisition once a month, six months in advance. The paperwork had to wind its way through Saigon, Japan, Washington, D.C., and who knew where else. I could only ask for four or five pins in any one order. Even though I stayed under the limit, headquarters often cut my order further. The pins were expensive and Saigon knew we would give them away. They were like money in a land without cash.

But, they were more. To the ARC girls they were a sign of the identity we had chosen, a small indicator that we were in Vietnam to make life more tolerable for the warriors, our younger brothers. I always kept an extra for fear of losing one from my uniform.

Everytime someone went home we put one on a plaque for a farewell present. Everybody took turns donating a pin for that. Otherwise, we gave them away only on special occasions. When I was in Korea, nine of us had gathered in our office at the end of the day. I noticed that one of the girls didn't have her pin on her collar and I pointed it out.

She was embarrassed, lowered her eyes, looked away, and mumbled, "I know."

The girl who had been with her, explained. "A Military Policeman stopped us. We knew we were going to get a ticket. The MP said how much he admired her Red Cross pin. She gave it to him, and he didn't write us up."

I had never heard of a Red Cross girl getting a traffic ticket. Because everyone watched everything we did, nobody ever did anything so bad as to get a traffic ticket. The Red Cross didn't just threaten to send us home: a girl in Korea was sent home because she *looked* like she broke a rule. People at our headquarters determined that she didn't care enough about how her actions appeared. Avoiding a traffic ticket was important enough to give away a Red Cross pin.

Sunday August 28, Nha Trang

Captain Windsor had been in the field for several weeks. He was allowed a day off, and I met him in Nha Trang shortly after noon. We both missed lunch because my plane was late, but I was so excited I wasn't hungry. The captain took me to a beach and introduced me to a handful of people, a few lieutenants and nurses, all lower ranking than he. They had a civilian speedboat and water ski equipment. It was amazing for a combat zone. They must have had high-placed connections.

When I first saw the people, I smiled to myself. The nurses looked good in their bathing suits, but the men, including the captain, were tanned only from the waist up. They had been wearing fatigues without shirts. I mentioned it to the captain and we shared a secret laugh.

The men prepared the boat and equipment. I expected that the captain and I would take the first turn on the skis because he was the highest-ranking officer. But the captain directed one of the other men to go first. When we moved away to a blanket, I expressed my surprise, "Shouldn't we go first?"

He answered, "No. It won't work the first time. Let them figure it out, then we'll take our turn." He was right. The first man got up on the skis and the motor quit. The man sank. That would have been embarrassing for the highest-ranking officer, but less so for a lieutenant. The men gathered around the boat in the shallow water. The captain joined them for a few minutes, and then came back and sat with me on the blanket while they worked on the problem. After two false starts the motor ran smoothly. The lieutenants took their turns, and then the captain said, "It's our turn now. You go first." I had only been water skiing a few times, but I didn't fall down. Then the captain took his turn and he was skilled. On his second pass he even came around on one ski; I loved to watch him. Nonetheless, the turn passed to another couple. All I wanted to do was sit next to him and be close.

The afternoon provided a perfect few hours. We had been apart a long time and wanted to be together. We didn't pay attention to the group. We sat at the side on an Army blanket enjoying the beach—powder-snow sand in a ring of jungle. We wanted to touch one another, but we couldn't kiss, even innocently, in front of junior officers. The captain's dignity was at stake.

My sister, Phyllis, a WAC captain, told me that training warned, "An officer is always on time and never in a hurry. An officer never carries packages or children." She explained, "We have to be dignified." The captain could never be seen kissing a Donut Dolly. The senior officer set the standards for everyone's conduct.

The captain astonished me with a perfect, private beach. He had insured that the outing was correct by inviting the proper number of guests. Water skiing in the South China Sea made the moment mystical. He was a general's aide and had to be good at many things.

I recalled the time in Korea when I first learned about the job of aide-de-camp, general's aide. In a mess hall I sat across from an officer who was absorbed in a book. He put it down to eat his supper and I asked him what he was reading.

"I'm studying etiquette."

"Etiquette?"

"Yes. There's a job opening for a general's aide, and I have to pass a test in etiquette to get it."

A few days later I saw the officer again. I asked, "How did the etiquette test go?"

"I didn't get the job. It went to a man who didn't have to study etiquette. He grew up with it."

In Vietnam, the captain's Southern charm showed. An image came to me of antebellum ladies flirting over their fans. I imagined Southern gentlemen bowing and kissing the ladies' hands. Far from demure, I used to like to climb trees and catch frogs, and it took an adventurous type of girl to come to Vietnam. This Southern gentleman seemed to be polished, to value a wide range of people's qualities, and so I felt he understood me.

The sun burned hot in the afternoon, but we had suntan lotion. The captain and I oiled our arms and faces, and then I invited him to turn so I could put lotion on his back. My hands lingered on his muscular shoulders. I reached behind him and allowed my breast to press against his arm. He pressed back. He gently took the bottle. His look said I couldn't touch his chest even though the other people were 40 feet away. They watched everything we did, and we had to be careful. He smoothed the lotion on my back and then returned the bottle to me. "I wish I could do more," he said. In my mind I saw the officer bow and kiss my hand and could feel my face burning.

He caught me watching him, but showed only calm. He spoke softly as he spread the oil on his cream-colored thigh, "Back when I was at Pleiku, one night I tried to get a line through to you on the telephone." My eyes met his. "Just as you came on, the general came in and decided to do some work. So rather then hang up, and to avoid bothering the general, I took the telephone out on a long cord into a field," the captain glanced up at me, "and sat under a poncho in the driving rain yelling into the phone, 'I love you!'" My heart burned as we sat on the scorching sand. All that afternoon Bob and I couldn't take our eyes off each other. We stayed as close together as we dared. We brushed lightly now and then and held hands where people couldn't see. Warmth flowed between us. He was the first man in my life to touch my heart.

On that tiny beach at Nha Trang the afternoon came to an end too soon. We had worn our bathing suits under our uniforms, since there were no facilities to change. In such hot weather bathing suits dried quickly, and we slipped our uniforms back on over our suits. As the friends headed to the parking lot, Bob slowed and let the others walk ahead. They rounded a corner out of sight. Unexpectedly, he pulled me to him and kissed me long and deep, a kiss I will remember for the rest of my life. He held me in his arms. I didn't want to let him go, but we had to hurry; the others would be looking for us. Neither of us said a word. Without even thinking about what I was doing, while he still held me, I reached up and took the Red Cross pin off my collar. I pinned it on his jungle fatigues, underneath the pilot's wings, below the pocket, where most people wouldn't see it. I couldn't let him go and had to send a piece of myself with him. That was the only Red Cross pin I ever gave away. Bob and I caught up with the group in time to shake hands with each other. He smiled at me, "Thanks for coming. I enjoyed and appreciate seeing you very much." We parted for our transports to return to the war.

Thursday, September 1, Dong Ba Thin

I was delighted when Bob told me in his daily phone call that he would come to see me at Dong Ba Thin. "I'm changing jobs and I have two days off. I'm going to Phan Thiet (pronounced "Fan Tee-et") to be commander of D Company 2nd Battalion 7th Cavalry." *Typical modesty.* He had received a big promotion. But, he was going to the hard luck battalion. "I'll come from Nha Trang in a 1st Cavalry Caribou. I should arrive at noon on Thursday." He would go from general's aide in the safe general's office back into combat. General Norton must have had a lot of confidence in him. I learned years later, that Delta Company, 2/7th Cavalry had taken heavy casualties at Ia Drang when the North Vietnamese Army (NVA) ambushed them on the march from LZ X-Ray to LZ Albany to be air lifted back to An Khe after the battle. They lost 31 men.[3]

With three girls in the Dong Ba Thin unit, I would have to work on Thursday in order to be off on Friday. But, I could welcome Bob at the Caribou ramp on my lunch hour. I borrowed a jeep and driver and waited beside the deserted airstrip, struggling to hide my excitement. Bob and I had been water skiing four days before, though it seemed like months. Memories of the warmth and the frustration crowded my mind. We had sat side by side on the beach all afternoon yearning to hold hands. Now I would see him again, and we would embrace at last. At the airstrip the sky was empty. I told the driver, "I hear an aircraft."

He listened, "You're hearing things. Relax." Moments later an aircraft appeared, and we watched it come nearer and nearer. It was a Caribou, but it turned and continued toward Saigon. I sighed, and then tensed again as I heard another aircraft. The driver laughed at me, "This time you're hearing things." But I wasn't. More aircraft came and went, separated by tense intervals of silence, until the driver started to believe me. We searched the sky. Faint engines droned, dots turned into planes, and then passed by. The lunch hour dragged. No Caribou. Finally, late for work, I gave up. Bob had somehow been delayed. He would have to call or get another ride in from the ramp. I didn't dare think he might not arrive at all.

I told the driver, "We might as well start back." I continued to strain my ears and watch the sky. Well down the road, I heard another Caribou. My heart leaped. I shaded my eyes against the sun, but I couldn't see anything.

Finally the driver spotted it. He shouted, "It's a Caribou. It's coming from Nha Trang." He slowed. I didn't breathe. The big plane came into the landing pattern for Dong Ba Thin. It began to lose altitude. This was it! I was going to be late for work, but I didn't care. The driver didn't wait for an order. He turned around in the middle of the road and raced back. The large olive-green Caribou floated down as we arrived at the parking area. As it taxied up I could see the big yellow Cavalry patch high on the proud tail.

Three or four men now gathered at the edge of the runway. They had emerged from the operations tent as if to watch the aircraft land. I knew they drew close to glimpse a Red Cross girl. I pretended I didn't know they were there. The jeep slammed to a halt and I leaped out. A man in a dress uniform jumped from the open ramp under the tail of the aircraft. The sun flashed off the insignia of a general's aide on his shoulders. My heart sang. He had bags in both hands. When he saw me he put them down, and I ran into his open arms. He lifted me off the ground and whirled me around. It felt like we were dancing. He gave me a warm, loving kiss that said, "Hello, I missed you." Time stood still. Then reality hit. *Remember, you are a Red Cross girl; you live in a goldfish bowl.* Bob swung his bags into the jeep, we hopped in, and the driver floored it. He drove me to work and then took Bob to the bachelor officer's quarters, where the friends had assured me they would take good care of him.

After work, as usual, each of us three girls ate in a different mess hall so we could see more people. I took Bob with me, and we enjoyed a leisurely dinner together. Everyone could see the big, yellow Cavalry patch on his shoulder from across the room. They knew he was a visitor from a distant combat unit. They pretended to avert their eyes, but took pleasure in watching us. They gave us rare, precious privacy to talk, to be together, and to hold hands under the table. Bob revealed that the evening after he got home from the beach, after I gave him my Red Cross pin, "I wore it to the general's mess for dinner. The G-2 saw it." That was the general's intelligence officer, Lt. Col. Bobby Lange. I thought, *Leave it to the intelligence officer to notice everything.* Bob smiled, "He said to the general, 'Do you see what this young captain is wearing?' The general said, 'No,' and he really couldn't see it because he wasn't wearing his glasses. 'But, I'll bet it's a Red Cross pin.'" I blushed. I thought, *Everybody really does see everything we do. How could the general know I would give Bob my pin? I didn't even know it myself.* Bob continued, "The next day after we went swimming, I discovered that the tops of my feet were sunburned. I was barefoot on the beach all afternoon. I limped around the office in pain all the next day."

Friday night, September 2

A jeep and driver took us to Cam Ranh Air Force Officer's Club for dinner. It was dim and quiet, like a moment back home, like a good restaurant in the States. Afterwards, the driver returned us to the house. We sat together under the almost-full moon on two reclining lawn chairs on the little patio in the back, with the privacy fence on two sides. We held hands with a warm touch and talked quietly.

Then I was stunned when he said, "I love you. I want to marry you, but I don't want it to be here." He had told me many times in his phone calls that he loved me, but I never thought about marriage. I was thrilled: at that moment I realized that to marry him was the one thing I wanted most, but, I was so shocked I couldn't answer. All I could think was, *He didn't even ask me.* I knew on that starlit, sweltering night in September that Bob and I would always be together. I knew he was the man I had waited for. No one I had ever met was so bright, so honorable, and so much in love with me. I had never loved anyone. That night the velvet, tropical sky rained down diamonds on us. He embraced me and sealed his proposal with a kiss. I didn't need to answer. My heart swelled. We kissed again and again. I held him tightly, and our passion burned. I felt my body begin to surrender. Then the other girls came home.

Bob and I ate breakfast together the next morning in the mess hall. We sat alone at the table for a long time. I felt a peaceful sadness at his departure. Then the jeep arrived to drive him to the plane. We couldn't kiss in front of everyone, but I saw love in his eyes. He squeezed my hand. Then he left for combat.

Friday, September 9

Bob called me tonight. He told me, "I got a phone patch [a telephone connection] on my field radio." He sounded in good spirits. He said, "I have to conduct some business." He left the connections open, and I could hear calls coming in, though I couldn't tell what the people were saying. He would excuse himself, I would hear him talk to someone, and then he would come back and talk with me. He had allowed me to stand beside him in combat. Although our conversation was brief, I was delighted and relieved. Maybe he wasn't in as much danger as I feared. I think that was what he was trying to tell me. Because Bob couldn't call me from the field every day as he had from the general's office, I began to call him. The reception was often poor, but when I could get through, I was happy to hear his voice.

✶　✶　✶

Why were Bob and I so attracted to each other when we did not know each other well at all? Was it purely sex? For me, there was sexual attraction. I enjoyed the attention of a desirable man. But our relationship was based on friendship and sharing our mutual interests, as were all my relationships with men. I believed that sex belonged in marriage. Archaic by some people's values, but in my opinion it's none of their business what my mores are. Bob and I were separated most of the time, and we could only touch each other by our carefully crafted words on the telephone. The few times we were together platoons of eyes watched.

Bob may have developed the bond with me that men have in combat. Thanks to my Red Cross service, I had had the opportunity to observe hundreds of men, and I knew the kind of man who appealed to me. Captain Windsor had all the qualities I wanted. I felt flattered when he pursued me, and I encouraged him to see where it would lead. I enjoyed his friendship, but I wasn't thinking about anything more permanent. That's why it was a shock when he told me he was.

Monday, September 12

Food events were big winners at the recreation center. Susie planned a pancake supper. The mess hall cooks contributed everything we needed—pancake mix, butter, syrup—and they loaned us their portable grill and a gas generator. Susie did something to make the Army's pancakes taste homemade. The crowd was bigger and more eager than usual. A line of men waited at the grill for every pancake. Some early arrivers were already back for seconds when the generator sputtered and stopped. From across the room I heard Susie exclaim, "The generator just ran out of gas. I have a grill full of half-cooked pancakes here."

One of the men answered, "I know where we can get some gas," and bolted out the door on the run. A few minutes later, before the pancakes could be ruined, he returned with a can of gasoline from the mess hall. It seemed the Army cooks were plagued with the same problems we experienced. They worked under difficult circumstances. By our estimate, 75 soldiers ate all we had, a mound of pancakes that was designed to feed 150 men, after their regular meal. We recalled that most of these men were still in their teens. They could eat more than the Army could cook.

September 18

Susie rotated home. Her replacement was Maddie, a petite girl with curly hair, older than the rest of us, from Alhambra, California. She had served in Morocco, France, and Korea.[4] We discussed the schedule of trips to Tuy Hoa in her first planning meeting. We explained that everybody had to go in rotation. She pointed out the rule that every unit followed: "We should always let those go who want to go."

In one voice we answered, "Because nobody wants to go." Maddie had served in all those countries and had never encountered a place where not even one girl wanted to go. It was such a bad trip that one of the girls wrote a song about it. People started to add verses, and we sang it at the next informal gathering.

> Put on your red dress, baby,
> The sorest eyes you ever saw.
> Put on your high heeled sneakers,
> We're goin' up to Tuy Hoa.

Saturday, September 24

Today I got Bob's first letter. He wrote it the day after he called me. He told me he missed me, it was good to talk to me, and everything was going well. From Phan Thiet to Dong Ba Thin it took his letter 14 days to get here. I was happy to receive it, even after that much time, to know that he was all right.

Thursday September 29

The biggest success we had, we all agreed, was a talent show. Maddie was in charge, and Fif helped. She was from Long Island, and had just arrived from the Philippines to replace Gini. Fif, like Maddie, was also small and older than the rest of us, but had short straight hair instead of curly hair. Their longer experience probably accounted for the program's success. Maddie and Fif put out a call for performers, and plenty of volunteers signed up. The acts rehearsed in secret—we had no idea what to expect until they actually performed. When show time neared, we ran out of chairs and places to put the audience. The room buzzed with anticipation. We estimated we had a crowd of about 130 people.

All the acts were excellent. Some looked better than amateurs to me. The bill that night was complete with singers, musicians, and creative goof-offs who made everyone roar with laughter. One man from New York in particular sang a song that transfixed the house. He had a strong, trained voice and a relaxed, natural stage presence that he could have learned on Broadway. When he sang he walked around and moved his whole body with the grace of a dancer. At one point he bent over and lifted one knee to emphasize a phrase. When he finished, the crowd erupted with applause.

The surprise of the evening turned out to be a group of orphans from an orphanage our men supported. We expected about 40 children to sing and dance and watch the show. Our eyes went wide with delight when more than 100 shy, scrubbed, Vietnamese children arrived on a big Army truck. The children neither sang nor danced. They didn't have to. They had to sit on the men's laps, since there was already standing room only. Men eagerly reached for the children and boosted them up onto each other's laps. Oh, the disappointment when there were not enough children to go around. Some men had to share a child. In the US Army there is nothing like homesick servicemen when it comes to children, especially orphans. To touch a child, to hold a child, transported a man home to his own family. He felt the little hand, heard the little voice, and remembered children he had left behind. He was home with them for a few, happy moments.

We sat one little girl on a man's lap, and she grabbed him around the neck and wouldn't let go, even when it was time to go home. The man's face was a wreath of smiles. Another little girl fell asleep. The man who held her came to me, carrying her carefully. He whispered, "It's so hot. Do you have anything I can fan her with?"

I whispered back, "How about this piece of cardboard?"

"That's great. Thanks." The man held her gently and fanned her all evening.

When it came time to say good-bye you would have thought the men were saying good-bye to their own children. At the end of the evening the truck drove away with the sleepy orphans all packed together in the back. The men quietly, sadly gathered to watch them go. They talked about it for days. I thought, *How lucky these orphans are to have a home and someone to care for them. There are so many children on the streets everywhere, dirty, hungry, sleeping wherever they can.*

I understood how different Americans are. These men's humanity never left them. With no thought of anything in return, they would do whatever was in their power to help people they didn't know. That included caring for a child and fighting an enemy. Their job compelled them to fight. I had seen the true face of the soldiers whom even some errant Americans called baby killers.

Years later, someone told me, "such images of US soldiers as being concerned about children were propagated by the government as part of its effort to drum up support for the war effort." Shocking. I disagree.

Those with an agenda must subserve to the truth and use history as history rather than history as opinion.

From the first day I arrived in Korea to my last day in Vietnam, I saw that the soldiers were concerned about children, not only their own, but the ones around them in those remote lands. The soldiers established and supported orphanages and talked about children in everyday conversation. And not only children, but animals and women. Soldiers had pet puppies and monkeys. Later, I worked among men for five years in a Detroit auto factory. I witnessed the pride and love those men had for their children, wives, and pets. I saw that men are just as soft as women, maybe more. But, they show it rarely and guardedly. They allowed me to see it only after I earned their trust. My male boss and my husband coached me to see it, and my effectiveness as a trainer increased.

Not long ago a Marine I've known since seventh grade emailed me a valentine of pictures of cute babies. He asked, "Would you believe a Marine sent me this?"

I answered, "I'm not surprised at all that a Marine sent you this. You sent it to me, didn't you? I get more pictures of cute babies and animals, flowers and poems and pictures of everything from scenery to bugs, from you and other veterans of all services and ranks, than I do from women. You are all soft with a thin, candy shell." I have said the same to other veterans. None has disagreed with me.

Another veteran emailed me: "Joan, I'm not surprised you get them, either [emails of puppies], after all, you are just one of the guys . . . you know, a Vietnam War Veteran!

> Bill
> SERGEANT MAJOR,
> AUS, Retired
> PS: You girls were UNARMED! I am in awe!"

Is that man talking about sex? No. Interaction between men and women is more than that.

I didn't find this out by reading a book.

Just as it's possible to eat too much chocolate, in Vietnam I observed that men get tired of too much men. They seek relief; they look for balance. They miss the parts of normal life that they don't have, the things that make life complete: children, pets, and women. Not just in war. I saw the same in Korea, where there was no war, only loneliness and homesickness. I saw that men have a nurturing instinct, just as women do. They need children, animals, and women, to care for and protect, and to give love and receive love. Civilization needs men to do that, for our survival.

However, men also know that to protect; they must sometimes fight and kill. They need that hard outer shell.

I do not believe that the image of soldiers as selfless is propagated by the government. It is real.

Sunday, October 2

When I first got to Vietnam I was at least a little frightened most of the time. As the days passed, however, I adjusted. The more I learned about the Army and the war, the less afraid I became. Within a few weeks I began to enjoy myself. I learned to distinguish between real danger, which I rarely saw, and imagined danger. Being in Vietnam was a tense, nerve-wracking experience. However, everyone found a way to cope, and before long they began to function normally. Many people looked back later and laughed at the way they reacted when they first got "in country," even though at the time they thought it was anything but funny!

Early October, Dong Ba Thin

An air base sat next to Dong Ba Thin. The number of people in the combined Army and Air Force made the area so secure that civilian entertainers could visit now and then. Once, the Air Force unit, with permission of the commander, booked an American stripper for one of their monthly parties. I saw a few American woman freelancing in both Korea and Vietnam. Their marketing programs were strip shows or singing and dancing acts. They earned extra money by sleeping with the soldiers. This young woman, about 23 years old, flew in on an Air Force transport because no commercial airline served the base. The commander, a lieutenant colonel, asked if she could stay overnight with us. I had met him before and he had invited us Red Cross girls to one of his parties. He was older than an Army colonel would be, with some gray at his temples. He probably had a desk job, because his girth spilled over his belt. His smile was easy and warm. The Air Force was more relaxed than the Army.

Our house and the nurse's quarters were the only women's housing anywhere around; I didn't think that would matter to a stripper. I guess it did to the colonel. He and two Air Force captains escorted the performer to our house after her show, before 10:00 at night. I noticed the time, because I was curious about an exotic dancer. We had no curfew, and I wondered whether she did. I was surprised, because I expected her to stagger in at maybe 2:00 or 3:00 A.M. When she arrived, Maddie and I were home. Our guest was about my age, medium height, attractive, with flowing blonde hair. The dark roots showed, but not much. Her makeup was a little heavy. She wasn't wearing revealing clothes. She was dressed right for a sweltering, tropical evening and to display her assets.

I welcomed her as a guest. I didn't think I should just take her to her room and leave her there. Besides, I was curious. What was she like? Maddie went to bed. She had served in Morocco, France, and Korea. I guessed she knew all she wanted to know about strippers. I sat in our living room with the stranger. The sweat rolled down our faces and the lazy ceiling fans turned above us. I didn't ask questions. I listened to what was on her mind, and encouraged her by being attentive. She smiled pleasantly. We were comfortable with each other.

I offered, "Would you like a soft drink? It's warm. We don't have a refrigerator."

She asked, "Do you have any milk?"

Surprised, I answered, "No, we don't get milk very often," and got up to retrieve a can of pop from the shelf.

She complained, "There are a lot of places where I can't get milk. I'm losing my breasts because I'm not getting enough." She sighed and lifted them slightly. They filled both hands. They were big. I was jealous. Sweat glistened on her shoulder.

"I need milk to keep my moneymakers up." She accepted the warm soft drink.

I thought, *It's the fat in the milk that she needs. But, she's a professional. Who am I to tell her what to do?*

She took a sip of the soft drink, "The local girls do shows and side jobs the same as I do. I'm in competition with them, but my service is better than theirs." She smiled with pride.

I wondered *How is she better? Exotic, oriental entertainers are legend, but around here they're common. She is an American. That would be enough.*

She saw the question on my face and continued, as if she were explaining how to make a sandwich. "I douche between customers. The local girls don't do that. Different men's sperm interact with each other and cause infections. My customers won't get infections from me."[5]

I didn't know that. I tried to act as though this was everyday conversation. In fact, I just about choked. I wiped a drop of sweat off the end of my nose, composed myself, and then smiled. *She's like the men. It's been a long time since she's had a chance to talk to an American girl. She feels at home.* The conversation caught me off guard. I didn't remember anything she said after that. We finished our soda, I showed her to her room, and we both went to bed. The next morning, the same officers picked her up in a jeep. They took her to another airplane.

A couple of days after the dancer's visit, one of the guys confided to me, "The Air Force had a stripper at their club, and she stayed over night with some of them."

I corrected him, "No, she didn't. She stayed with us at our Quonset hut. I was there when the Air Force men brought her in. It was 9:45." That was a problem that plagued the Red Cross girls. Rumors persisted that we made money on the side. We fought a constant battle to preserve our image. We had to keep saying to ourselves, "We do what we're supposed to do. And we have to *appear* to do what we're supposed to do."

One of the girls had said, "If we were the Virgin Mary, people would still spread rumors about us." The soldiers loved rumors. They were among the most interesting things that happened. The soldier didn't want to believe me. He gave me a blank look, ignored what I said, and changed the subject. I remember my father saying, "You can have your own opinions, but you can't have your own facts."

I was so bored in the comfortable, rear area that I asked Saigon to transfer me back to a combat unit. I got a prompt notice from Saigon that they were sending me to the 1st Infantry Division at Di An. I went back to the war.

Part III:
Di An

✚ CHAPTER 6 ✚

Bring a Case of Beer

Saturday, October 15, 1966, Di An, South Vietnam

Maybe it was my country-girl upbringing. Maybe it was because I had to live up to my father's job as a school superintendent, but I never saw it coming. I was abducted. The 1st Infantry Division had acquired their nickname, the Big Red One, during World War II. Their motto, "If you're going to be one, be a big red one," left me wondering if I should blush. The 1st Infantry Division had arrived in Vietnam just one year before, in October 1965, and only one month after the 1st Cavalry.[1] Six girls made Di An a large Red Cross unit. Dee had a black puppy, Sam; Peggy had a white puppy, Horatio. When I opened a door, I never knew when one of them was going to explode to greet me. Our house, a spacious, new, permanent building, had a cement floor and screen and louver sides. It sat in a comfortable area in the shade of a grove of trees.

On my first workday, Linda, the unit director, taller than me, gentle and modest, led me down a short path and then a few yards along a gravel road to the recreation center. Excited, I anticipated my new assignment and the adventures it might hold. My heart beat a little harder and a little stronger than usual. I would have never guessed the surprise that waited for me. Linda and I rounded a bend, and I caught

Di An girls. Top: Peggy (with Horatio) Brook, Joann, Dee (with Sam).
Seated: Linda, Eileen. Army Public Information Office photograph.

my first sight of the Di An recreation center, a faded, old canvas tent shaped like a Quonset hut. I understood why this rear area made do with hand-me-down equipment: combat requirements took priority. An entrance flap as wide as the tent, rolled up out of the way, made an opening big enough to drive a truck through. I had never seen a tent like that. It might have been a maintenance tent. Inside, water stains around the windows and on nearly every seam showed its battered history, like wrinkles on an old man's face. The just-passed rainy season had revealed this to be a canvas sieve.

A huge, new, permanent recreation center under construction a few yards away made the division's apologies for the current sub-standard accommodations. The unfinished, framed walls outlined the building on a cement pad. But for the time being, we crammed ourselves into the

*Interior of the Di An Recreation Center tent. Water
stains are around the windows and seams.*

sad, ancient tent. I saw round tables inside, ringed by lawn and folding
chairs. The tent held an overflow of GIs, but why did they sit in silence?
Why did they stare at one corner near the front? Could it be? Yes, it was.
That center had a television, the first one I had seen in five months.

My eyes grew wide, and I smiled. Apology for the small, fragile tent
accepted; I stepped closer, careful not to block anyone's view. The men
watched a football game, oblivious that a new Red Cross girl had arrived. I scanned the rest of the tent. Then one team scored. The men
exploded in a cheer. The TV camera caught a shot of the band as they
struck up a fight song, and my heart skipped two whole beats. I jerked
my head around to lock my eyes on the television. I knew that song.
Hail to the Victors . . . Twin base drums filled the screen. The block
letters on the drums spelled out MICHIGAN. I froze in shock and
surprise, and then a wave of fond memories overcame me. I could see
the stadium, the bowl of 101,001 focused fans on a warm autumn day.

Visions of a recent past merged with the crushing heat of this faraway land. I watched my school, the University of Michigan, play football on television in Vietnam. I strained to see more, and I stood there for a long time. I suddenly understood why the guys loved football. The men sat there, in the middle of the war, as if they watched the game at a friend's house back home. Our center was supposed to bring the soldiers reminders of home. That television brought the real thing.

Saturday, October 22

My first day off came a week after I arrived at Di An. The division compound sat less than ten miles north of Saigon. I decided to go for the day to see my sister. Di An was five miles west of the main road in the country. Highway 1, a modern four-lane thoroughfare, ran from Saigon to Bien Hoa and continued north. I rode down to Saigon on our truck with Eileen, who was going on vacation. The nature of the war, with no battle lines, forced the Army to declare the whole country a combat zone. Wherever we went we checked with commanders to learn what security we needed. At that time regulations said that any vehicle on the highway north of the Saigon Bridge had to travel in a convoy, two or more vehicles, and had to have someone riding shotgun. That meant someone with a weapon, other than the driver. That modern phrase had colorful antecedents from our country's history.

We made good time through light traffic on an early, sunny, Saturday morning. The grass shoulders of the roadway extended far out on both sides to deny cover for an enemy ambush or sniper. The endless pavement and absent trees and bushes intensified the relentless heat. We passed a handful of military trucks, a rare private car or two, a cyclo, and a number of motor scooters and bicycles. Just north of the city we crossed the Saigon River on a four-lane elevated super highway. It could have been any major bridge in the States. This was my first trip into civilization in six months.

I met my sister, Phyllis, a captain since the 4th of July, at her Bachelor Officer Quarters hotel. We went to lunch along with her roommate, Mary. After lunch Phyllis went back to work, where she supervised a room full of Vietnamese translators. Mary and I went to the PX. I carried a shopping list of requests from each of the girls. We had a good PX at 1st Infantry Division Headquarters, but Saigon was like Stateside. Inside the store I felt like I was back home.

When I finished shopping I planned to ride the military bus to Di An, which would join the 5:00 convoy at the Saigon River Bridge. I boarded the PX bus just as a monsoon downpour began. The windshield wipers barely kept up with the bone-soaking rain. I got off at the gate, expecting to hop on the Di An bus as it came through. As the transport pulled away, I hurried up to the air policeman on duty. I asked, "Has the bus to Di An come through yet? Does it come through this gate? What time does it come?"

He looked at me and said, "Uuhh what bus?"

I said, "It must go out the north gate. Is this the north gate? Which one do you go out to get to the Saigon River Bridge?"

He said, "Uuhh Saigon River Bridge? Ahhh let me call the next gate."

After a long time on the phone he said, "You can go to the next gate. It's just over there. You can walk to it."

I splashed my way 200 yards to the next gate; my arms ached with the load of packages. The rain poured down. I had no raincoat or cover for my head. I could feel the drops landing on my shoulders and back. Rivulets ran down my cheeks and down the back of my neck. My loafers squished water around my toes. I rushed up to the air policeman (AP). The day was so hot that I wasn't cold, just embarrassed at how bad I must look. My makeup had to be destroyed. Out of breath, I asked, "Can I catch the bus to Di An at this gate? Has it gone through yet?"

The AP looked at me and asked, "Uuhh what bus?"

I thought, *This sounds familiar*. I struggled to control myself, re-membering, *You can catch more flies with honey than with vinegar*. To the AP I said, "The guard from the next gate just called you and told you I was coming."

He said, "Yeah, well, I don't know." This was one of the drawbacks of being a Red Cross girl. People gave us extra privileges, like airplane rides, but they also sometimes delayed us so they could spend more time with us. The first air policeman couldn't help me. He knew his friend at the next gate couldn't help me either, but he sent me over there so his friend could spend some time with me, too. I stood in the rain, out of ideas.

A covered pick-up truck with markings from the Non Commissioned Officer's (NCO) Club at the replacement center stopped. The driver leaned out the window, "Can I help you?" The 1st Infantry Division patch on my shoulder had told him that I was from out of town. He was an Army sergeant, a little thick in the middle, a little older and hopefully a little wiser than the young Air Force privates at the gates.

I told him, "I'm trying to get to Di An, and I've evidently missed the bus."

He said, "Come on with me to Camp Alpha. We have something go-ing up there. I know we do. We'll get you there." In the past when I had turned myself over to someone to get me where I needed to go, it hadn't always gone well. I had learned that other people were not as interested in my goals as they were in their own. I knew all that, but I also knew that I had no choice, so I thanked him and got in. We still had plenty of time to get to the Saigon River Bridge and meet the convoy by 5:00. Camp Alpha was only a short distance. When we got there the sergeant went inside for a few minutes and came back. "We have a truck going to Long Binh [pronounced "Long bin"]. You can ride that far and get another ride to Di An from there."

I knew rides weren't that easy to come by, but I thought, *When that truck joins the convoy at the bridge I'll just get on my bus.* So I said, "That will be fine." I waited in the truck as men loaded it with supplies. I realized, *The truck that's going to Long Binh is this one. Well, I guess that's all right.* Time slipped away as the sergeant and a couple of other men continued to work. I didn't know how long it would take to get to the bridge, but I figured half an hour would be enough. I asked the sergeant once, "Do you believe we'll make the convoy?"

He answered with his mind on the loading, "I think we will." I couldn't hurry them; I was a hitchhiker. When we finally got started another NCO joined us. Each sergeant had strapped on an Army-issue holster that had a .45 cal. I thought, *Good. We have a man riding shotgun.* As we neared the bridge, military trucks streamed bumper to bumper along the congested road. Finally, we arrived. I expected to see a convoy, perhaps 25 military trucks lining the highway. I saw no trucks, and there was no place for them to wait. One roadside vendor after another, maybe a hundred, crowded both shoulders and crammed every inch. The farthest ones disappeared in the rain. Each was a little shelter that reminded me of the farmers' vegetable stands along country highways in the summer in Michigan. The owner sat behind a counter that displayed goods for sale. The driver pulled off the pavement. He blocked one of the shacks. The wrinkled woman inside gave him a dirty look through the rain. He volunteered, "We'll wait here for a few minutes to see if maybe the convoy is making up late today. It arrives at 5 P.M. and leaves at 5:15." My watch said 5:05. We should have seen signs that the convoy was forming.

The men didn't seem resourceful. They sat in the truck for a few minutes, then got out and walked, without resolution, a few feet in the direction of the bridge. One stopped and talked to a stand owner for a moment. The two sergeants returned to the truck, eager to get out of the rain. "We didn't find anything out," the driver mumbled. I wasn't satisfied. Someone among this many roadside stands would know enough English to tell me something. My blue Red Cross uniform could get me anything. All I had to do was show up. I got out of the truck and went to the nearest stand. I asked the middle-aged woman, "Can you tell me please, where does the convoy get together?" She gave me a blank stare and shook her head. I went to the next stand. This time I asked, "Convoy? Here?" The clean-cut man looked sympathetic, but shook his head. I went to several booths, but got the same response. I had been wrong. No one could understand me. That was hard to believe.

I decided to flag down a military truck and get a ride. I could rely on my blue uniform; the first truck that spotted me would stop. The now-thinner traffic flew, as everyone raced to get home before dark. At high speed, bumper-to-bumper, in monsoon rain, I couldn't catch even one bumper number to tell me where any of the trucks were headed. If someone had seen me and wanted to stop, he couldn't. Defeated for the moment, but still not worried, I got back into the truck with the two sergeants, out of the rain. I had dried out since my last drenching, and now I was soaked again. This time I didn't care how I looked. The convoy had left, or had never arrived. I had a choice: ride with the unprotected supply truck through VC territory to Long Binh and get a ride from there or stay here alone in VC territory in the dark. Ambitious Vietnamese vendors anxiously hawking their goods to American soldiers surrounded me. When night fell, it was likely but ironic that these momentary allies would become Viet Cong sympathizers. Searchers might never find my body. It wasn't much of a decision; I went to Long Binh. On the 45-minute trip we were watchful, but nothing happened. We saw no one for the shotgun to shoot.

When we got to Long Binh we drove to the NCO club. The sergeant took me inside an office with half a dozen Army desks. Sergeants and privates came in and out, phones rang, and everyone busied himself at work. The sergeant motioned to a straight chair next to an empty desk.

"Sit down, we'll take care of everything." I watched the two sergeants supervise men unloading the truck. I thought, *The supplies have to come first. The truck didn't make the trip just to bring me.* While the work progressed, the sergeant sat down at one of the desks and started to make phone calls. I thought, *Good, now he's going to get me a ride to Di An.* I could hear him on the phone. He called someone about food. I thought, *OK, he's a supply sergeant. He has to take care of business first.* Then he called someone else and said, "I have a Red Cross girl. Bring a case of beer and come to the NCO Club." I could hardly believe my ears. "Bring a case of beer?" I was pretty steamed. He was planning a party. He was not going to get me to Di An. In fact, I was the only one who was concerned about that.

When I first saw this sergeant back at Tan Son Nhut, I guessed that he was older and smarter than the Air Policemen who had just jerked me around. I was right. The sergeant knew how to manipulate with more finesse than the airmen. I angrily got up from my chair and walked to the nearest desk that had a phone. I asked the sergeant, firmly, "May I use the phone, please?" I gave him a look that said *You had better let me.* Before he could nod, I lifted the receiver and dialed the Di An Red Cross unit. Linda, my unit director, answered. I told her where I was and what had happened. Then I used a phone book that lay on the desk to call the Military Police. I told them who I was, "I'm AWOL. How can I get back to Di An?"

The voice on the other end said, "No way." I began to have a twinge of doubt for the first time. I still wasn't worried that I might not get back. I did start to worry that it might be harder than I thought.

It took a while for the MP's words to sink in. I asked, "No way?"

He answered, "Yes, the roads have closed for the night." I had never been defeated. The Red Cross on my uniform was a universal key that opened every door. I had to find the right door. Then I remembered the soap I had bought at the PX for the unit. I could call the trip a supply run. Then I would be authorized to fly. I started to call aviation companies. I told each one, "I'm stranded. I have to get to Di An." No luck. Nobody had anything scheduled to go to Di An until the next day.

Somewhere along the line, someone among the people I had spoken to called the headquarters commandant. It was probably the Military Policeman.[2] The commandant was responsible for lost souls like me, so he called me. "The Red Cross girls are on their way to come get you with a police escort." He did not mean the Di An girls; he meant the girls from the local Long Binh unit. I still had a couple more numbers to call, but there was no use. I would stay the night. I had been defeated.

Within minutes four Military Policemen, all armed with .45s and wearing armored vests and steel helmets, burst through the double doors and surrounded me. A Red Cross girl stepped out from among the towering men. Short, cute, brown curly hair, shadowed by a burly MP sergeant, she ordered, "I'm Sherri. Let's go." They hustled me outside. Two more MPs, armored and armed with M-16 rifles, waited. They guarded two open, marked MP jeeps.

When something like that happened, I was never sure how much of it was show and how much was necessary. My first clue was that Sherri did not wear an armored vest or helmet herself; and she didn't bring them for me. On the other hand, maybe this wasn't a combat unit, and the girls didn't have combat gear. Everyone began to climb into the jeeps. The sergeant offered, "One of you can ride in the lead jeep, if you have the nerve."

Sherri shook her head, "No thanks, the second one will be fine." She and I jumped into the jeep. Running without sirens and without red lights, we raced through the gate and roared down the road. I figured the theory was that we were safer if we didn't let anyone know we were coming and kept moving fast. But, we nearly crashed into a crowd of pedestrians, animals, and various vehicles. Sherri kept me entertained. She told me about all the mines that had blown up in the road within the past few weeks and how dangerous the area was. I wasn't impressed, because I thought most of it was put on for my benefit.

About 20 white-knuckle minutes later we arrived at the Red Cross girls' house in the American compound in Bien Hoa town. Sherri phoned my unit in Di An and talked for a while. She seemed stiff. Then she called me to the phone. Linda, my unit director, was on the other end. She told me, "Sherri thinks you have gotten yourself stranded on purpose, for the excitement of it. I told her you aren't that kind of girl, but I'm not sure she believed me. I'm glad you're safe. We'll look for you to be home tomorrow." The next morning I rode the bus with the Long Binh girls about 20 minutes to their recreation center and waited for a couple of hours. Their driver took me to a nearby helipad and put me on a chopper. I was home in ten minutes. The lesson learned here was, take care of yourself; no one else is going to.

Wednesday, October 26, Cam Ranh Bay

The bay at Cam Ranh, a neighboring base, was a natural deep-water port. Ocean-going ships could come to shore rather than anchoring far from the land and unloading their cargo onto smaller boats to be ferried in. It was the same as I had seen at Hong Kong, a wealthy center of trade. Until the US military arrived, Cam Ranh Bay was undeveloped: there was no port and no shipping commerce. It could support a thriving trade that would rival Singapore and Hong Kong and make Vietnam rich in the future. Little Viet Cong activity threatened the area. Cam Ranh Bay was so secure that it was the only place in all of Vietnam where we could go off the compound at night.

When President Johnson came to Vietnam to visit the troops, he went there.[3] Troops from all over Vietnam went to meet him. I talked to one man after he came back. He remembered, his eyes bright with pride, "We went in a troop transport airplane. We all wore our best fatigues. They rushed us onto the plane in a big hurry. A lot of us didn't have all

On a trip out of Di An, another girl and Joann (right) wear combat boots in mud.

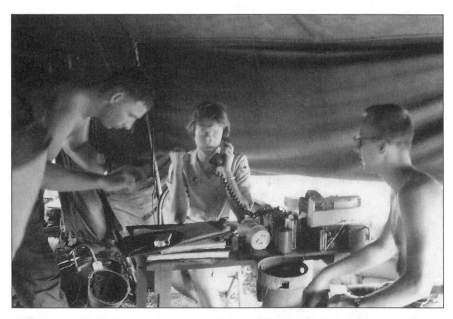

Joann makes a phone call in an Artillery tent. The gun crews were expecting a fire mission. Instead, Joann said, "Hello," causing both concern and surprise.

our patches on our uniforms. While we were flying we were hurrying up, sewing patches on each other." Many people were too busy to sew patches on new uniforms. Lots of people went around without patches that had fallen off or with patches that were loose and partly hanging. The man continued with excitement, "We were going to represent our unit in front of the president. Everybody had to be just right." I was sure the president chose to come to Cam Ranh because it was secure.

November 3 and 4, Tan Son Nhut Air Base

Two months after that special night in September, when I had last seen Bob, we tried to arrange another visit. My excuse for traveling was to pick up two trunks that I had left at Dong Ba Thin. All the girls offered to trade with me so that I could have two days off in a row whenever Bob was free. On the phone he suggested, "Try to come on Thursday." I spent several hours calling aviation companies to find a ride to Phan Thiet.

I finally rode a courier helicopter from Di An to Bien Hoa first thing in the morning on Thursday. I had several hours to wait, so I found a ride to the Red Cross unit there and saw two girls I had known in Korea. We caught up on the local gossip, and then their driver took me back to the airfield. I boarded a C-123 Air Force twin-engine cargo plane after lunch that would stop at Phan Thiet. As we flew over, the pilots told me, "We tried to contact the ground, but all five radio channels seem to be out. We can't stop." My heart sank. I thought, *I'll just have to keep trying.* We continued up the coast to Nha Trang and landed there in the middle of the afternoon. After dinner, I finally caught a flight to Dong Ba Thin to pick up my trunks. We arrived in gathering darkness. That evening I spent about an hour visiting with old friends and the rest of the time trying to find an aircraft going to Phan Thiet and then to Saigon where I could get a ride back home to Di An. I located a CV-2 Caribou, the light, twin-engine, Army cargo plane. I hoped I could persuade the pilot to stop at Phan Thiet and pick up Bob. I phoned him and he said he could be waiting at the runway.

I wondered why, when Bob arranged transportation, like the water skiing trip to Nha Trang, it went off smoothly. Then I realized that I had access to aviation units that served 1st Division but not 1st Cavalry. Besides, Bob was working out of the general's office. The Red Cross had luck, but the general had power.

The next morning I went out to the airfield early, hoping to get on the Caribou. Several men stood around, trying to go to Saigon. A pilot arrived, and I asked about going. He said, "The other pilot has the say. He'll be here in a few minutes."

When the pilot in charge came, he looked as if he were in a bad mood—not a good sign. I asked him, "Can I go on this flight?"

He grumped, "Yes."

I held my breath. "Can you stop at Phan Thiet and pick up another passenger?"

He scowled, "No, there isn't time."

I thought, *He can't say no. I have to make him understand.* "He's my fiancé. Can you *please* stop?"

He closed the conversation. "No." He ordered another man, "Get on the radio and arrange for another aircraft to pick up the passenger at Phan Thiet and take him to Saigon." I thought, *That's the best I can do.*

We had been airborne for several minutes when the crew chief yelled to me over the roar of the engines, "The pilot is going to call Phan Thiet. If the passenger is there, we will land." *Great. He's had a change of heart.* Every few minutes the crew chief told me, "They're calling Phan Thiet, but they can't make radio contact." Each time the crew chief told me they couldn't get through I thought, *They have to. All five channels can't be out again. This can't happen again. I'm running out of time.* Finally, when we were almost on the ground, he told me, "We're going to land." I felt wonderful. *At last, after a day and a half, I'm going to see Bob.*

Just as we touched down, the crew chief admitted, "We were going to stop all along. We were just teasing you to have some fun." I thought, *I'm not too surprised. It's a small price to pay. The pilot was probably putting on an act from the beginning.*

The plane had barely stopped rolling when Bob jumped onto the loading ramp. He wore combat gear. I thought, *There he is! Finally.* The plane began to taxi again, and then picked up speed. Bob worked his way up the aisle and leaned over me, his face close to mine so I could hear over the engines. "Where are we going?" Translation: "Hello. I love you. I wish I could kiss you. You worked hard to get this flight. What plan did you finally work out?"

I yelled, "Saigon." I thought, *Hello. I love you. I want to kiss you, too.*

His eyes returned my kiss. He yelled back, "OK," and brushed against me as he settled into his seat. Translation, "I want to take you in my arms and hold you." It was two months to the day since I had last seen him. I forgot about the struggle to be with him. He looked so good I wanted to hug. We sat among the people and the packages as the plane flew to Saigon. We couldn't touch; it wouldn't be proper. I thought, *This is so frustrating.* We could talk a little above the noise of the aircraft, however. When I spoke to him, he turned to look at me and leaned closer to hear. My heart jumped and I almost stole a kiss without thinking. He saw me lean toward him and almost kissed me back. We stopped ourselves from embracing at the last minute, as everyone looked on.

I stared at my feet. My bare knees peeked modestly from under the hem of my skirt. One knee was an inch from Bob's. The green cloth of his tropic-weight fatigues showed the outline of his strong thigh that moved as he shifted in his cramped seat. I checked my skirt. It remained tucked down. I ached to move my knee ever so slightly to touch, or even brush, Bob's. I glanced at the six or eight other passengers. They sat along the sides of the plane among the cargo, facing the center. They were privates first class, a few with their rifles, probably most of them 18 years old. Their commanding officers would be captains like Bob, many ranks above them. It would be bad for morale for them to see a combat leader with his knee against a Donut Dolly. They all looked in other directions, except the young soldier across from us. His eyes locked on my knee. I pretended I didn't see. I knew if I even took a deep breath, everyone would know. I glanced at Bob. He had observed everything. His clear, blue, approving eyes met mine, the warmth well hidden. I smiled. My eyes fastened on his. I couldn't move. He looked away to break the mood, because I couldn't. His hand lay on his lap. I longed to touch it, but I restrained myself.

A moment passed. I felt Bob's elbow press against my side behind my arm, out of view of the passengers. I stiffened and pressed back to answer him. His expression didn't change. He watched the jungle pass under the open ramp at the back of the plane a few feet away. I viewed the jungle for a short time, too. His arm hesitated and then moved away. My heart raced, and I gave him a slight smile. At cruising altitude the cargo plane felt cool. I could sense the heat of his body as he sat almost touching me, yet so far away.

An hour later we landed at Saigon, Tan Son Nhut Air Base. Bob reminded me, "I'd better start now to get a ride back to Phan Thiet." We went from one counter to another for an hour. He located a flight to An Khe. From there he could get to Phan Thiet the next day. He needed to be back that night, but there was no other option.

The flight was scheduled to leave at 1:45 P.M., but the clerk warned, "It might leave early. You should stay in the terminal." It was 11:30. We stayed, standing, because the seats were filled. More people stood than sat. Everyone looked preoccupied, but we knew they watched us: a captain from 1st Cavalry, armed and carrying his steel helmet, with a Red Cross girl from 1st Infantry Division in a blue dress in a sea of green uniforms. Both, a long way from home. We might as well have been in a dark theater with a spotlight on us. We couldn't go to lunch for fear the plane would leave. I never missed a meal when I could help it, and I was hungry because I had eaten breakfast early.

I had a reservation on the 4:00 bus to Di An. Bob and I stood in the terminal not knowing if he would leave in the next five minutes or in two and a half hours, or longer. We shared an almost hot soda pop from a stand nearby. He said, "This is a crazy way to run a romance." I thought, *He's just as frustrated as I am.* We couldn't even talk to each other, because in the busy terminal a stream of people stopped to talk to us. They were waiting for flights too, and had time to kill. I watched him, longing to feel his arms around me. *I wish everybody would go away and leave us alone.*

After an hour, at 12:30, they called the flight. Bob and I hastily shook hands. I couldn't kiss him. The frustration that had built up over two days was ready to boil over. He turned and strode away, putting on his steel helmet as he went. The crowd swallowed him on the third step. He was going back to the war. I treasured the image into my memory, where I could recall it when I missed him. I didn't know if I would *ever* see him again. He might lose an arm, a leg. He might be killed. On the other hand, he might come back unharmed. I wondered if I would still love him if he lost an arm or a leg, then I realized my father had lost his leg to cancer, and he was still my father. Yes, I would still love Bob if he lost a limb. All we could do was wait. Two days of planning resulted in an hour meeting, but it had been worth it.

Mid-November came, and I was eligible for a vacation. In the combat zone, everyone received twice as much vacation time as people holding other Army assignments. Those vacation trips gave more than rest and relaxation. It was safe to say that in 1966, more than 90 percent of the men who served in Vietnam would never in their lifetime have the opportunity, or the means, to take a vacation in Hong Kong, Japan, Thailand, Singapore, or any of the other choices the military offered. I had already been to Japan, Thailand, and Hong Kong, so I chose

Singapore, a former British colony. The military provided transportation on a chartered jet. Again, I was the only girl on a plane full of soldiers. I laughed when I heard the announcement, "Gentlemen and Miss Puffer. This is the captain speaking. We will be flying. . . ."

The vacation started with a bang when the lunch came with real milk. Not the kind made from powder that we got in Nam—real, fresh milk. Everybody missed fresh milk. We all drank milk because we loved it, but we never got used to the powder. When we landed in Singapore we traveled by military bus along a broad, four-lane highway to the Shelford Hotel, a modern structure leased by the military. The guys, without delay, discovered next to the pool an invention that kept them entertained night and day for the four days and three nights we were there: a jukebox that played a movie with the music. No one had ever seen anything like it, and they played it nonstop, for 25 cents a song.

Singapore was a beautiful, modern, comfortable city. It was so clean that you could not only drink the water, you could eat anything, even from the street vendors. I had a plateful of fried rice in a sidewalk café at 2:00 A.M. Two soldiers from the plane and I wandered around the city all day and night, free of the stress of Vietnam. Singapore is in the same time zone as Vietnam, so we didn't suffer from jet lag. The climate was similar, possibly more comfortable than Vietnam. The bulletin board at the hotel announced a number of activities. I chose a deep-sea fishing trip and a walking night tour of the city. Singapore offered goods from around the world. I bought an elegant tablecloth of Venetian lace and Irish linen, and a 35-mm camera that would have cost me a fortune in the States.

The deep-sea fishing trip took us through the harbor on our way out to sea. We steered around two huge ships that lay partially submerged. The boat captain told us they sank during World War II. The bay was a deep-water port like Hong Kong and Cam Ranh Bay. Established as a free port like Hong Kong, where imports and exports paid no taxes, untold wealth poured into Singapore. I was on board a small fishing boat with perhaps 15 GIs from my plane. The whole boatload caught a total of three fish all day. The lucky fishermen gave their catch to the crew. It rained, and most of us got wet, but nobody cared. It was comfortably warm, and we were in civilian clothes on a fairytale vacation.

The night tour was the high point of the trip. About half a dozen of us started at the Raffles Hotel, named for the founder of Singapore. That wedding-cake, Victorian hotel had included among its guests the rich and famous, novelists, and movie stars. In the bar we had a famous Singapore Sling, a cocktail invented by the bartender. A walk through exotic neighborhoods followed. The opium den fascinated me—the British answer to drug addiction. The guide told us the government bought up all the opium. They gathered the addicts, gave them free room and board and all the opium they wanted, and waited for them to die. Once the government cornered the market on opium, they reduced the price until the competition went out of business. Anybody who wanted opium had to get it from the government. We saw a dimly lit, clean room. Bunk beds lined the walls. A dozen dressed and groomed men of various ages lounged here and there on the beds and on Chinese-style cushions on the floor. They did nothing. That was it. No music played, no one spoke, no one read a book. No social workers interviewed them, or tried to rehabilitate them. No one did anything. Other rooms housed other men, all addicted, all waiting to die. I thought, *It sounds like a good idea. It appears to work.*

Next, we saw a neighborhood where the women worked as the breadwinners of the family and the men stayed home and took care of the children. At 9:00 at night we saw a woman carpenter who worked on the sidewalk in front of a shop. She used a hammer to pull some nails out of some pieces of wood, while the foot traffic surged around her.

On the last night the hotel gave a free buffet dinner around the swimming pool. The food was great, the beer was free. It was what every soldier would consider a perfect evening. Free food, free beer—everybody would make it to the plane in the morning.

One man got drunk and fell into the pool and almost drowned. People pulled him out and took him to the hospital. It happened long after I went to bed. The guys told me about it the next day. As we boarded the plane, the highest-ranking man, a general, carried a portfolio of papers for the sick man, who would miss the flight back to the war. I joked with the general as we boarded. I indicated the portfolio under his arm and said, "Too bad you have to work on your vacation."

He replied as a generous gentleman, "Well, someone has to take care of people who need help."

Monday, November 21, Di An

I was tired at the end of that day. I dragged myself to the mess hall for supper to join the three friends. Lieutenants Jones, Peterson, and Wilks sat in alphabetical order at their usual table. I loved to eat with them; they always laughed. Lieutenant Wilks was ready with another story: "We were in a field position. Everybody knew there would be a mortar attack that night. You could feel it in the air. Everyone was scared." Jones and Peterson looked sober. Wilks cast his eyes from side to side as if he looked for the enemy. "As soon as we came into position we started digging holes as fast as we could. Night came, and right on schedule the mortars started raining down. All hell broke loose. It was a heavy attack." Jones and Peterson were quiet. They had probably been with Wilks at the time. He continued, "I fell into my hole as the first round landed. I stayed at the very bottom for a long time before I got up nerve to stick out just the top of my head and look around." Wilks craned his neck and looked as though he were peering over the edge of the hole. "There on the ground, not ten feet away lay my radio telephone operator, fast asleep. If the mortars landing all around couldn't wake him, calling wouldn't help, even if he could hear above the noise.

There was nothing I could do but crawl out and shake him. That's what I did. Finally, he stirred. I yelled into his ear, 'We're being mortared!'

"The boy beat me back to the hole." The three friends, Jones, Peterson and Wilks laughed. I had the good laugh I needed to wash away my fatigue. No one mentioned that Wilks had put himself in danger to save another man's life. They figured anyone would do it. That story at supper, told for amusement, answered for me the question: Why do some people suspend the basic instinct of self-preservation? They put their lives in danger to perform acts of courage. The answer was: they had to.

Everywhere we went, security was a constant concern. If an area was safe for us to go into, sometimes different commanders required different levels of security. When I was in the 1st Infantry Division, if we traveled on the Bien Hoa Highway, 1st Division required us to have someone riding shotgun. The 173rd Brigade never required the extra man.

Once when we had an escort from the 199th Military Police, they sent a second jeep to drive 100 yards ahead of us. We didn't know where we were going, but most of the time we didn't know where we were, anyway. The officer riding with us explained that the road was mined, and the MPs were driving far enough ahead so that if they hit a mine, we would not be affected. I noticed that our driver tracked the lead jeep exactly. If they passed over, around or beside a bump, we did too. It seemed like a long, long road. I was relieved when we came to the end of it. I knew the MPs were playing the odds, but I didn't like it.

✛ CHAPTER 7 ✛

A Veteran under the Desk

Thanksgiving Day, Thursday, November 24, 1966, Phu Loi, South Vietnam

On Thanksgiving we got caught in the enemy's crossfire. The authorities in Vietnam confined most women to relatively safe rear areas. However, in Vietnam, commanders allowed the Red Cross girls to go where few went. We traveled to visit the men everywhere, even to the foxholes, as Sandra and I had done at Buon Blech. Thanksgiving Day, Dee (DeMaris) Walton and I planned to visit the 1st Infantry Division's 2/2nd Infantry in their field position at Phu Loi. As soon as we arrived, our escort, the Battalion S-1 Personnel/Administration Officer, Capt. Jerald D. Fuhriman,[1] found that we would have to wait. He told us, "B and C Companies are in a firefight, and everyone else is in an awards ceremony." Even Army Chief of Staff Gen. William C. Westmoreland was there. "We can't see units in the field or in base camp until after the ceremony." We knew we could not present a recreation program on this visit, but we hoped to serve Thanksgiving dinner at as many places as possible. It would give the men a chance to talk to an American girl, probably for the only time in their year in Vietnam.

A smattering of personnel moved among headquarters buildings. Dee and I joined half a dozen men gathered around a field radio on a jeep. They welcomed us. We discovered that they were listening to the conversations going on among the elements engaged in the fighting that was making us wait. The men brought us up to date, "A unit of our infantry has engaged a group of VC at one end of the valley. The VC broke off and fled down the valley. Our scout helicopters spotted them, and told the commander their strength, position, and movement."

Another continued, "The commander directed another infantry unit to intercept the VC. He ordered the first unit to withdraw, but watch out the VC didn't double back and ambush their withdrawal."

Over the radio Dee and I heard the commander give the order: "Pull out bag and baggage and all your wounded. Make sure there's somebody covering your ass!" He called for artillery and for a "dust-off," a medical evacuation helicopter, for the wounded. I was pleased to learn that the heroic stand-to-the-last-man, leave-me-behind-save-yourself story line was a Hollywood fiction. The soldiers who listened to the radio cheered and rooted for each unit, even more excited than if they were listening to a ballgame. Their friends were out there. Men like those, who drove for officers, earned a break from combat by showing how good they were in the field. One man almost shouted, "Yes, get the artillery in there, level that house, get that sniper!"

Another man asked, "Why aren't they using the tanks? They've got four tanks out there."

A third man exclaimed, "Here comes the dust-off. I see it, over there." He pointed. The fight was so close we could actually see the medical evacuation helicopter in the sky above the treetops, with a big Red Cross on the side. In agony, I watched it creep. It searched for colored smoke to show where to pick up the wounded. The enemy, no doubt, had plenty of time to take aim at it.

"There it goes," shouted the first man. He pointed to the ship again. It dove into the trees. "Those people will go anywhere. They're going to draw a lot of fire on that one." Everyone nodded, their eyes wide. On the radio the chopper confirmed lift off with the last wounded soldier.

Dee and I were relieved. A Hollywood happy ending could be real. We went over to the awards ceremony with the rest of the people. General Westmoreland was there, also the premier of South Vietnam, Nguyen Cao Ky ("Win kow kee"). The awards ceremony filled the parade ground, which looked like a high school football field. A reviewing stand at the 50-yard line extended about a third of the length of the field on the right side. The crowd overflowed and spread outward, standing all around the field, as at the big game on Thanksgiving. This *was* Thanksgiving. Dee and I joined the throng on the reviewing-stand side of the end zone. Everyone made way for us to move to the front. We wouldn't have been able to see much otherwise, because the crowd—all men—towered above us. Rows and rows of soldiers covered the field.

Dee exclaimed, "This is big."

I asked, "How many men do you think are out there?"

A lieutenant who stood nearby replied as if we were in our hometown: "There are about 2,000 men on the field in review today." All during the awards ceremony, artillery boomed and whistled over our heads in support of the fight we had listened to on the radio. We experienced during the daytime what I had heard in the bunker at night at An Khe. I looked up. I couldn't see the shells, but I could follow their path across the sky by the sound. We saw two Distinguished Service Crosses (DSC) presented that day, one step down from the Medal of Honor. Five other soldiers received Silver Stars. The G-3 (Operations), Lt. Col. Alexander M. Haig, Jr., from Oderbrook, Pennsylvania, received the Republic of Vietnam National Order Medal Fifth Class.[2] Reporters and photographers, Vietnamese and American, engulfed those real heroes while the commanders pinned on the DSCs and Silver Stars.

While commanders awarded the other medals, the photographers looked around for something else to shoot. As soon as one took our picture, the rest surrounded us. We smiled and turned so our Red Cross patches would show, as Washington had trained us. Soldiers took my picture often, but by the time those newsmen finished, my face was frozen. When they moved off, every serviceman in the area took our picture. How many people photographed us, I never knew. When the soldiers took my picture, I knew I represented a piece of home for them to cherish.

The commanders presented the last medals and the ceremony ended. Now we could see the men. We hurried back to the Officer's Club, where the personnel officer had arranged for the cooks to serve us ahead of everyone else. We ate our Thanksgiving meal as fast as we could. Next, we attended a fifteen-minute Thanksgiving church service in an outdoor chapel, conducted by Capt. Tom Carter, the chaplain. The service gave us a chance to see more men, and in the combat zone we could use all the help we could get.

Chaplain Carter's sermon title was "Abundant Life," using Scripture John 10: vs. 7-21, "I came that they may have life." Carter asked for the troops to share what they were thankful for, even in war. He said, "God gives not just enough life to keep going, not just enough courage, but overflowing and abundant." "On this day of Thanksgiving, my prayer is that you will seek the abundant life offered by God and share your thanks with those around you." Attendance at that service was 55 men. Many years later his memory of the day was clear. "I do remember you all being there. It was a happy day and lots of food. I ate a little at each company when I went for services."[3]

After the church service, we helped the cooks serve the dinner for base camp. We had just finished, when Captain Fuhriman received word that the battle had ended and the area was now secure. We could go visit the soldiers we had listened to on the radio. We left in two jeeps escorted by the battalion commander, Lt. Col. Jack L. Conn, Sergeant Major Harry Sanders, and the S-1 Personnel Officer, Captain Fuhriman.[4]

The Company A Commander, Capt. Francis J. Thompson, gave us unit patches and made us honorary members of 2/2 Infantry. The cooks at A Company had just started to serve dinner, an overflowing cafeteria line outdoors and we stepped in to help. The men had not taken part in the action. They were clean and pressed for the occasion, right down to creases in their fatigue trousers and on the sleeves. We greeted each man with a smile, as we did whenever we served chow. "Hello. Happy Thanksgiving. Would you like some fruit salad?"

The soldier replied, "Same to you. Yes, thank you Ma'am."

"How much would you like? Is this enough? A little more?"

Sometimes we could make a joke, "There's no room on your plate. Shall I squeeze it in next to the cranberry sauce?"

The man replied with good nature, "Yes, thank you, Ma'am. That will be fine." We both laughed as I carefully placed the salad. Others in the line laughed with us.

I asked another man, "Isn't this a great dinner? I hope you're hungry."

He replied with enthusiasm, eyes wide at the heap of food he carried, "Oh, yes Ma'am, I am." I remembered the pancake supper we had served at Dong Ba Thin, when 75 soldiers ate enough pancakes for 150 men, *after* they had eaten their supper.

I said, "Have a good dinner."

"I will. Thank you." I heard a burst of laughter from the end of the line where Dee served the pumpkin pie. The men always responded to her with warmth. Each man got as much as he could eat. Afterward, we walked around and talked to everyone. They sat here and there in groups on the ground. They shared each other's company and enjoyed the food, picnic style.

Years later I had a phone conversation with Jim Huggins, who had been there at Company A for Thanksgiving dinner. He emphasized that he was a young lieutenant at the time. "When I saw the Red Cross girls, I thought they were the most beautiful women I ever saw in my life."

I interrupted him, "Jim, that was me." I thought he was going to choke.

He confessed, "We might have had some impure thoughts at times. . . . We were young. . . ." I asked how the war affected the men's lives. "Chaplain Carter baptized me. I was a heathen . . . " "We thought the bullet, if it came, it would be for somebody else." "Total fear . . . kept the adrenalin pumping." He added, "The VC hit us right after you left. We had no idea you girls were in so much danger."[5]

Next, we served the dinner at B Company as we had at Company A on a clear Thanksgiving in the first year of the war. However, these men had just returned from the fight. They looked as if they had been crawling around in mud. Most of them wore no patches, no rank, and even no nametags.

It struck me that everywhere we went that day the cooks had just begun to serve dinner. I was sure the cooks had orders to hold the meal until we got there. After we finished serving, Dee and I each took some food and ate as we talked to the soldiers. For a few minutes I sat and finished my dinner with a group of people who relaxed in a circle of logs under some trees. A sergeant arrived to escort me on a tour of the camp. Instead of a rifle, he carried a machete. It had to be a trophy belonging to someone in his unit, maybe even to him.

I knew he expected me to notice it. "That's quite a machete you have there."

"Yes." His chest swelled. "It's from the fighting this morning. Let me show you our defenses." We walked almost all the way to the perimeter. I stood and admired the bunkers and other fortifications. Suddenly, we heard a burst of small arms fire, then another and another. The sergeant yelled, "Get down!" He almost shoved me into a bunker and ran, calling back over his shoulder, "I have to get back to my unit." I skinned my elbow when I landed.

Years later I understood that I was hearing the VC hit at Company A. It was the attack that Lieutenant Huggins told me about years later on the phone.

I could see and hear men as they dashed. They snatched up weapons and steel helmets. Everyone yelled, "Ammo over here! Ammo! Ammo!"

I heard one holler, "Two miles away." They jumped into trucks and roared out of sight. Then the men were gone, the perimeter was empty, and I was alone. My escort was gone. I crouched down as far as I could in the small bunker and froze like a cornered rabbit in the stifling heat. I remembered that the colonel at An Khe told us scorpions had stung two men when they dove into bunkers. I looked around to see if I had startled any crawling creatures. I cursed my light blue uniform, so easy to see against the dark green jungle. The Red Cross pin on the collar and the patch on my shoulder were tiny shields to hide behind, little comfort and less protection. I didn't remember my "If Captured" card that said I was a civilian non-combatant. I held my breath. At any moment I expected a VC in black pajamas and a cone-shaped hat to thrust a Soviet AK-47 in my face and say, "You come with me, Led Closs Lady."

I remembered later that the VC couldn't speak English. I asked Gerald Burns, of counterintelligence, if the VC took prisoners. He answered, "Sometimes they took them but usually did not. They had no facilities for holding prisoners. I found one they took, young, E-2, garbage truck driver. He, of course, had lots of Intel about coming battles. They held him for a few days before we found him. They had punched out his eyes, cut his fingers, toes, and ears off, cut out his tongue, knocked out all his teeth, beat him almost to death and roasted him alive on a spit over a fire. Found one hanging in a tree that I did not recognize as a human." Nasty thoughts. Even the most callous US soldier would be repulsed by the extent of Viet Cong torture. Good thing I didn't know about it at the time.

I didn't dare look out of the bunker. If I could see the VC, they could see me. I squatted awkward, motionless, almost. I tried to stay out of the way of hostile creatures, but a spider bit me on the neck. It felt like a long time. The fight grew louder. It got closer. I wasn't panicked; I wasn't even really scared. I had dived into bunkers so many times it was part of the routine, but I felt lonely. To be alone gave me a special vulnerability. I saw when I arrived at Ton Son Nhut, how the group could give me courage. Even to have one other person with me in the bunker would have made a difference. To be alone felt like I was naked. Finally, I heard an American voice calling softly, "Joann, Joann, where are you?" Relief flooded over me. The loneliness evaporated.

I called back, almost in a whisper, "Over here." I hadn't heard him approach. He moved without a sound.

He almost whispered, "Follow me, run! Keep down, over this way!" His uniform introduced him. It was rumpled and dirt-stained with sweat rings under his arms. He wore sergeant's rank on his sleeve, three chevrons, although one corner hung loose. He carried his M-16 in his right hand. His self-assured manner inspired my confidence. He led me at a run, away from the sound of the guns. Even when he ran, he moved like a ghost. We burst into the field position. He pushed me into another, much bigger bunker and ordered, "Keep down." I landed on that same, skinned-up elbow.

Dee sat there on the dry, clean, scorpion-free dirt floor. She exclaimed, "I was on the other perimeter when the fighting broke out." She looked relieved. "Everyone was frantic when your escort came back without you." I thought, *It was extremely dangerous for me to be out there alone.* I looked through the doorway of the bunker. A handful of men lounged here and there as though they didn't have a job. A dozen other men surrounded us behind sandbag walls. I heard a scrape and click. Several people inserted clips into their rifles. Weapons loaded and ready, unhurried, long-practiced, they watched and listened to the rustle of the trees and the fight nearby.

Two men gave us their helmets. They looked serious. "Put these on if mortar rounds start coming in." I didn't learn until many years later that "Everyone in the area prepared themselves with weapons and steel pots because the enemy would target the mortar if they could identify where it was located."[6]

A few minutes later the jobless men burst into action. They snatched up steel helmets and ran, yelling "Fire mission." Within minutes,[7] *boom, swish,* mortars started going out from next to us. The VC must have been headed our way and less than a mile out, the range of the weapon. The frantic mortar crews fired non-stop for five or ten minutes.[8] *Boom, swish, boom, swish.* Dee and I couldn't see anything or hear anything over the sound of the guns. All we could do was get down and stay down.

The booming of the mortars finally stopped, and a sergeant came to the doorway and told us we could come out now. My ears rang.

Dee and I planned to visit C Company next. Captain Fuhriman broke the news, "This is the company that has seen the most action during the day, as well as during the past week. The fighting that just took place was about a quarter of a mile off the road between here and C Company. It won't be safe for us to go through there. Even if we could, we wouldn't be able to get out and back along the roads before dark [when they close]." Disappointed, Dee and I loaded up in separate jeeps, spaced far apart for safety, and started toward 1st Infantry Division Headquarters at Di An. We met the battalion commander, Colonel Conn, on the road as he returned from the battle. He stopped us and spoke to our escort several yards away. I could see the colonel seated next to his driver. His helmet moved from side to side and jerked up and down. He said something to his radio telephone operator in the back seat of the jeep. They made a call. The colonel spoke again to our escort, gestured, and pointed down the dirt road, back in the direction he had come.

The captain drove his jeep over next to Dee's and then to mine. He looked worried. "The colonel still wants you to visit C Company. He has ordered his four escort jeeps armed with machine guns to turn around. They will join our three, and together we will take you to C Company." The colonel set a fast pace, our best defense. The road passed through a wood. Tense, I watched everywhere for shadows. We came out of the wood and entered a village. Armed Vietnamese men stood in groups of four and six, in front of shops.

I asked Sergeant Major Sanders, "Who are those men?"

His disapproval showed. "Those are called 'Black Shirts.' They are Vietnamese soldiers who were supposed to be fighting with us. They're hiding in the village until the fighting stops." GIs in jeeps raced up and down the road to secure the area. I thought, *That's great. Whose war is this, anyway?*

At C Company Dee and I joined the cooks in the mess line. This time I served the pie and she gave out the fruit salad. Adrenalin and dirt still clung to the infantrymen. We greeted and joked with each one. Morale soared. The noise level in the mess line climbed, and laughter pierced the quiet jungle non-stop. The battle won, everyone safe, the heaped-up plates of hot Thanksgiving food shouted celebration. The reminder of home that Dee and I represented added a spark, like fireworks. I saw Colonel Conn, for a moment, way in the back. He looked over the scene, nodded slightly to himself, and disappeared.

The dinner served, Dee and I split up and walked around as we ate. We joked and laughed with everyone as they sat in groups on the ground. Finished, we discovered some 20 officers who stood clumped together at one end of the compound sharing a bottle of champagne in paper cups. They divided the last of it between Dee and me. Another officer arrived. Several people poured a little of their champagne into a cup for him. The combat officers, for their safety, wore no nametags, few wore rank, and no one saluted. They communicated with glances, not speech. I greeted the chaplain, Captain Carter. He had arrived ahead of us at each stop all day. I learned later that Carter had preached his sermon to each company, 265 men in all.[9] A captain remarked, "We have a lot of admiration for him. He makes a big effort to reach the men in the field." The officers raised their cups in assent.

The chaplain looked at the ground. He joked to me, "Your presence here has set back my pacification program three months." That was a pun on the Army's mission in that sector: Pacification. It meant to drive the VC out, secure the area, make it peaceful, win the loyalty of the people, and then turn the area over to the Vietnamese to defend against further VC infiltration. Everyone gave a long laugh.

I wondered who these officers were. What were they doing there? This was C Company. I didn't think they were all the C Company officers, because there were too many. Years later I got my answer. Tom Carter told me, "The additional officers were from the battalion headquarters. They went from one company to another also to bring Thanksgiving greetings. They were members of the battalion staff."[10]

A fresh-faced lieutenant complimented us, "Your being here has raised morale 90 percent." A chorus muttered agreement and nodded. I laughed at the exaggeration.

Another said, "If Charlie tries to attack tonight he's in for real trouble."

The group glanced agreement at each other. Several repeated, "Yes, he's in for trouble." As we joked and laughed and shared the champagne, a helicopter appeared in the sky. Down came 1st Infantry Division Commander Maj. Gen. William E. DePuy (pronounced "De Pee-oo"). His chopper landed outside the earthwork berm of the camp, a few yards from where we stood. Then Assistant Division Commander Brig. Gen. James J. Hollingsworth's chopper settled down beside General DePuy's. Then a third chopper.

Anxious people started to glance at a clump of palm trees some 200 yards away across the gray, November rice paddies. A round-faced lieutenant asked the officer standing next to him, "How long can all those choppers sit there, a nice juicy target, before the VC open up again?"

Someone barked his answer. "Get down! Get down!" Everyone dropped. Champagne and cups flew.

I hugged the ground. "What is it?" I had heard no explosions, no small-arms fire.

The round-faced lieutenant answered, "A sniper. Probably from that clump of palm trees." Yes, in my memory I heard *crack, crack, crack*. I felt bare. I looked around. Everyone was down as low as he could go, except for one tall, intense captain. The captain looked this way and that, at the tree line where the shots had come from. Could he locate the sniper? He looked at the people around him. Had the rounds hit anyone?

I had dropped beside his feet. I looked up, "Why don't you get down?"

He stared straight at me, his jaw set, resolve in his voice. "I came to Vietnam to get killed." He looked away.

I indicated Captain Intense and cast a glance at the man next to me on the ground. He nodded and whispered, "It's true. Something about his wife leaving him." That must have happened back in the States. I almost never heard men talk about marital troubles. Some joked about "Dear John" letters, but not their own. The captain's wish was opposite of everyone else's in Vietnam. I wondered, would he be spared? Captain Intense was disappointed that he was still alive, but there would be other times. He started to run.

We all strained to listen for more shots. Silence. Men ran, keeping low, and shouted. An officer a few feet away explained, "They'll form up a squad to go after the sniper." He got up and ran, bent over. The sniper had probably already hidden his weapon in the brush. A moonlighting local farmer by now, he trotted back across the rice paddies to his village for supper. Tomorrow he might be selling souvenirs to the soldiers he shot at. But, just to be on the safe side, everyone would assume the worst until the danger was past. It looked like chaos, but it really wasn't. Every runner knew his destination and his assignment.[11] The helicopters had not shut down. They took off like startled dragonflies. The generals, all of us, were stranded. If this was an attack, we had cast our futures with those soldiers.

Our frantic escort officer yelled to me, "Get in a hole! Run! Keep down!" I got up and raced after him. He threaded me through the crowd dashing bent over in every direction. He ordered, "Get in here. Stay down!" and vanished.

I couldn't see which shelter he indicated. I asked, "Where?"

Dee answered, "In here." She had beaten me to safety, again. A sergeant appeared, drew his .45 and knelt in the doorway. I crouched in the bunker, intent on the moment, concentrating on staying down out of the way. A sniper attack, the enemy so close, brought a rush, but it didn't last long. Reality crowded it out. Getting shot at could get you seriously dead.

After a few minutes an officer stuck his head into the bunker. "You can come out. No more rounds have come in. It was just a sniper." The sergeant in the doorway holstered his .45 and disappeared. The helicopters returned.

I found Captain Fuhriman. "Thank you for taking us to see so many men, and especially for getting us to Charlie Company."

His shoulders drooped. He didn't smile. "Yes, but I'll feel a lot better when you get on that chopper and get out of here." Moments later Dee and I ran to the third ship and took off. The chopper that had started all the ruckus had come for us. We climbed into the sky, and I looked out over the company's field position to the clump of palm trees. Beyond it and all around stretched miles of dry rice paddies. I strained my eyes in the dusk. Could I see, at the far end, a farmer who trotted toward the village? It was too far away; I couldn't tell.

I didn't learn until years after that Capt. Francis Thompson Company A, 2ND BN, 2INF, who gave us unit patches at the beginning of the day, was killed in action two months later, on January 24, 1967. Captain Thompson and two enlisted were killed and one officer and five enlisted were wounded by a Claymore mine and firefight near Tay Ninh.[12]

I wondered what more I could find out about that day. Chaplain Carter remembered,

> My memory is somewhat foggy. I do remember the champagne :-) I was probably hanging around with the group that had gathered. I do remember a crack and that is what got us all on the ground. I'm not sure how many rounds. The account is accurate from what I recall of the day. Good writing![13]

Sergeant Fulps, who knelt in the doorway of the bunker, had a clear memory:

> At the moment the sniper fire erupted, I was indeed conversing with General Depuy. We were standing to the right, as you face the bunker, which you and Dee later occupied. I distinctly remember hearing the sniper's initial gunshots and I would also describe the sounds as "cracks" rather than a "swish" or "pop." The next thing I remember is ushering you ladies into the bunker and posting myself in the doorway. After we were given the "all clear" I returned to my Platoon area.[14]

What was the significance of the sound, "crack"? I learned that:

> On Oct. 25, 2007, Medal of Honor recipient, 22 year-old Army Spc. Salvatore Giunta [pronounced "Joon ta"]

raced head-on into an enemy ambush. He observed, "There were bullets all over the place . . . Sometimes they whistle, sometimes they crack . . . Then there's the whiz. That's a little bit further away than the crack."[15]

Sergeant Fulps commented:

I would say at least three or four shots. In my mind it seems that there was an initial shot followed by several more in rapid succession. It had never crossed my mind, but it is entirely possible that your light-colored uniform would have made a very distinguishable target.

If that was the case, God surely had his hand on you that day. Take care Lady Veteran.[16]

Thanksgiving, Thursday, November 24, Di An

Dee and I got home to Di An that evening bruised and battered, but pleased to have had such a successful day. I called Bob to wish him Happy Thanksgiving. We wrote letters to each other almost every day. I attempted to call him every evening that I could, and talked to him whenever I could get through. The phone lines were inadequate. We had to yell, and still couldn't make out what we said to each other. I was frustrated because communication problems interfered with my work. On the other hand, I knew there was no use complaining. Everyone struggled with the same difficulties. There was nothing to do but work around it and try to be patient. Whenever I called Bob I started and ended by saying "I love you." Sometimes the lines were so bad that was all we could understand, and sometimes we would get cut off without warning.

That evening he came on the line, "Cold Shower 6." My heart leaped when I heard his call sign, and I felt the blood rush to my face. My heart leaped again when I realized that tonight the phone lines were faint, but we could understand each other for the first time in weeks. I could recognize his voice. I didn't have to yell.

"I love you. Happy Thanksgiving. How are you?"

He answered, "I love you. I can hear you!" His voice jumped in surprise. "I'm fine. How are you?" I knew he couldn't tell me much because there were people all around and on the phone lines, including the VC, who listened to everything.

I was so excited I rushed to tell him about my day, before we could get cut off. I told him, "We went to church and we went to an awards ceremony, and we ate four Thanksgiving dinners." We both laughed. Not wanting him to worry, I skipped all the parts about diving into bunkers. It was so good to hear him laugh. I felt warm all over. I told him what the chaplain, Captain Carter, had said about his pacification program. We both laughed again. I felt closer than ever to my best friend.

Bob told me as much as he could on the telephone, "We had a big Thanksgiving dinner, and everyone is stuffed." Then he asked me to do something no other officer had ever asked me to do. "Would you mind talking to the people who are here, my first sergeant, my three RTOs [radio/telephone operators] and my driver?" He knew I would be glad to. His men knew he talked to me whenever he could, and when they were nearby they participated in the affection. They might have listened in, as the telephone operators did. It was like a call to relatives on a holiday back home. We passed the phone from one to another, and talked to everybody. True to military fashion, Bob began with the highest rank. "Here is the first sergeant."

"Hello. This is Joann. Happy Thanksgiving."

The seasoned soldier's voice resonated, deep and businesslike, "Thank you, same to you."

"Is it pretty quiet there today?"

"Yes, nothing much going on." I knew that troops in Vietnam did not sit around, even on Thanksgiving. I had seen that earlier in the day.

They hunted for the enemy, engaged the enemy, or pulled guard duty while they rested from combat.

"Nothing much going on here, either. Did you have a good dinner?"

He replied, "Turkey and all the fixin's. Ate too much. Here's the 1st Platoon RTO, Cold Shower 1 Alpha."

We exchanged a few words, and he passed me to the 2nd Platoon RTO.

That man sounded young and enthusiastic. He shouted across the weak lines. "We like the captain for a boss. He treats us well."

I laughed, "What would you say if the captain weren't standing there?"

He raised his voice. "Can't hear you, Ma'am." His good-natured chuckle echoed as he handed the phone to the 3rd RTO.

He yelled into the phone, "Hello!"

That man also volunteered in a cheerful, Thanksgiving Day mood, "We think the captain is a good boss. He treats us well."

I laughed out loud this time and repeated my jest.

He joined the tease, "Can't hear you, Ma'am," the grin audible in his voice. He passed me to the driver before something could happen to the great reception.

The driver, with a soft Southern accent said, "Nice to talk to you, Ma'am. We appreciate the chance to say hello. Here's the captain."

He came to the phone laughing. "What did you tell them?" My explanation heightened his humor as I shared his laugh, a good release from the tension of the day. We concluded the call and hung up the phone. Years later I learned that the first sergeant's name was Van Allen, and the three RTOs were Curt Anderson, Shank, and Barry Holden. Another RTO, Alec Lyall, not present at the time, operated a radio that communicated with battalion headquarters.[17]

Something unusual about the conversation made me think. No commander had asked me to talk to his staff, a thoughtful gesture that these men appreciated. On the phone call that day two men had paid a compliment to their captain. What they said to me, they were also saying to him.

My friend Lt. Jim Brigham of 2/7ᵗʰ Cavalry gave me some insight. "RTO is considered a good job. RTOs and COs become close because they are together all the time; and they have time to talk at night. With the CO there, the comments were from the heart. They must have gotten along good with him. Troops are not afraid to speak their mind. They liked him and respected him. If the CO was Dip Shit you probably would not have gotten any comment."

Everyone knew that to command an Infantry company put my captain in more danger than most jobs. I got my mind off the thought as fast as I could and concentrated on the joy from our conversation. I forced it to squeeze out the empty feeling I always had when I hung up the phone from someone close to me.

Friday, November 25, Saigon

The day after Thanksgiving, I went to visit my sister, Phyllis, in Saigon. She told me, "Guess what. I saw you on TV last night."

I laughed. "What? You did?"

"A bunch of us were sitting in the hotel lobby watching the evening news. They were showing an awards ceremony. All of a sudden, somebody said, 'Look. Two Red Cross girls.' I looked just in time to see another girl and you!"

All I could say was, "Well, what do you know." I thought to myself, *We made the evening news on television in Saigon, just because we were there.* I didn't tell Phyllis all the hair-raising things we did that day. She didn't need to worry.

I planned to stay the night with my sister, but she didn't have any place for me to sleep. I could barely squeeze between the two beds, the room cried for paint, and I noticed fingerprint smudges around the light switch. The Vietnamese style bed was a wooden platform, smooth from years of use, covered with a thin mattress. I didn't know that beds were almost impossible to find. My sister told me, "You have to start right away to find a place to sleep." Regulations required that I stay overnight only in a women's housing unit, not just for appearances, but for protection. The 9:00 P.M. curfew kept all military personnel off the streets at night, buttoned up behind guards in military housing. Otherwise, to stay in a Vietnamese hotel would have been suicide. With no protection, I had a good chance of waking up dead with a bayonet between my ribs. I also knew that to break the rules meant an instant plane ticket home.

My sister and I sat together on her hard bed, "You have to go down to the front desk in the lobby. There, you have to see the sergeant in charge. He is responsible for getting people rooms. He will give you a room or a place to sleep." My sister warned me: "The sergeant is a crotchety old guy who has a miserable job as a desk clerk in an officers' billet. Being a sergeant, all the officers order him to do things, like give them a room. Sometimes he can do what they order, and sometimes he can't. When he can't, he gets yelled at. Military protocol says that an officer can't actually order a sergeant to do anything unless he reports directly to that officer. But, that doesn't stop this hotel full of officers from making his life miserable."

I had no other choice. I had to get the sergeant at the front desk to give me a bed. I couldn't take no for an answer—I couldn't even consider it because of the danger. So I went to see the sergeant. I could get anything I wanted from anybody. We girls used to say to each other that all we had to do was bat our blue eyes and smile and everybody would give us whatever we asked for. We were conscious, however, that we only asked for what we needed, never took advantage of anyone, and always remained professional. We knew that it was too easy to be misunderstood and that would hurt our reputation and our effectiveness in our job, not to mention put us in physical danger. Failure never crossed my mind. The sergeant had a frown and sandy-blond hair that blended into his khaki uniform. He was starched and pressed from head to the top of the desk. No sweat stain marred his perfect uniform, even in the swelter. He wore a chest full of combat medals and new lines on his face that said, "I didn't do anything to deserve this punishment." Like all the military men in Vietnam, he was lean, fit, trim, disciplined, and proud. He looked up from the desk briefly, but only to be polite.

"I need a room," I said, with my sweetest smile.

"I'm sorry, there are no rooms." His answer was firm, detached. He studied the papers on the desk.

"But I really need a place to sleep. I'm here visiting my sister." I tried to look vulnerable, but innocent.

"There's nothing. I haven't anything for anybody," he repeated with added firmness. He showed no sympathy. It was Thanksgiving weekend. He moved some reports from one side of the desk to the other, and then looked up to end the conversation. My gaze fell on his chest-full of medals. I thought, *This poor man. He's a genuine hero. Someone tried to do him a favor. They brought him out of a dangerous foxhole to Saigon to give him a break from combat, and he ended up in this miserable job where people scream at him all day.* I was sure he wished he was back in combat.

I said out loud, "Boy, you must have the toughest job in the world." He hesitated and studied me. His long-practiced eye went right past the Red Cross on my uniform that usually stopped everyone. He recognized the patch from a combat unit, the 1st Infantry Division, on my right shoulder. He spotted the stain on my sleeve, the day-old skinned-up elbow, and the spider bite on my neck. I had passed inspection. He became a new person. The lines on his face softened, but he couldn't let anyone see him smile. He disappeared silently into the back and returned with an untidy, dusty bundle, which he laid in my arms. It contained the pieces of a folding, canvas Army cot with a wooden frame. I gave him my biggest, warmest, blue-eyed smile, in the pseudo-air conditioned swelter, and the most heartfelt "Thank you." I had, with a WAC to help me put it together, the last bed in Saigon.

Monday, November 28, Di An

What a surprise. Tonight Jessica Hunter, the big boss, called from Saigon and told me I am being promoted to program director and transferred to Bien Hoa. I will report there on December 7. I wondered if I would be able to fit my new job. I like Di An. I asked to come to a combat unit. Bien Hoa is more secure than Di An. I hope it won't be boring.

Wednesday, November 30

My replacement came today. She is a nice redhead transferred from Korea after five months.

Saturday, December 3

Yesterday I received two boxes from home, made of wood, about three feet long. One end was open, and inside I could see two live Christmas trees. A few decorations arrived along with the trees. My parents had offered to send them, a gift to me and to the soldiers. Mom and Dad knew that we would need a lot of help to have a real Christmas in Vietnam. They guessed that the trees would be a wonderful piece of home. They were right: the Christmas trees caused a sensation. My family owned a Christmas tree plantation near Traverse City in northern Michigan. Among the thousands of trees that grew there, Mom and Dad had chosen two perfect Scotch pines and ordered them cut and custom packaged.

When I was a kid we bundled up, and my dad took the three of us girls to pick out a Christmas tree. We romped through the knee-deep snow and rejected one tree after another until we found the perfect tree. My parents knew how much I treasured Christmas trees. They did not want me to miss out on that joy while I was in Vietnam.

The second Christmas tree in a box.

I decided to take one tree with me to my new assignment at Bien Hoa. I had a couple of the guys carry the other one to the recreation center, where I invited everyone to help. Eager hands pulled the boards apart. The soldiers stood back in awe as the branches sproinged open to reveal a real, live Christmas tree. My Mom and Dad had sent a wonderful gift. The men fashioned a stand for the tree and moved all the furniture to give it the featured place of honor. All the men loved the Scotch pine. One after another, they went up to it. They felt it and smelled it. Some drew their chairs close to it. They sat and remembered their childhood Christmases.

Sunday, December 4, Can Tho (pronounced "Kan Toe")

My promotion to program director in Bien Hoa meant that I would coordinate production of the programs, write the work schedule, arrange transportation, and chair the production half of the weekly staff meetings. Saigon sent me on a trip with Dee, the program director at Di An, to help me learn the job. We would see what we could do to set up visits to the Special Forces in the Delta. Two 1st Infantry Division Military Policemen picked Dee and me up at our house at first light in a jeep mounted with a machine gun. The trip from our house to the helicopter pad wouldn't require a machine gun, but it conveyed the importance of the mission.

The courier chopper to Saigon waited on the helipad at 7:15 A.M., shut down in deference to our hair. We really appreciated it. Our flight took us above the peaceful and dangerous countryside. The cool, pre-dawn light grew. The sun, low in the sky, turned the rice paddies into an array of mirrors that followed us as we flew. Golden sunlight washed us. The sunrise cast shadows as we landed on the helipad at Tan Son Nhut (TSN) Air Base. We ate breakfast in the TSN officer's club, then walked the short distance to an Army Caribou cargo plane (CV-2). It would take us to Can Tho in the Mekong ("Mee kong") Delta. Dee and I would conduct our business, and then ride the same plane back to Saigon at the end of the day. To conserve our strength for the long hours ahead, we dozed in our seats to the hypnotic drone of the engines. The plane cruised south over endless, flat rice paddies. We flew from one airstrip to another around the Delta for 2 and a half hours. We landed at Can Tho just in time for lunch. A perfectly turned-out lieutenant met us with a jeep and driver. Both men wore the distinctive green beret. The jeep drove us to Special Forces Headquarters. We ate at the C Team, where the food was excellent. Dee seemed to know half the officers.

People everywhere admired them. The "Ballad of the Green Berets," high on the music charts in the States, had echoed across An Khe. It was a great song.

Fighting soldiers from the sky.
Fearless men who jump and die . . .

Our contact turned out to be a captain with dark skin, dark eyes, and black hair, probably from Spanish ancestry. He was an officer of the fearless sky soldiers, but he wasn't fierce. We discussed visits to the men. We explained what we could do for them, looked at a map of their camps in the Delta, and explored transportation. While we talked, a puppy whimpered. We cast a quizzical look at the Captain. He laughed. "Those are the puppies." The officer pushed back his chair and bent down to the floor beside his desk. He removed a loose board, and revealed a litter of multi-colored puppies that squirmed in a little nest. He reached in and picked one up, nuzzled it and stroked it. "We heard a noise a few weeks ago, here under the floor. We took up the floorboards and discovered that a mother dog had had a litter right there. Nobody can resist them." That day introduced me to the real Green Berets, taught to be merciless, yet compassionate.

Finally, we looked at the base facilities, and then our escort took us for a drive through Can Tho. Everyone thought it was a peaceful, prosperous, small city in the center of the Delta, far from the war. We passed a market. At another corner a pedicab stand held a jumble of gaudy, three wheeled, pedal-driven vehicles for hire. We followed a palm-lined road along a canal; we crossed a bridge where we could see down into the houses. And, for a short distance, we followed a red star painted on the back of a Texaco gasoline truck.

The driver glanced in the rearview mirror. He stiffened. "Oh, oh. We'd better pull over." He steered the jeep to the shoulder. I turned in the back seat to see what was the matter. Half a block up the street behind us, in the middle of the city, a herd of water buffalo bore down on us—fast. They hurried four abreast, a dozen black beasts as big as horses. Their swept-back horns, longer than a man's arms, looked dangerous. Pedicabs and bicycles moved to the side to let them pass—business as usual. The animals came shoulder to shoulder with us where we waited beside the road. I could feel the power in their bodies. They paid no attention to us as they sped along. Some of them had rings in their noses with short ropes attached. A small boy, maybe eight years old, rode one of the beasts in the center of the heard. He stared at us as he passed, and we stared at him.

I asked our escort officer, "Are they dangerous?"

He laughed, "No. All the adult water buffalo are docile. As they grow up, if they show signs of meanness, they are killed and eaten. So, you never need to fear being charged by an old one. Young ones, perhaps. Children ride them and take care of whole herds of them." Not an ordinary street scene for a girl from Michigan. Our idyllic day in what everybody thought was the safe, peaceful Delta finally ended. Our jeep roared out to the airstrip, and we hopped back onto the Caribou just as it was starting its engines. We had been on the ground for two hours and 15 minutes. The Caribou dropped us off in Saigon, and we caught the 4:00 bus from Tan Son Nhut to Di An.

Monday, December 5, Saigon

Seven months into my tour, Dee and I had been called from Di An to a meeting at Red Cross Headquarters in Saigon. It was for the unit and program directors from Bien Hoa and another 1st Division unit. I had worked and traveled with Dee almost all the time since I learned about my promotion, because she had the job here. We sat with the director and assistant director around a table in the morning in a peaceful, walled garden. Eight of us discussed the information that Dee and I had gathered the day before on our trip to Special Forces Headquarters at Can Tho. We traded ideas enthusiastically. I went to the meeting to learn as much as I could. By the time it was half over I realized that Dee and I were the only ones who had anything to contribute. When they first told me I was going to have a new job I wondered if I could do it. Now I had more confidence.

I also met Lori, whom I will work with. She seemed nice. I looked forward to going on Wednesday to Bien Hoa. I believed we would set up regular visits to the Delta soon. At the meeting we concluded that the Green Beret A Teams, elite 12-man units, were so isolated that we couldn't travel to them from Di An. The Bien Hoa unit would make most of the runs because transportation would be easier from there. That meant it would be my responsibility to schedule and coordinate the trips, in my new job. I was eager to visit remote outposts.

That same morning, a class of five new girls, fresh from the States, went through processing and orientation in the office. They exclaimed about everything, reminding me of how I had felt in my first days in country. I couldn't wait to get started on my unknown undertakings, grabbing onto every new event with enthusiasm, and at the same time fighting the jet lag that shrouded everything in fog. That fervor was still sharp, but I was thankful the jet lag had gone. During a break, the girls from both groups mingled and milled around in the office. Suddenly, more than half a dozen deafening explosions erupted in the street, one after another. The walls of the building rocked. I dove under the nearest desk. In the isolated shelter, steel furniture blocked my vision. The cramped knee-well forced me to sit on the dry season's dirty floor. I straightened up and bumped my head. The cement under me punished every bone of my spare frame. I was uncomfortable, alone and blind, but not scared, just careful: calm and confident. The only thing left to do was wait for whatever had happened to end. My senses sharpened. Bumps, shuffles and crashes sounded around the room. The experienced members of the staff had dropped to the floor, some in the open, some behind desks. We assumed it was a terrorist attack.

The new girls cried out. Their footsteps ran in the direction of the window.

"What is it?"

"I can't see anything."

"What's happening?"

"Move over. Let me see, too." The new girls enjoyed the excitement. A little jealous, I longed to share the fun. Yet, I knew the girls could see nothing from the window, and they risked exposing themselves to danger. I wanted no part of it. A wave of loneliness tried to overtake me. Vulnerable to everything as a civilian, I had no way to defend myself. To be in a group, or with just one other person, would have made me feel safer, even if I really weren't.

Footsteps arrived from the other office. They jolted me back to self-control. The Red Cross director barked, "Get down!" I heard thumps. The director's voice commanded from floor level, "If you hear an explosion of any kind, the first thing you do is get down. You don't care what it is or what is happening. You stay down!" By then the street was quiet. No sirens shrilled, no small-arms fire crackled, no more explosions rang out. We heard no one run or shout, as I had heard after that first explosion in the street when I was new in Saigon. The normal sounds of motorcycles and bicycle bells reached us. The explosions were not serious. The director listened. "It's a false alarm. You can get up."

I crawled out from under the desk and tried to brush myself off. I thought, *Now all of my uniforms have stains on them.* I was relieved that everything was all right. I had done the right thing. Glad to be no longer blind and alone, I joined the safe group. Later that day we learned that the Vietnamese were having a festival. The explosions were a string of firecrackers. That didn't change anything. All explosions were serious, regardless of their cause. By then I had dived into so many bunkers that it was second nature to dive first and think later. I had forgotten what it was like to be a civilian. No longer a new girl, I was a veteran under the desk.

Wednesday, December 7, 1966, Di An, 25th Anniversary of Pearl Harbor

The drab flight operations center looked like a bus station in a backwater town, except that everyone wore a soldier's uniform. The worst heat of the day had passed; it was probably less than 90 degrees. The sun was going down and cast a yellow path on the floor from the open doorway. Dust swirled in its beam whenever anyone walked through. I saw shoulder patch insignia from units everywhere, like license plates at a tourist attraction back home. Men sat uncomfortably here and there on rows of wooden seats waiting for flights. Everyone wore green. I wore blue and stuck out like a snowman at a picnic. The Red Cross on my shoulder was a neon sign. Everyone knew I could have anything I wanted, go anywhere, and do anything I wanted.

Sunday, I had been to Can Tho in the Mekong Delta, Monday to the meeting in Saigon, and now on Wednesday I traveled from Di An to my new assignment at Bien Hoa. I waited for a flight like everyone else. Officially, I was off duty, but I continued my charge to speak to everyone, to smile, and to help them remember Home. As I moved about, the commander of the flight operations center, a captain, came up to me. He smiled, but the stiffness in his shoulders told me he was trying not to look anxious. Accustomed to deciding what to do and ordering people to do it, he had no authority to order me, a civilian, to do anything. But he had made the decision that I was the only person who could do what he needed.

As one friend to another, he asked, "Do you think you can help us?" He knew I would. "See that soldier over there?" The young soldier looked like all the others, lean, strong, healthy, tanned. Slumped down in one of the hard seats in the center of the front row, he slept with his arms curled around his rifle. His legs stuck out straight in front of him, crossed at the ankles, perfect for someone to trip over. He cradled his weapon across his chest, muzzle pointed just past his left ear. His cheek resting on the barrel, he cuddled it like an old friend.

"We need to have him move over here," the captain pointed to another seat out of the way. "The problem is that he's drunk, and we're afraid to wake him. If we startle him, he might shoot us." Everyone knew the soldier could fire his weapon with accuracy, drunk or sober. I didn't know why the soldier had come to the terminal. He might be on his way to a new assignment, as I was. He might be returning to his unit from a few days of leave. Maybe he wasn't traveling at all. Maybe he had been to a local village bar. In those remote areas, soldiers took their weapons wherever they went, even to a bar for a drink, or two, or more. Maybe he just came into the terminal to sleep off a drunk, because it was a safe place.[18]

Whatever had brought that boy there, no Viet Cong could have been more deadly. He was as dangerous as a land mine in the middle of that crowded air terminal. The slightest misstep, a bump from a newly arrived passenger, could have startled him awake, and set off a blast of withering fire from his lethal, fully automatic rifle. People who passed him were careful to walk wide around him.

Some would argue that the officer put me in too much danger when he asked me to wake a sleeping soldier. The captain's choice was clear. He could leave the man where he was and risk startling him. He could try to wake him and risk startling him. Or, he could ask the Red Cross on my shoulder to work magic. If I failed, and startled him, I faced the same consequence as everyone else. It wasn't my fight, but I had magic.

I once saw Major Hayne, at An Khe, move a drunken soldier. The major put on his cap with the gold oak leaf rank squarely in front. He positioned himself so that the soldier would see the rank the minute he opened his eyes. The major ordered, "Soldier, look at me." The kid opened his eyes wide and froze. "Go back to your unit, on the double." The man got up and ran, instantly. I don't think he was awake. The scene had stayed in my unconscious memory.

Everyone in the terminal saw the officer speak to me and some heard what he said. Those who had been moving stopped where they were. Heads followed us as the captain walked me over to the sleeping soldier. I waited until the officer stepped clear, then positioned myself so that the drunken combat veteran could see my blonde hair and blue-eyed American-girl face close to his the minute he opened his eyes. I greeted him sweetly, "Good morning." The man awoke. The instant he saw me he smiled a huge, sun-drenched smile. I appealed to him, "Will you move over there, please?" He got up, his eyes fastened on me. Without relaxing his grip on his rifle, he walked with me as in a daze, to where I indicated. Then he settled down, that smile still glowing on his face, and fell instantly asleep. I believe he thought he was dreaming. I heard a long exhale from around me. I hoped someone would tell the sleeping soldier what had happened, after he woke up. He might not have believed it. I didn't remember until long after, that Major Hayne had moved a drunken soldier who *was conspicuously unarmed*.

Part IV: Bien Hoa and the Voyage Home

✛ CHAPTER 8 ✛

Rabies

Wednesday, December 7, 1966, Bien Hoa, South Vietnam, Pearl Harbor Day

The last gift I wanted for Christmas in 1966 was rabies. I arrived at Bien Hoa with the second Christmas tree that my parents had sent from their plantation. I thought the girls would be thrilled to put the tree in the recreation center. Everyone at Di An had loved the live tree. I was shocked to learn that not everybody at Bien Hoa agreed. They already had something in the center that I considered just short of sacrilegious: a plastic tree. I struggled to understand their attitude. I took my tree to the officer's club. The manager, a lieutenant, reminded me of the sergeant at the hotel, and before him, Sergeant White at the Enlisted Men's Club at An Khe. The lieutenant looked dignified but harassed; however, he had the right attitude. He thanked me when I offered him the tree, and gave me a broad, enthusiastic smile. He cradled the treasure in his arms and carried it straight to his office. I saw him set it next to his desk and pick up the telephone.

The next day when I went to dinner, the tree greeted me in all its three feet of good wishes. The lieutenant had found the perfect place for it, at eye level. It sat on a custom-made stand on top of the half-wall in the entryway. It wished a Merry Christmas to everyone, and

The Bien Hoa girls, Saigon, December 1966.
Top: Lori, Jan, Barb; Front: Becky, Cal, Joann.

was visible from everywhere in the dining room. Diners delighted to watch officers come into the club, dragging from fatigue and hunger. They would see the tree, and then do a double take when they realized that it might be real. One after another, people reached out and took the needles between their fingers. They rubbed the needles together, then put their fingers to their nose and smelled the fragrance. They had to convince themselves that they actually saw a live Christmas tree in Vietnam. I received expressions of gratitude from the officers.

"You brought this? It's real?"

"It's great to have a live tree."

"I can't get enough of the evergreen smell. It's so strong. It lasts so long."

No one put decorations on the tree, but that only emphasized the tree's most important features. It was perfection, and sealed the case for a live tree.

December 8, Bien Hoa Air Base

The Bien Hoa unit had received a request to meet several plane-loads of soldiers from the States. The 9th Infantry Division had been ordered to Vietnam from Fort Lewis, Washington.[1] They would arrive, one planeload per night, over the course of several days, and we would receive notice a few hours before each aircraft landed. We made tentative plans to send as many girls to each plane as we could. Late in the afternoon, the day after I arrived, word came that two planes would land at 9:00 that night. We scrambled. The mess hall took the short notice in stride, sending plenty of hot coffee in five-gallon insulated cans and lots of chocolate cake, a treat. I hadn't remembered seeing chocolate cake in Vietnam, ever. The coffee had to be black, because we couldn't handle cream and sugar on the runway. The cooks had cut the sheet cake into man-sized squares. They didn't put any frosting on it, because frosting would melt in the heat. Any field trooper would wolf down both. Actually, any field trooper would wolf down anything we offered.

The airstrip aviation unit provided our transportation. Our driver guided the truck without lights, on blacked-out dirt roads to the dark runway. We set up our coffee on the ground and the cake on a table outside the small transportation building, just off the runway. Nighttime usually offered a respite from the withering heat. But, that night brought a cold, piercing wind. My ears ached, rain bit my face, and my hair whipped without mercy. I blessed the darkness, *I'm so glad no one can see how terrible I must look*. The refreshments set up, we found a place in the terminal to sit and wait and try to overhaul our appearance. The first plane arrived pretty much on schedule, an Air Force cargo plane. It looked just like the many cargo planes that came in and out of that landing strip all day. I thought, *What a good way to camouflage the arrival of thousands of new troops*. The plane rolled to a stop a short distance from our coffee. A larger than usual number of men from the ground unit helped the plane's crew chief open the door and put down the steps. I thought, *I can just imagine that the ground crew is anticipating the surprise waiting for the men inside that plane.* All five of us stood at the foot of the stairway.

In the pitch dark, at 9:30 at night, we shivered. The cold wind sliced through our tropic-weight uniforms. A man filled the doorway. We smiled and greeted him, "Welcome to Bien Hoa." The senior officer, first to come to the door, couldn't see us until just before he stepped over the doorsill and onto the stairs. Then he saw five American girls, four blondes and one brunette, in blue uniforms with red crosses on the shoulder, speaking English. Stunned, his gaze locked on us, his eyes couldn't move. Momentum carried him forward; he caught his toe on the edge of the doorsill and tripped. He grabbed the side of the doorway to keep from diving headfirst down the stairway, stumbled down the seven or eight steps to the perforated steel planking (PSP), and then regained his balance. I noticed that the second man tripped, too. He couldn't see past the man ahead of him, and had no warning that we were there. Then the third man tripped. As more and more men came off the plane, I took note. They were so startled that every one of the 150 men stumbled.

I remembered how I felt when I first stepped off the plane from the States. Fear tried to press in on me, and on everyone else. I knew these new men expected something terrible, just as I had. It took a lot of guts to be the first man off. It was the commander's job to lead from the front, but that didn't make it any easier. Instead of a sniper, the soldiers were staggered to see five American girls. Every man forgot to look at that extra-high step. The ground crew and we girls all delighted in the surprise, but not one betrayed our glee.

I noticed that the men we were used to were different from these new men. They came off the plane slowly in new fatigues and new boots, each with a little, sad smile. Once everyone had managed to get off the plane, we began to pass out the refreshments. We used a cup as a ladle to dip coffee out of the insulated containers on the ground, and invited each man to take a piece of cake. The hot coffee tasted good to us in the cold, but the new troops felt hot. Only a few took the coffee, and only a few wanted the cake without frosting. We realized our mistake. We had offered what seasoned soldiers would love. These men were fresh from the land of hot coffee and chocolate cake with frosting, and they had just eaten on the plane. That wouldn't have mattered to veteran troops. Their stomachs were bottomless, as I had learned at the pancake supper at Dong Ba Thin. We made a mental note to bring Kool-Aid to the next plane, and to ask the mess hall for cookies instead of cake.

The first thing the new arrivals had to do was change their money to Military Payment Certificates (MPC). No one was allowed to have dollars in Vietnam. Also, it was against regulations to give MPC to Vietnamese people, so the men had to change some of their MPC to Vietnamese Dong. The money-changing line went past our cake table, but we couldn't get any of the men to take our refreshments until they finished changing their money. That was easy to understand, too. These men didn't know how rare chocolate cake was in Vietnam. Also, I didn't think about it until much later, but maybe the men had heard stories that the Red Cross charged for what we gave out, and thought we were selling cake and coffee. Some myths die hard. The new men then moved off and waited for whatever would happen next. The only ones who wanted cake or coffee were the MP escorts from Long Binh and a few men who waited for other planes. Those men showed their appreciation, though. One MP said to me, "I've got to hand it to you girls for being here."

Old troops would have taken anything we offered, just for a chance to see us. New troops weren't interested. They didn't know how rare American girls were in Vietnam, not to mention five of us all in one place. Old troops would have remained at a respectful distance from us, but all would have faced us. They wouldn't really stare, but would watch us just the same. The new troops were shyer than even the oldest field trooper. They grouped with their backs to us. We were surprised, but understood. These men had just come from the land of American girls. I had to admit that by stateside standards, wind-whipped, dirty, shivering and tired, we lacked glamour, even on the dark runway. As soon as the new troops took all the food they wanted, the few men who stood around finished off the rest. Actually, the small ground crew devoured more cake and coffee than the whole planeload of new troops. They had probably never seen more than two of us at a time, if they had ever seen any of us. The food vanished, and then all five of us circulated. We talked to the new troops until they moved out. They spoke to us politely, but showed no eagerness. We adjusted without any trouble.

One man told me, "The plane didn't have real seats. We sat on cargo webbing."

I asked, incredulous, "Cargo webbing?"

"Nylon straps." I knew. I had ridden on it, but only for a short distance. I remembered the comfortable airline seat I enjoyed on the commercial airliner when I arrived. I couldn't imagine how uncomfortable it must have been to sit on nylon straps for 23 hours.

Another man told me, "The crew chief gave us one cup of coffee after another through the whole flight." I could see why so few men accepted our coffee. Curiously, I overheard in the conversations around me, that these new soldiers pronounced their destination "bean hoe." I had forgotten that the French priest who first wrote down the Vietnamese language spelled it in French. Bien Hoa was supposed to be pronounced "Ben Wah." The new troops all looked a little overweight. Too many stomachs poked over their belts and compared to the lean, hard, tan old troops, the new men looked pale and puffy.

The new troops moved out, and we stood together to wait for the next plane.

*Joann (left) and Lori at Bear Cat, in early December. Crews are
building latrines and shower houses before troops arrive.*

Saturday, December 10, Bien Hoa

My new unit had five girls and belonged to the 173rd Airborne Brigade. They guarded the Bien Hoa Air Base just north of Saigon. When I
had missed my bus back in October, I had stayed overnight at a different Bien Hoa unit located inside the town. Lori was the unit director at
my new assignment. I had known Becky, the outgoing unit director, in
Korea at St. Barbara, and had seen her a few months before when she
visited An Khe. Now, after a full year's tour in Vietnam, she neared her
day to rotate home. Cal, new from the States, related that trainers in
Washington, D.C., warned her class that they would have no privacy.
They told this story: One of the girls called her boyfriend. He complained, "When we hung up last night you didn't say 'I love you.'"

She said, "Yes, I did."

He said, "No, you didn't."

The telephone operator cut in and said, "Yes, she did." That girl was
me. The trainers were right. We had no privacy.

Saturday, December 10, Bien Hoa

The Bien Hoa unit had a recreation center smaller than our quarters. The center was only large enough for three tables. We spent most of our time visiting regular Army and Special Forces in the field, and Air Force units at the air base. We used the center's cement patio in front for our Sunday morning coffee hour. Our living quarters and the recreation center were both permanent, wooden buildings with louvered sides over screen, and a tin roof. A fence encircled the house and a small yard of bare earth. A street light illuminated the area. The front door of the house entered into a central living room with two bedrooms on each side.

The sergeant posted two armed guards at our house inside the fence every night at about midnight. By the time we got up in the morning they were gone. We rarely saw or spoke to the guards, but we knew they were close by. No one could see into the house because of the angled louvers, but the walls were made of screen. The guards could hear every sound we made and every word we said. My life in a goldfish bowl took on a new aspect. We learned not to leave any food outside overnight because it would disappear by morning. If we had anything edible left over from an activity, we would put it on a bench next to the house for the guards. I only heard them make a noise once. We had a couple of gallons of champagne punch left after a celebration at the center. We put it on the bench and went to bed. In the night we heard a clatter. The next morning we decided the guards must have had an accident. They probably tipped over the bench and the metal washbasins. We didn't find any damage, but the two gallons of champagne punch were gone.

December, Bien Hoa

Captain Hoza, of the Cowboys gunship unit, pushed back his empty dinner plate and took a long swallow of coffee. He recalled the excitement in the cockpit of his helicopter earlier in the day. They had exchanged fire with the enemy. "That was some operation today. I yelled to Eager," he indicated his co-pilot on the other side of the table. "'They're firing at us! It's too close on this side. Move over to your side!'"

Lieutenant Eager, young and wide-eyed, replied, "And I said, 'No, it's too close on my side! Move over to your side!'" A dozen of us looked at each other. We pictured the pilots as the VC fired on both sides of the chopper, and no way for Hoza and Eager to get out of the way. Grateful that they were all right, everybody had a laugh.

I liked to sit at dinner with the gunship pilots, 335th Aviation, the Cowboys. They told the best stories. They numbered among the few in Vietnam who faced danger daily. December through April, most of the time I was at Bien Hoa, I passed many evenings at the pilots' supper table. Pilots took risks. They walked with a swagger, and loved to tell tales. A slightly older Captain Hoza led the most vocal group, a dozen young lieutenants. They would push back their plates after supper and sit for an hour or more with their coffee, laughing and talking. Captain Hoza led the discussion. The stories came one after another, night after night like a television adventure series. I thought they had more fun than anyone. Then at the end of the evening, three or four of them would walk me the two blocks back home while they continued the banter. The captain, short and stocky with dark, straight hair, had a complexion both clear and fair. He was almost indescribably handsome.

Pilots didn't come and go in the group, and no one was killed. Two were slightly wounded. They turned up with bandage patches, one on a hand. The other pilot had a bandage on an arm, and was grounded. He joked, "I'll see the doctor in a few days and I'll be back flying, if I'm healed. I'll have the scab picked off by then."

My doctor-boyfriend at St. Barbara in Korea had told me, "Pilots will do anything you say. All you have to do is threaten to ground them."

That night after the VC had shot on both sides of Hoza and Eager, another pilot, Jamie, with freckles across his nose, questioned, "Did you see Carl? From where I was I could see that he had been hit. It must have been in the fuel tank. He was leaking fuel by the bucketful. I called him on the radio and told him, 'Hey, you're leaking fuel.'" I didn't know who Carl was. I had never met him.

Jamie imitated a slow, matter-of-fact response. "Carl answered back, 'Yeah, noticed it on the fuel gauge.'" It was so good, Jamie repeated it, "Man, that's about as cool as you can get. 'Noticed it on the fuel gauge.' It must have been going like that." The lieutenant made a motion with his finger like the needle on a fuel gauge going from full to empty. Everyone took a moment to appreciate coolness. Some looked into space, some shook their heads.

One night Captain Hoza talked about his daughter. He said she was a beautiful little five-year-old. He asked the men if they had daughters. Only Eager and Jamie were bachelors. One by one the others went around the table, a dozen pilots, telling how many children they had. Every man had at least one daughter. Most had more than one child, but no more than three. Pride and love shone on their faces as they recited their children's names. Hoza included another captain, sitting alone at the next table. "Hey Andy, do you have any daughters?"

Andy replied in a strong, proud voice, "Two boys, six and eight years old." Hoza smiled, and resumed recounting the antics of his little girl. Those men missed their families.

December 15

Today Lori and I gave seven programs. I believe that five or six programs a day should be the maximum, and not every day. Our job is to smile and be nice to people 24 hours a day. We can't do it if we are dog-tired. It will be my job to write the schedule, and I think I'll lighten the load as soon as I can. At the end of the day, I was so tired, I felt ill. I lay down for a short while, and then had to get ready for a party. Becky, the former unit director, is leaving Vietnam, and there will be two farewell parties. Tonight at our house is one for enlisted men and non-commissioned officers. Tomorrow is one for officers.

Sunday, December 18

Today when I made my regular phone call to Bob, the RTO who answered told me, "All the RTOs wish you a Merry Christmas." I was thrilled. How thoughtful. This morning we had Sunday Coffee Call at the center. Lori and I served over 100 men with coffee and coffee cake, and then I went to church at 9:00. I thought of Bob and his men in the field and wondered if they were able to go to church. I manage to go about every other week, the way my work averages. This afternoon I tried to get a tan and then fell asleep in the shade. This evening we had a decorating party at the center. We played Christmas music. I climbed up on chairs and hung things everywhere. The place is loaded with decorations. Then we played bingo and had popcorn. It looked like all the enlisted paratroopers had a good time.

December 21

This evening, as on every evening, a handful of soldiers had dropped by our living room to sit and talk. They didn't come to see anyone in particular. They just liked to be around, to participate in anything that was going on. We heard some unusual sounds and all trooped outside in the dark and watched an uncommon sight. An aircraft circled and circled at a fairly high altitude. It dropped flares and shot its machine guns at something on the ground. Someone said it was *Puff the Magic Dragon*, an Air Force fixed-wing gunship.[2] I ran and got the new camera and tripod I had bought in Singapore. I took six or eight time-lapse pictures, the first time I had tried to use it.

I forgot to keep track of where all of our visitors were and what they were doing while I concentrated on figuring out the settings on my camera. Some of the men gathered around to watch. I didn't notice that

Puff the Magic Dragon *circling, dropping flares, and shooting targets on the ground.*

one fellow took advantage of my distraction. He edged closer than the others until he was inches from me. And then, as if he wanted to look at the camera settings, he pressed his face close to mine and tried to kiss me on the lips. I realized what he was doing and eased away just as he brushed me. I moved just enough to interrupt his kiss, but not enough to draw others' attention and embarrass him. I smiled at him to let him know that I was flattered, but he couldn't do that. He moved back and kept the proper distance. I made sure to be more aware after that, and not let anyone get close. I reminded myself that paratroopers are bolder than other men.

Saturday, Christmas Eve 1966

Merry Christmas.

Yesterday and today were two of the most hectic days I've had yet. The centerpiece of the program we are giving this week is a Christmas-theme charades game where the men draw the clues on an acetate board.

They play enthusiastically. Yesterday, two of the girls were out with the new program, two girls were in the center, and I had only a couple of stops with last week's program. I spent the rest of the day in the office with a million things to do to set up a schedule of visits for Christmas Eve and Christmas. All five of us presented a Christmas program at the hospital after work and then went to a farewell party for the commanding officer of our aviation company.

Today was even fuller. At 10:00 Lori and I did the Christmas program. The men had all ready started celebrating and were unusually cooperative. They hollered and shouted and laughed at everything. We served in their chow line and ate with them. Back at the office alone, I made one phone call after another on the impossible lines, still working on the schedule of visits for today and tomorrow as fast as I could go, then a party for one of the sections in the administration company. Back at the center we had a Christmas Eve program, which I had written in about half an hour during the week. In Korea we used to allow six weeks to write a program. For this one I took the most successful activities from recent programs and put them together in a "best of" collection. We had a version of the TV tic-tac-toe game, *Hollywood Squares*, a couple of crowd-pleasing quiz games, a version of the game "Battleship," and a take-off on the TV show *Concentration*, where people matched pairs of pictures hidden behind numbered squares. I knew it would work because all the girls were familiar with the activities, and nobody needed instructions or rehearsals. I was right; it was a hit. Besides, I had no choice. This was an emergency. Three of us were supposed to go to another battalion party after the center closed, but I never got there. I hit the bed and couldn't get out again.

Christmas 1966

Today was a full day. I slept until 9:45. I made myself presentable, and Cal and I went to 17th Cavalry for our first program. The fellows had all assembled when we got there. They cheered when we walked in. They hollered and hammed it up in enjoyment. Everyone laughed until we hurt. People kept poking their heads in to see what all the noise was about.

Dinner was at 12:00. The tables were laid with white cloths and silverware. It was sit-down. Everyone was served. The six or eight Vietnamese waitresses were all prettied up. They started to serve and Cal and I jumped right in and helped. When we first appeared carrying the heavy trays of food the whole mess hall erupted in a cheer. Major Sutton presented each of us with a recognition plaque. At dinner I talked to a warrant officer who had been in 8th Cavalry in Korea while I was there. He said, "Yes, I remember the Donut Dollies. They came every Tuesday. We would see them coming in the gate. Everything would stop and everybody would start heading for the mess hall." That made me feel good to learn that the people in Korea thought that much of us. There was a short wait, the second sitting started, same routine. Then we presented another program. The fellows gave us a five-pound fruitcake. We had a cup of coffee with the major, and one guy from my hometown rounded up about four others from Flint, and we took some pictures. All day long people kept snapping pictures. They took a lot of us when we served dinner. Everybody really got a kick out of that. The Vietnamese help were astounded. In their culture, there is a serving class and a ruling class, and they never trade places.

After dinner, Bryan, our driver, came over to the house. We all opened our presents from home together. We had also drawn names. Everybody got humorous gifts for each other.

Monday, December 26, the day after Christmas

Tonight with the pilots, I listened to a tape they had made in a gunship during a particularly dangerous operation. It was the sounds of men under fire. One co-pilot was wounded, and another got a piece of shrapnel in his flak vest. Weapons were firing in all directions. I have started to lose some of my fear of the unknown, as I learn more about the battle situation. I'm getting a better grasp of the probabilities of getting wounded or hurt in these operations. As long as the VC are such bad marksmen, a lot of rounds can fly back and forth before anybody gets hurt.

December 28

Three days after Christmas, I went with Lori to the Bien Hoa Air Base. On the cement pavement next to the aircraft, it was almost too hot to breathe, too hot to think. We scheduled regular visits to our Air Force neighbors at the Bien Hoa Air Base, always with plenty of Kool-Aid. We drove across the huge base on good roads, but we usually couldn't cover it all in one day. Most of the time when we visited Army units in the field, they were able to find some shade or some other shelter. The air base offered scant shade in a few big maintenance buildings and open hangars, but there were no trees. The sun pounded down on the cement pavement of runways, aprons, aircraft parking areas, and the vast flight line. The airmen always welcomed something to drink and gathered around wherever we stopped. No one on the air base carried a weapon, and I saw no bunkers. The cooks wore un-camouflage white. No enemy threatened for miles around, as our Air Force pick-up truck traveled the moonscape. We stopped everywhere to pass out Kool-Aid, and we took recreation activities. We drove in and out amongst the parked jet planes and stopped wherever we saw crews working.

In the maintenance yard, each plane occupied a U-shaped area surrounded on three sides by a corrugated metal wall at least 15 feet high. It looked strong enough to protect the plane from an explosion in the next bay. The barriers also prevented all air movement. A proud airman invited me to climb up and sit in one of the planes. These jets had thrilled me when they flew over An Khe back in July. Now I sat in the

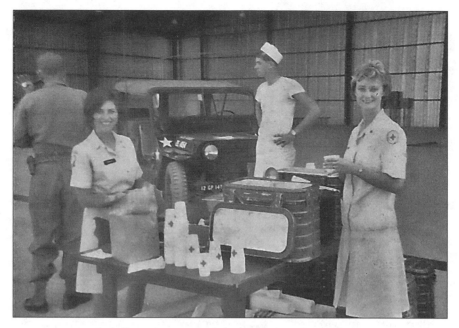

*Camilla and Joann (right) serve Kool-Aid in a hangar
at the Air Base. Note, the cook is wearing white.*

cockpit of the F-100 Super Sabre swept-wing jet, the first supersonic
fighter in the Air Force.[3] These aircraft took off and landed during all
daylight hours. Whenever they went over, the air cracked, and all conversation had to stop.

Out on the flight line at the maintenance ramps that day we served
Kool-Aid and played Concentration too many times. My eyes burned
from the light and heat. I was tired when I started, still recovering from
Christmas, and kept getting worse all day. To do the same thing over
and over is boring, but the people we saw never ceased to appreciate us.
I noticed one man who sat apart, and I tried to get him interested in the
game. I thought he was shy and needed encouragement. He said, "No,
I want to just sit here and look at an American girl." He had reminded
me again why I was there.

We scheduled regular stops at the jet engine repair shops during
our visits to the air base. One of our activities illustrated the kind of

talent those mechanics possessed. We had somehow acquired several copies of the same issue of a *Playboy* magazine. Barb had a good idea. She was careful to keep the activity innocent. She found a full-page pin-up, the only modestly clad, least revealing one in the issue. She glued two identical pictures to cardboard and cut them into identical puzzles. For the activity, she divided the men into two teams and let them race to put the puzzles together. The men loved the game. They were especially pleased to watch the picture turn out to be a pretty girl in a bathing suit. We used the activity everywhere, with both Army and Air Force units. The unconventional shapes of the pieces made it a difficult puzzle and gave the men time to enjoy it. Not at the jet engine shops. The mechanics put the puzzles together so fast it wasn't fun. Barb finally put an important piece of the puzzle into her pocket. That increased the skill level so they could enjoy it. I marveled at how the military had found so many men with the skills needed for that critical job.

I talked to Dee, from Di An, on the phone tonight. She said they saw 3,000 men during the week before Christmas, about twice the usual number. She also said they worked so hard they all got sick after Christmas. I guess being all dragged out, we at Bien Hoa didn't fare so badly. I arranged to spend New Years at Di An. I never would have guessed the danger that waited for me on my in-country New Year's vacation.

I keep thinking about the wives of the men here and in the Army in general. Life for them is full of separations of anywhere from a week to a year. Generals like DePuy are away from their families for extended periods. It looks like a hard, lonely life.

December 29

Tonight I listened to Hanoi Hannah on the radio. She said the US Army was a tool of the government, and that we lost 3,000 men in Attleboro. She played good music, though. I learned later that Operation Attleboro ended on November 24. Enemy killed were 1,106 in the largest

US operation to date.⁴ The best thing about the Christmas truce was that the jets didn't wake us up in the morning. Funniest thing, nobody missed them. We only noticed it when they started to fly again. Nobody got to see Bob Hope on Christmas because 173ʳᵈ wasn't allowed to go. They had to guard the airfield; we were part of them, so we couldn't go, either.

Monday, January 2, 1967, Di An

Saturday morning, New Year's Eve, I sat in the living room with Dee and Linda talking about my new job. Brook announced that she had purchased a civet cat in town. A sweet-natured city girl, Brook had a round, open face framed by short, curly blonde hair. We all gathered round. The more I looked at the animal, the more it resembled a yellow tiger-striped domestic kitten, except that a pair of black stripes ran down each side of its back, with spots between the stripes. A stream of visitors moved in and out of our living room throughout the day. Within a few hours, a couple of fellows told us that our new addition was just a half-grown, gawky kitten. Someone had used a magic marker to enhance its appearance, and its price. Con schemes like that cropped up everywhere. Lots of people got caught in them. The kitten was only partly tame, frightened, and nervous.

I slept all afternoon and through supper to around 8:00 or 9:00 in the evening and then sat in the living room with Dee and Peggy. I held the kitten in my lap. Suddenly, someone opened the door to the bedroom area. Peggy's white puppy, Horatio, exploded into the room. The kitten bit me on the hand and streaked under a chair. Peggy apologized. I didn't blame her. I thought anyone could see that the puppy would scare the kitten. I didn't give the incident another thought.

I was about to fall asleep for another nap, when I learned there would be a *shoot-out* at midnight to bring in the New Year. I was a little worried that some drunken GI would wind up killing somebody, but I guess no one did. Gerald Burns from counter intelligence told me later,

"Everyone went outside that night and emptied their weapon into the air. It was mass pandemonium for about ten minutes." Someone threw a tear gas grenade behind the house, but the wind blew the smoke away. A drunk climbed the signal tower across the street and hollered for 30 or 40 minutes that he was going to jump. Someone talked him down and sent him to the social worker. And so ended my 1966 adventures in Vietnam, I thought.

Sunday, January 8, 1967, Bien Hoa

A week after I went to Di An for New Year's, the phone rang at 2:00 A.M. All the girls woke up and gathered around, clutching their robes like zombies in curlers. The call was for me, from Dee, at Di An. At that time of the night? The telephone connection surpassed terrible, from only ten miles away. I could barely hear her. Static punctuated every phrase.

"Do [crackle] remember kitten [crackle] aa bit you [crackle] Eve [crackle] Di An?"

"What?"

I had to imagine about half of what she said and ask her to repeat almost everything. She told me that the kitten that bit me had died. I pieced together, "We don't know if it had rabies. It was never examined. They burned it in the trash. There is no way to know whether the kitten was sick when it bit you. You will have to get the series of 14 shots. First thing tomorrow, you have to go to the doctor and start them. If you don't start the series, you might get rabies. It would depend on whether the kitten was rabid. You will die. There is no cure."

There were no options. We had nothing to discuss. Everyone went back to sleep. The next morning I saw the doctor, Captain Davis, at the 3rd Surgical Hospital across the street. He told me, "Dee is right. Rabies is common in Vietnam because this climate is perfect for growing all kinds of diseases." He examined my left index finger. The bite remained barely visible. "You must start the series within 10 days." *I was bitten on*

New Year's Eve. This is January 8. "The series is 14 injections, given in the abdomen." My heart sank, but I was resigned.

A nurse, a kind-faced young lieutenant about my age, greeted me at the hospital. She wore fatigues and combat boots. Her wavy, brown hair fell just above her shoulders. She took me to a row of examination tables separated by white curtains and asked me to climb up on one. She drew the curtain around the table and explained the procedure. "We give the shots in the abdomen because that is the largest area available. Small amounts of serum can be injected into an arm, larger amounts into the thigh or buttock. This one needs more room. Open your uniform so we can see your abdomen. Be sure to relax the muscles. If the muscle is hard, the needle will have to force its way in. That will be more pain-ful." *Oh, Lord. How do you relax your muscles when someone is about to punch you in the stomach?*

I felt the stab as the big needle broke the skin, then drove deep into my stomach. *Ow. About what I expected. So far, so good.* Next came a slight hesitation, and then the ache as the large volume of serum forced its way into the tissue. The ache increased and hung there. I thought, *OK, it's almost over, almost over, almost over. . . .*

An explosion of pain overwhelmed me. I had never known a more fierce, painful thing in my life. It stabbed like a snake bite, but worse. It engulfed my middle. Steady, sharp, relentless, it was agony. I couldn't breathe. I couldn't think. I couldn't hear anything. It wouldn't stop. I squeezed my eyes shut until they hurt, and pinched my face against the pain. The nurse grabbed my hand. I gripped her fingers so hard she must have lost the feeling. I had no concept of time. Finally, finally it stopped.

She explained, "It's not the size of the needle that causes the pain. It's the serum reacting with the tissue." I felt weak. I closed my uniform, climbed down off the table, and followed the nurse out to the desk. She gave me an appointment for 9:00 A.M. every day for the next 13 days, to come in and get my shot. I could choose either to get the shots or die. I could never know if I really needed the shots but I couldn't change my mind.

Every day for two weeks the shots were the same; the pain never let up. I never knew two weeks could be so long. At first, I had only slight nausea and fatigue. After five days, I began to feel the effects. The doctor had told me rabies is a virus, and I began to experience increased fatigue, like a viral infection. I started to react strangely. I felt as if I wanted to physically attack somebody, for no reason. The fatigue and nausea increased over the two weeks, and the shots made my stomach sore. I was able to work less and less, finally as little as two hours a day.

By the time I finished the full series of 14 shots, I had become so weak I could hardly work at all. Besides, I snapped at everyone so rudely that nobody wanted me around.

I had my last shot on January 22. I asked Doctor Davis to record the series in my shot record. He declined, "The shot record is for immunizations. This series doesn't give you any immunity. If you get bitten again, you will have to go through the series again." *What a desperate thought.*

I pleaded, "Can you record it anyway? This is too important. I want to have a record of it." He agreed, and my shot record bears his entry and signature: "22 Jan 67 Rabies vacc. 14 vials Capt. Davis, MC." I began slow improvement. After about a week I got over being combative, but I still couldn't work a full schedule. People around me were being wounded in a war, and I got bitten by a kitten. That threat to my life was no more than an intrusion, a footnote to the war.

January 20

Automatic weapons started firing at 11:30 at night. It sounded like dueling machine guns back and forth, one, then another. Not a little, a lot. And it didn't let up. It continued, nonstop, for several minutes. We never heard gunfire at our house, though that night it didn't sound dangerous. Artillery boomed at rapid intervals. My curiosity took over, and I looked out the door. I saw red tracers, ours, streaking along the horizon from one side of the perimeter to the other. Someone had once told me that for firing at night, our men loaded ammunition with a red tracer every fifth round.[5] The person who fired could tell where he was shooting, but the tracers gave away his position. We used red tracers; the VC used green. A red flare popped open in the sky near our house. It hung above the tracers on its invisible parachute. "Positive contact with the enemy," I remembered from some past dinner-table conversation. I studied the tracers, all red ones, ours—no green ones, theirs. Either the enemy was firing in another direction, or their tracers tracked behind trees, out of sight.

Then I remembered hearing that a unit of engineers had moved all of their people out from Saigon. They had begun to build a command compound nearby. Most likely, our new over-enthusiastic neighbors, fresh from the Saigon garrets, had heard an animal in the brush and were defending us. I watched for a while longer. The two men who were detailed to guard our house that night came swinging up the driveway. They slung their weapons carelessly at their sides. When they saw me watching the red flare, one joked, "Don't worry. We're here now. We'll protect you." I laughed and went back to bed.

I learned that real war can be random noises, fits and starts, false alarms, and sometimes nothing.

Tuesday, January 31

Two weeks after I finished the rabies shots I worked almost a full day. There seem to be a lot of people who have had the shots. Men have told me about half a dozen, and I've met three or four of them. We thought of ourselves as *quasi-domestic-pet casualties.*

Saturday, February 4

Yesterday I went to the area office because they wanted to see what a person looked like who was a rabies shot victim. I'm still weak, so

Saigon decided I needed a rest. They are sending me on temporary duty (TDY) to Cu Chi (pronounced "Koo Chee") on Monday the sixth. I'll be there for a week. They think the way to rest is to go work somewhere you have never been. I would have thought the way to rest would be to rest. They had planned to send me to the Marine unit at Da Nang ("Duh Nang") and let me get away. But, I was sure I could never hold up under the 11-hour plane ride. Cu Chi is closer, and I don't know anyone there, so they changed the orders. A week away would also give me a chance to see another Red Cross unit and another Army unit.

Monday, February 6, Cu Chi

I left early this morning to come temporarily to Cu Chi. I got up an hour before usual. I wouldn't have had to make all that fuss if I had been able to talk the pilots at Bien Hoa into taking me to Cu Chi. But, when I asked them one said, "Hell no. Last time I went up there I got my ass shot off." At the heliport I met a service club girl who was waiting for a flight. She was frightened about being in the war zone. I tried to make her feel better. The flight was about 2 and a half hours long. It went smoothly; I seldom get off so well.

When I got to Cu Chi the girls were on the road coming to get me. They had a welcome poster for me, and my name was on the door of my room and on a box in the office. Everybody was thoughtful. The Cu Chi post is a bit smaller than An Khe, but two-thirds of the tents have been replaced with tropical buildings. Our house and office are behind the Division Headquarters buildings and right next to the aides' tent. We are in the *best* neighborhood. They have a refrigerator and some fresh watermelon. It tasted like home.

Tuesday, February 7

The 25th Division originally came from Hawaii, so we have a lot of Hawaiians here. A big sign at the helipad says, "Aloha." Today I visited

25th S&T Battalion (whatever that is) Headquarters Company. Instead of tents they live in little houses with wooden sides and thatch roofs. This unit has six girls, three I had met briefly. Some of the men spotted my 173rd Airborne Brigade patch today. They hollered, "Airborne!" came up to me, and looked longingly at my patch. They miss being in an airborne unit. I answered them properly, "All the way!"

The housing is comfortable. Each girl has a private room in one of two buildings just a few steps from the shower house. A high wire fence encloses it all, and no men can come inside. The living room is attached to the office just outside the fence. I've never had so much privacy or so much security. This division takes good care of its girls. When they took me to visit the commander, Maj. Gen. Frederick Carlton Weyand, he said, "I have every confidence in our girls. It's the *men* I don't trust." He has imposed an 11:00 P.M. curfew on us. I'm safe and sound in the middle of a division of Hawaiians.

One of the girls at Cu Chi playing Twister.

Wednesday, February 8

I'm having a great time here. With little to worry about, I have all the fun and few worries. I needed the rest. My room has a dressing table with a big mirror. What luxury. Today I went on three visits with two different programs. The people here are friendly. The girls have one recreation program that demonstrates how strong and healthy our men are. It has a game, Twister. I learned later that it was first introduced in 1966 by Johnny Carson and Ava Gabor.[6] We spread a heavy oilcloth mat on the ground, with colored circles on it. Two men place their hands and feet on the circles according to a spinner. We are supposed to play until somebody falls down, but we can't get the men to fall down. They go and go. They are so muscular, so lean, so young and healthy that the game is a disappointment. Not only that, their combat boots are so rugged, they tear the mat apart. A person could walk on nails with those boots. Whenever a man twisted his foot, it tore a hole in the oilcloth. Years later I learned that Twister is famous at parties for getting men and women closer together. We never would have played the game with the men. I can't see how anybody would play it in a skirt.

Friday, February 10, Tay Ninh

Today I went along on a visit to 196th Light Infantry Brigade at Tay Ninh. It was a recon trip to set up visits out of Cu Chi. I was fortunate to meet Brig. Gen. Richard T. Knowles. He was at 1st Cavalry until a year ago January. He asked about my 173rd patch. I saw a cartoon picture in his office drawn by Sandra Fosselman, who was at An Khe when I was there. Joan McNiff and I made the trip today in a Caribou. Both the brigade S-1 (Personnel) and the Red Cross field director escorted us all day. We ate in the general's mess and visited the quarters that are being built for us.

Saturday, February 11, Cu Chi

I read in the paper this morning that the VC broke the Tet Truce, four times Wednesday morning northwest of Phan Thiet.[7] I thought about our Cavalry troops there.

Sunday, February 12, Bien Hoa

Today I came back to Bien Hoa. I caught the afternoon helicopter to the air base, and there sat one of the choppers from 173rd. I climbed aboard. The whole trip from Cu Chi was about 20 minutes. Sure beat the two and a half-hour trip to get there. At Cu Chi I had maintained a light work schedule, and came back to Bien Hoa feeling better.

✛ CHAPTER 9 ✛

Ambush in the Delta

Sometimes the places we thought were the safest were the opposite. One day I received an audiocassette tape from my parents. They talked about what was going on, and told me they had just added a new room, with a fireplace, to the farm house. On the tape, they had recorded sounds of my father stoking the fire. I played the tape on the equipment at the center, available for anyone to use. Guys came in every once in a while to play tapes from home. I felt bad for one man. He told me, "My wife is mad at me. She's not speaking to me, so she sent me a 90-minute tape that turned out to be blank, nothing on it." Telling me about it seemed to make him feel better.

I thought my buddies, the pilots, would enjoy hearing my dad stoke the fireplace. I took the tape to supper the next day, and sure enough, the pilots were eager to hear it. One man volunteered that he had a tape player in his room. The dozen pilots pushed back their chairs. The scraping sounds echoed through the empty mess hall. We all trooped the 50 feet to the man's room.[1] He was proud to show it off, one of a dozen cozy, two-man rooms that opened onto a central courtyard deck, in a new building. One of the pilots had planted a banana tree in an opening in the center of the deck. We squeezed into the room, some sat on the cots and some on the floor. They all insisted that I have the one chair at the desk. When we played the tape, everyone groaned at the part where Dad stoked the fireplace. We could hardly listen to it on that evening in January. The sweat ran down our faces, even though we sat still. When the tape finished, I asked, "I love to hear your stories. Will you tell one on the tape recorder for my parents?"

They responded with an enthusiastic chorus of, "Yeah. Great idea." Some shifted their positions as they settled in for another good story.

The man with the tape recorder turned it on, and Dusty, from Texas, asked, "Remember the time everybody tried to shoot the same VC?"

They all looked at him, ready for the story. "Yes," they chorused.

Dusty continued, "He was out in the open, running as fast as he could. Running across a field of dry rice paddies. How many of us shot rockets at him?" He looked around the crowded room at all the pilots, who laughed and nodded. "It was everybody. The whole rice paddy exploded." He waved his hands in the air to simulate clouds of dust that billowed up. "Dirt and smoke flew everywhere. You couldn't see a thing." He squinted as if he tried to see through the smoke. The chorus laughed with him. "Then, there he was. He came running out the other side of the cloud of smoke." Dusty's eyes opened wide and he pretended to startle in surprise. "It was unbelievable. Everybody missed him. He just came running out of that cloud of smoke."

Some pilots repeated, "He came running out of that cloud of smoke." Some shook their heads, "Right out the other side."

Eager took up the tale where Dusty had left off. "We all shot at him again, including my gunner. The next rice paddy exploded." He threw up his hands to emphasize the explosion. "Smoke was everywhere. This time, when the smoke cleared, he was dead. I really think it was my gunner who finally got him."

Captain Hoza nodded and finished the story. "The Air Force verified the kill later."

Eager added, "You know, that gunner is terrific. He can hit any-thing. I can tell him to give me a burst of five, and he can do it."

Another pilot added, "I'd hate to count up how many thousands of dollars in rockets and ammunition it cost Uncle Sam to kill that one VC."

I sent the tape to my folks. My mom wrote back and observed that the pilots had learned to de-humanize the VC so their minds could justify killing a human. I had no more information about the story. I'm sure it was unusual, certainly not typical. I'm sure the VC was a valid target. I never heard anyone say anything that led me to believe they bent rules. The pilots never talked about rules or complained about them, as the infantrymen did. The fact that the pilots commented on the cost, was typical. No one felt what they spent that day was justified. Soldiers in many different units often expressed concern that materials and equipment were expensive. They were careful to conserve.

Those pilots faced danger every day. They had to keep up their posi-tive attitude, or they would lose their nerve. As cowboys say, if a horse bucks you off, you get back on. I didn't see their vulnerability. I wasn't ready for the superstitions. I didn't remember the other situation, the carnival at Dong Ba Thin with the fortuneteller booth. Nobody would go near it. No one wanted to know his future. Those combat soldiers at Dong Ba Thin never knew what might happen to them, whether they would make it home or not. They didn't want to know. The pilots who called themselves Cowboys felt the same way.

Thursday, February 16

Today we were extra busy. I shuffled the schedule at least three times. The brigade came in from the field, and we tried to meet as many of them as we could. We did well. Plus, we met all our regular commit-ments. It took a lot of juggling. We have two girls fresh from the States, and we had to send them out by themselves to two separate places. They came through full of enthusiasm. They're going to be good. This week is also a round of parties. Last night was a farewell for a battalion commanding officer. Tonight was a celebration at the Military Police Company; tomorrow, a farewell for one of the girls; Saturday, a promotion party at the aviation company. I haven't been to so many parties since I left the Cavalry. I'm ready to go home at 8:30 or 9:00. But, I try to stay until 10:00 at least. I'm sure, if I left right after dinner, the host would be offended. I try to go to as many parties as I can, though, because it is part of my job, and great for morale.

The donut salute in front of our shower house at the end of the day.
Note the sweat rings under the arms and spots and splashes on our
uniforms. Left to right: Cal, Becky, Joann, Barb, and friend.

Saturday morning, February 18

The day started out with a normal round of visits to nearby units. This time I went out by myself because we were short handed. The 9:00 A.M. visit was with about 30 people in two batteries of the 3rd Battalion,

319th Airborne Artillery of the brigade. They had just come in from the field. I stayed longer than I was supposed to because they were so appreciative, so enthusiastic, and enjoyed the activities. I couldn't tell them the time was up.

The people at the next unit, A Battery, were making sandbag bunkers around the ammunition. The commanding officer, Captain Anderson, didn't want them to stop work, so he told two lieutenants, the executive officer and one other lieutenant, to escort me and "take her everywhere." They obeyed to the letter. I visited all the 105-mm howitzer gun positions. I also saw the motor pool, the communications shack, the orderly room, the ammunition storage, even a new litter of puppies. I greeted 130 men, one-by-one, for two hours. I was exhausted. I ate lunch with the commanding officer after that. The officers were uncomfortable through the meal. I think it has been a long time since one of us ate there, but I was too tired to put them at ease. I still hadn't recovered my full strength after the rabies shots. I fell into bed as soon as I got home. I got up again at 4:00 P.M. to do another program, but when I arrived the commander said they were too busy to take time out.

I went to a party at 5:30 at one of the mortar platoons in 2nd Battalion. It was the first party I had ever attended where everybody wore civilian clothes. They were all dressed in sport shirts and slacks. In uniform, all the people looked like warriors, but in civilian clothes, they all looked like high school kids. One man smiled, "I like wearing civilian clothes."

I asked, "Why?"

"Because they are lighter and softer. Uniforms are heavy and stiff. Civilian clothes are more lightweight, thinner material. They are easier to move around in." He lifted his shoulders and moved his arms around in circles. Some of the civilian clothes did not flatter the men, whereas the uniforms looked good on everyone. And their faces, it was easier to distinguish their faces as their choice of colors and styles expressed and emphasized their features. They were young. Then I remembered: most of them really are in their late teens. Just teenagers.

Tuesday, February 21

This afternoon I visited two hospitals. Gave a program in one and just chatted in the other, took names of men who wanted to call home. I came across a man from 173ʳᵈ Airborne Brigade. The paratrooper was tall and lean. A few weeks ago he might have been a kid in Detroit hanging out on street corners, imitating Motown. He confessed, "It seemed like a good idea at the time." He lay in an Army Surgical Hospital. Wounds from a machine gun covered his body. The Red Cross on my shoulder and blue eyes were a license to know everything. He explained, "People think we're all scared out there. After you get used to it, you don't care. You keep down as much as you can. Then if Charlie gets you, that's it." I understood what he meant. You can't stay terrified for months and months. At some point you have to mentally step back, take a breath, and accept the situation. You have to give your mind a break. There are hours and hours of boredom when nothing happens but it could at any second, like a baseball game. Being terrified doesn't help. That happened when I sat in the bunker at An Khe, when I was new in the country, and listened to the shells fly overhead. The men in that bunker had learned to relax, "keep their heads down, but if Charlie got them that was it," except for the extreme short-timer next to me. He had to work at it.

In other situations when something is happening, you have to be hyper-vigilant, to see everything in slow motion. You can't lose your concentration even for a second. The closest I had come to that was in the "fight" at the 9ᵗʰ Cavalry party. I was not aware of some of the things that happened. Somehow, my watch ripped off and the high heel on my shoe broke. I knew enough to glimpse into what the Detroit hero confessed and to sense what he wanted to tell me. I put on my "Tell me more" face.

*Joann (left) and Cal with troops in the field. At first
they don't know what to make of the girls.*

"We do crazy things. We charge at the VC yelling 'Airborne,' and
all kinds of things. Then after it's all over we get scared and ask ourselves, 'What did I do? What did I do that crazy thing for? I could have

Joann gives a program in a rice paddy. A patrol passes in the background.

We walked around greeting troops as they rested in the field.

gotten myself killed." I thought the same thing after the 9th Cavalry party when the escort officer told me I had challenged a combat leader. Detroit didn't tell me, but afterward, maybe his life flashed before his eyes. Maybe then was the moment he faced mortality, not the moment it actually happened. Afterwards would be the moment when he would lose his nerve, if he did. What he expressed to me in the hospital was the result of that re-assessment.

In the movies people get killed all the time. In cowboy movies, a man 100 yards away gets killed with one shot from a pistol. In war movies, whole rows of enemy soldiers get mowed down with a spattering of machine-gun fire. As Hollywood sees it, if you shoot a man, he's dead. Real war isn't that way. That was one of the first things I learned when I arrived in Vietnam. The Detroit soldier had amazed me. He was covered with bandages. He had charged a machine gun. Why wasn't he dead? In the movies, he might have captured the machine gun, but he would have been dead. He realized that afterwards—over and over again.

Friday, February 24

This morning at breakfast, one of the officers had just come in from the field. He told me that, not long ago at the airfield at Ben Cat a sniper came and sat at the end of the runway. He shot at the aircraft every day as they landed and took off. One day a new aircraft landed at Ben Cat. When the sniper shot at him, he returned fire. An article appeared in the unit newspaper shortly afterward entitled, "Please don't kill our Charlie." It appealed to the new pilots not to shoot the sniper at the end of the runway, because in the weeks that he had been there he hadn't hit anything. If someone killed him, the VC might replace him with another who was a better shot.

Sunday, March 5

Today I went to church. We prayed for those out in the jungles and for those who had been wounded.

At dinner a captain tracked me down in the mess hall. He wore field gear, steel helmet, armored vest, .45 pistol. He asked me if we could please visit his men. He was from 9th Division, the area guard troops for Long Binh, in their rear rest area for two days. He was anxious for us to visit. He sat there so concerned for the welfare of his men, I thought he must be a good commander. I feel so sorry for these men. I hope what we can do for them helps a little.

Thursday March 9

I heard on the news tonight that Hong Kong is tense right now. Political unrest or something.[2] I thought about our soldiers on R&R there. From one hot spot right into another.

Today the phone lines were fantastic. My call to Bob went through immediately. It normally takes anywhere from half an hour to an hour, if I can get through at all. When I got Typhoon I asked for Skylark, and the operator asked if I wanted Cold Shower 6, then chuckled, pleased with himself that he anticipated me. He stayed on the line and relayed for me without even being asked. Without those guys I would probably never get through. As usual, I couldn't tell what Bob was saying except,

"I love you," but I could hear his voice. That was enough. Conversations had always been short since I moved to Bien Hoa because there were so many telephone exchanges to go through. We never knew when we would be cut off, we couldn't talk about classified information, and you can't have a long discussion when you depend on someone else to relay your words. It's almost time for Bob to go home, and I won't hear his voice at all. We will only have letters.

Date between Wednesday March 15 and Friday March 24, Phan Thiet

On a rare full day off I managed to get a ride on an aircraft that would take me to Phan Thiet to see Bob. I would only be there a few minutes in the afternoon while the plane unloaded and loaded cargo and passengers, and then it would return to Bien Hoa. I had talked to Bob on the phone every night and we wrote letters to each other every day. It had been four and a half months since I watched him put on his helmet and stride away in the airport at Tan Son Nhut. I treasured the memory.

When my plane landed at Phan Thiet, Bob was there to meet me. I ached to kiss him, but the area was bustling. I felt giddy inside, my heart hammered, but all I dared to do was smile. We shook hands, and he smiled at me. I wanted him to take me in his arms. He was so strong, so good, so capable and loving; I was proud and blessed to know him and love him, and to have him love me. It was great to see him. Wherever we girls went, we always stayed in public places.

Bob and I walked a short distance from the runway to a cluster of tents. A few people moved here and there. He showed me around the small area and introduced me to a few people who emerged to greet us. Then he asked the group, "May I use an office?"

One captain offered, "Sure, take mine."

The office was the only structure that wasn't a tent. It was con-structed from wooden ammunition boxes, the contents lettered on the side, "105 HOWITZER." Louvers over screen on the top half of the little building allowed air to flow through. Inside there was only one chair. Bob insisted, "You sit in the chair," and he knelt beside me.

I couldn't have him do that, so I offered, "I'll sit on your lap." We talked for a few minutes. He tried to kiss me, but he couldn't from that position. I suggested, "Let's stand up." He took me in his arms and kissed me with the passion both of us were hiding. I tightened my arms around his broad shoulders and returned his ardor. I held my breath. I felt the full length of his strong body against mine.

Joann and Captain Windsor in front of the office made of ammunition boxes. Note, they are holding hands so no one can see.

Whoops and hollers erupted from all directions. Shocked, we startled apart. People could see us through the vertical louvered sides of the hand-made building. We couldn't see anyone, but they must have been in the tents around us. We sat down, embarrassed. We talked quietly for a few minutes. I told him how much I missed him, how good it was to see him, and how much I appreciated his letters and phone calls. We shared a hug and a few awkward kisses where no one could see us, and then it was time to go.

After that trip I stopped writing letters to Bob, because I knew they wouldn't reach him before he went home. I would have to wait until he got to his next assignment and could send me his address, before I could send him a letter again.

Joann greets a group of soldiers coming off a night patrol. They are waiting in a breakfast line in a rubber plantation. Note the cuts in the bark of the rubber tree (center) where it has been tapped to harvest the latex.

Wednesday, March 22

A warrant officer from 3rd/319 Artillery came into our office today. He told us, "Three people were killed in A Battery."

I jerked around and stared at him. "Those were the people I visited alone because we were short handed that day. That was the last time the brigade was in from the field, about a month ago, right?" He nodded. I remembered that I had spent two hours with them. I checked the schedule on the wall. It showed our visit on February 18. I told him, "Two lieutenants, the executive officer and one other lieutenant, took me around, because they were too busy to stop work. I walked around to all the gun positions. I even looked at the new puppies under Captain Anderson's floor, and I ate lunch with the officers."

The warrant officer went on, "The three people who were killed were the commanding officer Captain Anderson, his executive officer, and his driver. An artillery round landed in the area." I closed my eyes. I had ugly visions of that charming West Point graduate and the two other men blown apart. If you close your eyes you don't get rid of a vision in your heart.

The next day another man from the 3rd/319 Artillery told us, "Captain Anderson had been talking on the telephone. The 1st sergeant came into the tent after the round landed. He found Captain Anderson holding the telephone, slumped over in the chair." The man stopped a minute to compose himself, and then continued, "At first they thought he had fallen asleep. A piece of shrapnel had hit him in the back of the head. He never knew what happened." Then I suffered more than Captain Anderson had. His death was instantaneous, while I was left to dwell on it. Yes, death is sometimes harder for those who remain.

Once in a while, Green Beret Special Services Officer Captain Goodwin, invited us to ride along on the Airmobile PX run. That was a traveling store. It carried civilian-style goods for sale to those in isolated units. It was a good way for us to visit remote areas. Many of the units we visited were Special Forces. Goodwin took us along whenever he had a good run.

On one PX trip we dropped down to a unit in the middle of the jungle. Half a dozen shirtless, tattooed soldiers roared out of the forest, clinging to a bouncing jeep. It skidded to a stop at the helipad, and they jumped clear. The enthusiastic men swarmed around the boxes full of merchandise lined up on the ground. I imagined that those men could dispatch multiple enemies with their bare hands in the tradition of the Special Forces. Camilla and I hopped down off the chopper and mingled with the soldiers.

I said to the man beside me, "Oh, look. There's a corncob pipe for sale."

"Yeah, I bought one last time the PX chopper was here." He pulled it out of the pocket on one side of the leg of his jungle fatigue pants, and stuck it between his teeth. Another man came over to look at the pipes. I moved on and joined the men looking at the camera film. Captain Goodwin soon told us it was time to go. Camilla and I climbed back onto the helicopter and waved goodbye. All of the men had corncob pipes clenched in their teeth. I thought, *Nobody can tell me men don't like to shop. They just have to be in the right store.*

Left to right: James Garner, Captain Goodwin, Joann, and Camilla on a PX run.

One of the most memorable PX chopper flights was a trip with the movie star James Garner. Before we started, he posed with Goodwin, Camilla, and me for a picture. We flew together from one stop to another all day long. Most of the stops were to visit large units. Crowds of men poured around the popular celebrity. I had loved him since his TV series *Maverick* in the 1950s. I had seen every movie he made. He was just as charming in real life as in the movies, and more. Every time someone asked for an autograph, he obliged. Every time someone tried to take a picture of him, he invited them to give the camera to someone else and pose in the picture with him. He spoke to everyone, shook hands, and made all comers thrilled that they saw him. He didn't eat lunch. Camilla and I were starved. We split up and ate with the men while James Garner went off to another part of the base to see another group of soldiers.

Between stops, as we flew over the jungle, he told us about his hobby of race cars. He said his insurance company wouldn't let him drive any more, but he loved to watch. He also told us that the Army had wanted to give him a simulated rank of colonel for the trip. He declined because at the higher rank he would have to face special protocol that slowed him down and kept him from seeing so many men. He accepted the simulated rank of lieutenant colonel. I was sorry to see the day end.

Later, I learned that Garner had been a Merchant Marine. Then he joined the National Guard. He was drafted into the Army during the Korean War and received a Purple Heart.[3]

Once, on another trip with the PX chopper, we completed a stop and took off. About half way up, one of the boxes of cigarettes shifted and protruded from the open door. The wind snatched the box. As it fell, it got smaller and smaller. I looked at our escort. Above the noise of the jet engines I wouldn't have been able to hear what he said, but his return glance told me it was no use trying to chase the box. We were over enemy territory, and we might as well consider the cigarettes a gift to whoever found them. I never saw them land. We were a long way in the air.

The man next to me saw me watching the box. He explained, "Sometimes when we take prisoners, and we need information, we take two of the prisoners up in a helicopter. When they won't answer our questions, we push one of them out. After that, the other one sings like a bird." I was shocked. I remembered that a few months ago a soldier was driving us in 1st Infantry Division. He pointed out a bamboo cage sitting beside the road in the full sun. He told me they had a prisoner, and they made the cage to keep him in. Their commander told them that would be cruel, and they couldn't do it. If our American soldiers couldn't keep a prisoner in a bamboo cage, I doubt they would push a prisoner out of a helicopter. I discounted the story as a myth.

Later, I asked my military intelligence friend, Jerry Burns. He said, "Not sure. I wanted to do it, but none of my pilot friends would go along with it. I always heard they took three up, bound and gagged. All three were lying on the floor looking down. They asked the first one a question, he said *khom biet* (I don't know anything) and out he went. The second one thought they would throw one out but not two, so he wouldn't talk. Out he goes. As he is zooming in for a crash landing they ask the third one a question and he will tell them anything. Not sure if it's true, but probably true at one time or another."

Thursday, March 30, the Mekong Delta

Every day a supply truck from the 86th Engineers started from their base camp just north of us, passed us, and continued south to the Delta. It traveled without a convoy, delivering supplies and people all day, and then returned to base camp. Intelligence rated the Delta as a safe area, so we thought we could set up visits to a number of units there every week. I scheduled a ride on the supply truck for every Thursday. We planned to travel to the Delta, visit as many units as possible, and be home at the end of the day.

On the first trip, the truck arrived on time, a three-quarter ton, a little bigger than a pick-up. The canvas cover on the back was rolled up. Three or four soldiers sat on the wooden bench seats along the open sides among the supplies. The sergeant in charge sat in the window seat of the cab, the window rolled down, his arm resting on the door. He and another man jumped down and greeted the two of us. "Good morning, Ladies." We shook hands. He handed our big, canvas bag of program materials to the other man, who took it to the back. The sergeant indicated the cab of the truck, held the door open, and helped us up the step. Then he walked to the back and climbed over the tailgate to sit with the cargo, near the front, where he could give orders to the driver.

The Red Cross had trained us in military courtesy. Each person's rank dictates where he rides in a vehicle. In a three-quarter-ton truck the vehicle commander sits in the window seat of the cab. He has an unobstructed field of vision, he can give orders to the driver, and besides, it's the most comfortable seat. The open window catches the most breezes. The lowest-ranking people sit on the hard benches in the back. In training we had been cautioned not to sit in the commander's seat unless he offered it to us. The sergeant had given up the best seat to us. We would hurt his feelings if we refused. I sat next to the window, because I out-ranked the girl with me. This was a safe trip; to command the vehicle was a formality.

On the way to the Delta I asked the driver, "Aren't you going to take it out of four-wheel drive?"

"No, the rear axle's busted."

"It's what?!"

"It's been that way for a year. All we have is front wheel drive. You can't have everything at once."

When the two of us arrived in the Delta on that first visit, we checked in at Nha Be (pronounced "Nah Bee"), the headquarters. We discovered that we would visit a unique, historic unit. It was 2nd Battalion of 3rd Infantry, part of "The Old Guard (TOG)" Dating back to 1784, it was the oldest active military unit in the US Army. The men wore three-cornered hats, the first I had ever seen. We learned that elements of that unit guard the Tomb of the Unknown Soldier in Washington, D.C., one of the highest honors in the military. The units in the States actually wore a copy of the old, black three-cornered hat that George Washington wore. The men in Vietnam wore an OD ("olive drab," Army green) cotton camouflage version. The battalion commander, Lt. Col. Bill Healy,[4] gave us each a unit patch to identify us for the day. He introduced our escort, Personnel Officer S-1 Robert Wagner,[5] a tall, blond captain from the headquarters staff. I could see him playing high school basketball in Indiana. Captain Indiana would take us where we needed to go and keep us safe.

He told us, "Today, we're going to visit some engineers building a bridge." I knew that the Mekong Delta contained numerous rice paddies and rivers. Captain Wagner explained, "The Viet Cong don't bother the bridge until it's almost done, and then they blow it up. Then, the engineers build it up again. When it's almost done the VC blow it up again. In the meantime, there is no VC activity. There's no use blowing the bridge up while we can't use it." That sounded logical to me. Everyone agreed we could travel safely, the local military commander, the area military commander, and the Red Cross Saigon office.

Our escort officer took us first to visit The Old Guard Headquarters unit. Then we traveled to B Company, commanded by Capt. Paul Morgan,[6] some distance away. Our jeep passed through a unique tidal region of the Delta. At high tide that morning, water covered the area for miles around. The road ran along a raised bed three feet above the water. Grass and brush covered the banks. Palm-thatched houses sat on mounds of earth above high tide. A rowboat or sailboat floated nearby, and banana trees grew in the dooryard. Captain Wagner pointed to a flock of white ducks that swam near one of the houses, "Instead of chickens, the local people keep ducks."

That afternoon we traveled to C Company at Nhon Duc 2 ("Non Duck"), 20 miles from Nha Be, through the tidal area again, now at low tide.[7] We saw endless mud flats along both sides of the raised road. Twenty-five or 30 men and women, worked alone or in pairs on the flats and carried wire baskets. They wore black pajamas and cone-shaped hats. The driver sat up straighter and checked his mirrors. Captain Wagner shifted his weight in the seat so that he could reach his side arm. He adjusted his three-cornered hat more firmly on his head. He cautioned, "Those are clam baskets. The people dig for clams in the mud during low tide. We have to watch them. You can never be sure if they have hand grenades in their baskets with the clams. They might be bending over to pick up a clam, then stand up and throw a hand grenade at you." I sat up straighter and paid attention to every person we saw. No traffic ran on the road through the tidal region. Few people lived there. We saw no farms, fields, or crops, and only a few houses. It resembled one big, mud beach for as far as I could see. The many rivers, swamps, and tidal mud flats explained why the Army had no large-scale military operations there. However, with such an unpredictable population, hindsight later told me that we had underestimated the potential danger. The VC could ambush us from anywhere. At the end of the trip we crossed a wide river in a military motorboat next to the unfinished bridge. Captain Wagner told us, "The VC attach explosives to the bridge supports all the time. Divers have to check them constantly."

We waited on the other side of the river for 20 minutes in an outdoor café in a busy, crowded village at the foot of the bridge. Our rocky little table with four chairs, and two other tables, made up the whole café. It squeezed into the spattered shade of an over-worked, middle-aged tree,

*Joann and Personnel Officer, S-1 Captain Robert Wagner, walk
across the gunwales of several boats next to the bridge under
construction. Their military transport (right) pulls away.*

on a bumpy roadside, packed hard by foot traffic. A layer of road dust covered everything. We were the only customers in the café. Captain Wagner's knees couldn't fit under the round table, barely big enough for four cups of tea. We treated it like a patio drink table. The fragile folding chairs, big enough for the small adult Vietnamese, would have qualified as children's chairs in the States. We sat lightly, carefully. The travelers at our elbows, mostly pedestrians and bicycles, barely missed us as they swirled past. It reminded me of the carnival midway at a county fair back home. Bicycle bells rang. The people, all civilians, spoke the sing-song Vietnamese language.

The café blended into the bicycle traffic of the ill-defined road. An occasional small vehicle threaded its way through the chaos. Travelers more or less kept to the right, with no definition of traffic lanes, as at a carnival. People and vehicles trotted or strode on left or right as business or pleasure took them. The café perched at the top of a little rise above the river. We enjoyed a panoramic view of the bridge, the river, and the road that went down the hill. Captain Wagner had chosen a great place to sit and have a cup of tea and watch the people and the activity in the shops and on the road. We had the best table in the house to see—and be seen. We always aroused curiosity wherever we went, two American girls in blue uniforms that anyone could see a mile away, escorted today by a soldier in a three-cornered hat. I imagined that the whole village began to buzz, and for miles around, as far as the tide could carry. We didn't guess that the news of two American girls went straight to every VC within walking range.

The village was a grand experience to cap a memorable day. The perpetual tourist in me bathed in it. That day I had taken a trip to a far-away, exotic land. I journeyed back in time as well as distance, an excursion to an ancient, untouched place, unspoiled by a careful tourist, an expedition only a millionaire could afford. We met our ride and traveled home.

Our Red Cross unit of five girls meant that I scheduled two girls to go to the Delta each week. My turn would come up again a couple of weeks later. I was eager for it.

Friday, April 3

Bob is on his way home, where he'll be safe.

Monday, April 10

My EDPAC (Estimated Departure Pacific)[8] was exactly one year from the day I arrived at my first assignment, the 1st Cavalry Division (Airmobile) at An Khe, May 10, 1966. Today I had 30 days to my ED-PAC. I was "Short." People counted down their last days "in country" from thirty. They could tell you exactly how many days they had left. Commanders often excused them from dangerous assignments, even unimportant tasks that would annoy them. Everyone was extra careful when they were short. They would say, "I'm too short for this." To the Donut Dollies, however, being short meant no special treatment.

Wednesday, April 12, Bien Hoa

Twenty-eight days to my EDPAC.

I called 86ᵗʰ Engineers, the bridge-building specialists, to confirm our trip to the Delta for the next day. I looked forward to the trip, for it was my turn to go. A sergeant told me, "We're moving the base camp tomorrow. From now on, the supply run will originate from south of you, so we won't be able to take you any more." He wouldn't tell me anything more over the phone. That ended our trips to the Delta. I was disappointed. That was one of the best trips we had.

Sunday, April 23

Every Sunday morning we had Coffee Call at the recreation center. All five of us were there, some in civilian clothes, a treat for the men. We moved a table and some chairs outside to the cement pad in front of the door to make an outdoor café, and served coffee and refreshments. We had no recreation program. The guys just came to relax.

Two weeks after we cancelled the trips to the Delta, that Sunday was a typical, too-bright, sun-scorched morning. A sergeant from 86ᵗʰ Engineers sat alone at the outdoor table, slumped over. He stared at his untouched cup of Kool-Aid with the big red cross on it. Everyone else walked around and talked to the girls and to each other. We tried to boost morale, to help people forget about the war, even if only for a few minutes, so I went over and sat with the sergeant. I said, "You look down."

He raised his head. "My sergeant was killed." His eyes pinched back the pain. Eleven months in Vietnam had taught me that I could show sympathy in moments like this, but nothing more. My job was to bring morale up, not down. I struggled. He went on, "On the day you didn't take the trip, the VC ambushed the supply truck in the Delta."

My brain went numb. I thought, *The day we didn't take the trip? Ambushed?* I let my face show sympathy, but my gasp and cry stayed silent. *The Delta was safe. There wasn't any VC activity there. That's why we could go. I don't think anyone on that truck was armed. Nobody was riding shotgun.* I remembered the truck, a three-quarter ton. Several soldiers rode in the back to travel between units where the truck would stop.

I was supposed to be on that truck.

The sergeant continued, "They hit it from the right side of the road. The driver floored it and kept on going; 150 meters later they ambushed it again from the left side. The driver kept on going until they got out of range." In my mind I saw the truck race across the tidal mud flats on the elevated road. The sergeant took a drink of his Kool-Aid. "The VC fired about 20 rounds each time. Sergeant Harris was killed. He was the NCOIC [Non Commissioned Officer In Charge]. He was the only man hit. They never saw anybody."

His words stung my brain. I wasn't sure I heard him correctly. *Did he say Sergeant Harris was killed?*

My heart stopped. I realized that Sergeant Harris, the highest-ranking person on the truck, would have sat in the window seat of the cab, according to military practice. When I rode in the truck, the sergeant moved into the back and gave me the window seat. Was Sergeant Harris killed instead of me? I couldn't breathe; I couldn't speak. I realized that I was listening to what would have been the story of my death. I felt my soul elevate from my body.

I couldn't tell the sergeant at Coffee Call that I was the girl who would have been on that truck. At the least, it would complicate his feelings. He might blame me for Sergeant Harris's death. I had learned by now that the men had superstitious ways to look at chance happenings in a land of incomprehensible events. I remembered how the men avoided the fortuneteller booth at the carnival. The sergeant at Coffee Call finished his Kool-Aid and left. He felt better. I didn't. I couldn't tell the other girls about the ambush in the Delta. In the combat zone we could not become *too* paranoid. Every sound was not a threat. It was my job to arrange transportation, though. The full impact of this coincidence struck me. The Delta was a safe trip.

Joann serves a cup of coffee at Sunday Coffee Call at Bien Hoa Recreation Center.

I put together more pieces of the puzzle. Why did divers have to check the bridge supports all the time for explosives, if no VC operated there? Maybe the area held more danger than anyone thought. Maybe the VC watched for something to do while the engineers worked on the bridge. I remembered that on the first trip to the Delta we sat in the café at the foot of the bridge. We waited for transportation with our escort officer for about twenty minutes. That gave every VC in the area time to discover us. Not only that, the VC knew the supply truck traveled that route every day. They could have learned in the weeks after our first visit, that the Red Cross girls rode the truck every Thursday. Had the VC set up that ambush on a Thursday to kill a Red Cross girl riding in the window seat?

I knew why the first attack had come from the right side of the road. The first rounds would take everyone by surprise. From the right side the attacker had a clear shot at the highest-ranking person in the truck, the window seat in the cab. Sergeant Harris sat in that seat, the same seat that I would have been sitting in. That was why he was the only person hit. Then I knew. *When I was less than 30 days from going home, the VC would have killed me.*

That phone call to 86th Engineers that cancelled the trip had saved my life. Sergeant Harris had died instead of me. I was stunned. I felt the blood rush to my head. It began to throb.

A wide-eyed private who wore new fatigues, new combat boots and Paratrooper wings approached me. He held a cup of coffee in one hand and a mostly-eaten muffin in the other. "Do you have any writing paper, please, Ma'am?" He stuffed the rest of the muffin into his mouth.

I summoned up my Red Cross smile and swallowed my emotions. "Sure. Let me show you."

I learned many years later that two men usually carried out an ambush. They fired from cover, as far away as possible, spraying everywhere. They fired two clips, if possible, and were gone instantly. Attackers in the Delta used AK-47s, the old French MAT-49 machine pistol, and other handmade weapons common there.[9] The most-used VC weapon, the AK-47 Kalashnikov, carried a clip that held 30 rounds and had an effective range of 300 meters, 330 yards.[10] The truck was still within range of the first weapon, at 150 meters, when the second one opened up.

I pictured Sergeant Harris. As I remembered him, he was a little older, a little gray, of medium build, and a little heavy. He was a supply sergeant. I had taken care of supplies at 1ˢᵗ Cavalry in Korea and at Di An in Vietnam. Sergeant Harris had a vast inventory compared to mine. He didn't have a physical, combat job to keep the extra pounds off.

Remembering the ambush, I reasoned that the VC didn't hit anyone when they struck from the left side of the road because, by then, the truck was flying, and everyone would have dropped to the floor, *except the driver.* I knew: The target of the second attack was the driver. Lieutenant Neil Persinger, a sailor who had experienced an ambush, explained that the truck was harder to control when it was traveling fast. If the attacker could hit the driver, the truck would run off the elevated road and roll over. The people in the back would spill out into the open and become easy targets. Unarmed, the leader down, they would be inside the effective range of both guns. The attackers still had 10 rounds in their first clip and a fresh clip ready. All the people on the truck could have been killed.[11]

I had glimpsed a chilling picture of what the soldiers saw and felt.

✦ CHAPTER 10 ✦

The Cigarette in the Rain

Sometimes the wisdom of our decisions surprises us. Choosing between one form of death and another is no simple matter. Back in late August, for several days it had been hot at Dong Ba Thin. At dinner some of the officers traded war stories about the heat. One said, "Two days ago it was 110 degrees in the tent at the airstrip." I had experienced high 90s in a tent at Di An, but not 110 degrees.

The next one said, "In the sun it was 134 degrees."

The third one topped them all. "On the steel paving of the runway it was 145 degrees. I have people who have gotten blisters on their feet from walking on it, *through their boots*."

(About) April 25, Bien Hoa

Almost every night after dinner the company showed a movie on a screen they set up outdoors behind the officer's club. Everyone would bring a chair. One night, as usual, we pulled our chairs into rows and traded lighthearted jokes. We anticipated a story to entertain us and distract us from the tension that surrounded us. The movie was an old-fashioned western. In one scene the villain stampeded the herd. A hero good guy was thrown from his horse. We saw him go down under the thundering cattle. The man sitting next to me, one of the Cowboys gunship pilots, Jamie Gregg, stiffened and groaned. He said, "That guy's name was Jamie, and he got killed. My name is Jamie." I could hear the fear in his voice.

He had taken the story, a movie cliché, as a premonition. I said, "Ah, he's too tough to die. Watch, he'll show up later." I didn't know. I just tried to say something to make him feel better. Surprise, Jamie, the movie cowboy, lived and married the girl. Jamie, the Cowboy pilot, relaxed. But, I'm sure that if the man had been killed, Jamie would have been nervous for several days. That might have been what started my reputation as someone who could see the future.

I thought about the movie. I never saw a cowboy movie where a man went down under a stampede and lived. Usually, that was a good way to kill off the bad guy. I suspected that someone carefully chose the films we watched, edited them, and even rewrote parts of them, because the Army knew how soldiers would react to what the movies portrayed. This movie even had a cowboy who had lost an arm in an accident. We saw that he functioned fine with just one arm. Was the Army preparing men for the possibility that they might lose a limb? I thought there was precedent for that kind of censorship. Growing up in the North, in every movie I ever saw about the Civil War the soldiers wore blue uniforms and they were the heroes. When I lived in the South, the heroes wore gray uniforms. I was shocked the first time I saw a bad guy wearing a blue uniform.

I should have seen the clue, the superstition. These pilots lived on the edge of a fear that fought them. They battled back with the stories at supper. It proved the value of the non-mythical myth. They spent much of their free time in the lively group. They depended on each other to keep fear away. Like the conversation in the bunker at An Khe (his mother's bar stool?) it kept their minds focused. In that bunker I was so new I didn't know how to control my fear. I learned from the soldiers. The Cavalry officers at An Khe had used their song, "The Hand

Grenade at Plei Me" ("Thanks a lot, you SOB") to help them fight their fear in combat. To be alone made a person more susceptible to fear. I should have remembered how lonely I felt by myself in the bunker last Thanksgiving and under the desk in Saigon.

Shortly after we saw the cowboy movie, I got home from work about five o'clock as usual, tired. I walked the couple of blocks to the club to have dinner with my buddies, the pilots. I looked forward to some enjoyable stories at supper, then a couple of drinks and the movie, The *Navy Versus the Night Monsters*, before I turned in.

A few yards from the club I heard the helicopters and looked up. The Cowboys had come home for supper. They flew in their customary formation, single file. A few weeks ago at dinner, the pilots had told me that all aircraft flew in formation. "That way, we don't run into each other. The formation is based on the way a helicopters flies. As the helicopter's rotor turns, it pushes the air down. That is called the rotor wash. Each ship flies a little higher than the one in front. Its rotor turns in undisturbed air a little above the rotor wash of the one in front."

On that night the Cowboys came in trailing smoke. A smoke grenade attached to the skid of the last chopper spewed a plume of bright pink smoke. It announced a celebration. Pink signified kills. They must have had a good day. The stories would be great at supper. I looked again. The ships were flying too close together, and they were coming in too fast. They made the turn to the right to line up with the airstrip; the lead ship suddenly slowed down. The line flared out to the left to avoid a pile-up. Then they dropped out of sight behind the buildings. It worried me. They seemed too reckless. A few minutes later the pilots trooped in to supper. More animated than usual, they laughed about the day.

I scolded, "I saw you come in. You're driving like cowboys. You keep flying like that and you're going to run into each other." (I sounded like my mother.)

They laughed. Some of them waved their hand to brush me off. "Eh. No way. We know what we're doing." In the real world, if you make a mistake you could lose a customer. My months in Vietnam had taught me that, in a war, if you make a mistake, people die.

Bob had told me that on a helicopter the rotor blades perform the function of wings on an airplane. If the engine stops, an airplane will float, or glide to a landing. A helicopter will do the same to a point, if the rotor blades can maintain sufficient revolutions per minute. But, if the wings break off, whether it's a fixed wing or a rotary wing aircraft, it goes into free-fall. When it hits the ground, the fuel tanks will explode. Pilots didn't usually say an aircraft crashed. They said "crash-and-burn," all in one word. Everyone feared it.

The disaster happened a few days later. Two helicopters collided. The crash killed everyone on board both ships, possibly 30 men. A shudder went through the company. Sandy, the pilot with the freckles across his nose, told the story at supper. "We were escorting a forma-tion of loaded transport helicopters." A transport could carry 11 to 13 men. "I knew these 'slick' pilots. I had worked with them before." "Slick" denoted troop carriers. They were slick because they didn't have the full complement of armament like the gun ships. They didn't have the big rocket pods on their sides, though they had machine guns on mounts, in their doors.

A gunship door gunner, Phil Rosette, once declared, "Those guys [the slick door gunners] can shoot pretty damn straight. Those are the guys *we* look up to, ground level with good guys and bad guys and they have to stay cool under fire, sometimes shooting just inches over the heads of our guys to give them cover on landings. We gunners at least have the assurance of seeing where the tracers are coming from and knowing where we can shoot and where we can't."[1]

As we ate together that evening on the day when the two helicop-ters collided, Sandy explained what had happened. "There was this one slick pilot who liked to fly beside the next helicopter, so close his rotor blade was just above, and overlapping his neighbor's." He used his hands to demonstrate one blade overlapping the other. "The accident happened when the lower chopper turned away. As he turned, he banked. He tipped just enough that the blades of the two helicopters touched." The tips of Sandy's fingers touched. "Both blades sheared off and disintegrated. Both choppers went down. I was so close I could see the expression on one man's face when he realized they were going down." We all remained silent. I winced and tried not to imagine what that expression must have looked like. I wondered how long it would take for that image to fade from someone's memory. In a crash like that, no one expected survivors.

A few days later I went to the memorial service. The chaplain conducted a simple, dignified ceremony at an outdoor briefing area near the mess hall. Several hundred people, probably most of the personnel from the units that had lost men, both infantry and aviation, had gathered, and other friends like me. Rain poured. It obscured the scene and created a steamy mist. The men moved in silence through the vapor, like ghosts in their identical ponchos, to their places on homemade benches.

My raincoat was transparent with a hood, designed to draw attention to our blue uniforms and to identify Red Cross girls. I couldn't understand why nobody spoke to me. Nobody even acknowledged me, as if nobody knew me. I felt like a stranger, completely alone, an intruder. The people who sat beside me and around me on the wooden benches didn't even look at me. It seemed as though the hood hid my identity. But, I knew nobody could mistake me among all the identical, hooded green ponchos, a small person among all those big men. Anybody who didn't know me had to know I was Red Cross.

After that, no one in the gunship unit would talk to me. Not just during the memorial service, but afterwards as well. They treated me like a poison. The stress of living in that unpredictable environment of danger made people superstitious. I had predicted the tragedy, so they believed I had caused it. Like the fortuneteller at the carnival back at Dong Ba Thin, they were afraid I might predict something else.

Phil the gunner reassured me, "Don't take it personal that they wanted to stay clear of you after that. You said something that spooked them, and they were a spookier bunch anyway, those front seat guys."[2] I shouldn't have been surprised. The clues were there. The Cowboys' bravado was fear.

Thursday, April 27, Bien Hoa

Today Camilla and I served coffee and Kool-Aid to 120 troops, ten helicopters full. We knew the number because we used that many cups with the big red crosses on them. We met the soldiers on a helipad where they stopped for a few minutes between flights. When they went away, not one paper cup lay on the ground. The men had put them into the many cargo pockets of their jungle fatigues, up and down the legs and on the upper and lower front of the jacket. The troops put the cups into their pockets partly because their discipline had taught them not to leave the enemy any trace of where they had been, and partly as souvenirs.

The closer I came to leaving Vietnam, the more impatient I became. I wanted to go home. I was weary of going to one party after another, of making small talk with people I didn't know. I was tired all the time, I felt fatigued and beaten up; the girls weren't sympathetic. Later, after I got home, I tried to give blood. The technician rejected me. He said my red blood count was low, meaning that I was anemic. No wonder I had been tired all the time. I didn't know if the rabies treatment had made me anemic, or if the pace and strenuous life had taken its toll. I was never really concerned for my safety. I paid attention to everything and made sure to stay where it was safe. I was just tired. The commander of Headquarters Company gave me a small going-away party and a plaque. It meant a lot to me.

I counted down the last 30 days, because everyone else did. It was the worst thing I could have done. The days dragged. They felt longer than they should have. Thirty days were forever. I didn't have the sense to stop, so I was miserable.

> April 30, 1967
>
> Dear Mom and Dad,
>
> Visited some units of Special Forces today. They are A Teams working with the Montagnards, primitive people in the jungle. I took some great pictures. There are also some pictures of the Delta on this roll. I'm having them sent to you because I'll be leaving for home in ten days. I hope you enjoy them.
>
> Love,
>
> Joann

I never told my parents what had really happened in the Delta, or in Montagnard Territory.

Sunday, April 30, Montagnard Territory

I had ten days left in Vietnam. As soon as you woke up, that day didn't count. Camilla and I served coffee, cake, and warm Kool-Aid to about 300 troops in the morning. Some were people from the Aviation unit, and some were from 173rd Airborne Brigade.

Special Services Officer Captain Goodwin, picked us up at 12:30 to go on the Airmobile PX run. When we arrived at the soccer field, the III Corps chopper pad, the mechanics told us our ship was down for repairs. The radios were out. We needed a radio, because we planned to go deep into Viet Cong territory. We would have to contact the units we intended to visit to see if they could assure our safety before we landed. We also didn't want to be in the way if they had to fight off an attack. Not only that, we had gone to Duc Hoa on a previous trip to see some advisory teams, the elite, 12-man Special Forces units. When we got back a pilot told us that a helicopter had been shot down by small arms fire near Duc Hoa and all four aboard were killed. We couldn't go without a radio so the mechanics sent along a portable.

At the first stop we came in for a landing at treetop-level in a wide sweep. It felt like a carnival ride that whips you around. Inside the typical Army buildings of the small camp we chatted with the men for a few minutes. The commander showed us his skull of a tropical deer. I had actually seen two deer several weeks earlier. They were only as big as a small dog. As we said goodbye, the A Team commander asked me, "What was your pilot doing flying low level? That's Charlie's territory. If you fly low level around here he's likely to shoot you down." Our pilot overheard the exchange. He didn't have to be told twice. We spiraled up out of there so tight and fast it made me dizzy. And we did that at every stop for the rest of the day.

Next we visited a brand new camp. A three-star general, the only one I had ever seen, was just leaving. Long faces and bowed heads remained. One man told me, "The general just told us that a main Viet Cong trail passes only a few meters from this camp. Recently, the VC have been concentrating troops here. Right now he estimates that over 3,500 VC are in this immediate area."

The man next to him continued, "This camp only has nine American advisors and a couple hundred barely disciplined Cambodians, South Vietnamese, and Montagnards. They all speak different languages, and would just as soon fight each other as the enemy. The VC could wipe us out any time." As we left, we spiraled into the sky to gain altitude while still above the camp, and then headed out over the jungle. From 2,000 feet, the forest lay below as peaceful as if it remained empty.[3] I wondered, *How many enemies watch us as we fly above them. How many thousands of eyes follow us? Can they see our blue uniforms? Do they wonder what this helicopter carries?* I felt vulnerable as I sat in the open doorway. If the engine stopped now, there would be no hope for us. The VC would be on top of us in a minute. I put the thought out of my head. *How green the jungle has become after the recent rain. Do I see bananas down there?*

Next we stopped at Bu Dop, a Special Forces camp near a Montagnard village. Inside, the small group of Americans received us with surprise. A cordial man who wore only a towel greeted us. He disappeared soon after and returned fully dressed. He was the A Team commander. One of the men gave me a guided tour of the village. I took some interesting pictures of some most primitive tribal people. Mothers carried babies on their backs, and switched them to the front to nurse, without breaking stride.

That A Team had a unique store of Montagnard crafts. They kept a supply of crossbows, copper bracelets, and musical instruments to use for trade, mostly with pilots who came through. I bought a Montagnard guitar made out of a two-foot length of bamboo about three inches in diameter. I also bought a crossbow for $2.50, or the soldiers would have accepted a case of beer. The A Team also stocked a large store of captured weapons for sale or trade. They ran a regular trading post.

On our way to the next stop we flew over a Michelin rubber plantation. Large trees grew in neat rows that swirled and curved their way around the forest floor. A few miles farther on, bright pink smoke told us where to land. A battered deuce and a half truck waited. I noticed as Camilla and I climbed in, that the front grill was crooked where it had run into something. Goodwin, our escort officer, stayed at the helicopter to mind the store while we visited with the men. The driver steered the big, clumsy truck over the rough ground, not quite a road. He slowed when we reached the headquarters building, and rolled to a stop against a log in front of the door. He saw my quizzical glance.

"The truck doesn't have any brakes. The only way to stop is to run into something." *Oh, that makes sense.* I nodded.

There, we saw another remote Special Forces camp isolated in the jungle. As we sat in their mess hall, one of the men asked Camilla, "Would you like to see the new calf? We have a project to teach the Montagnards to breed livestock, to help raise their standard of living."

Another man asked me, "Would you like to tour the mercenary's camp?" He walked me around where families lived and cooked over open fires. I took a picture of a Cambodian man whose back was a mass of scars. He had suffered some terrible injuries while he fought with us against the VC. It looked to me like he should have been dead. I remembered what the doctors at An Khe had told me, "If we can get a wounded man to a hospital, we have a 98 percent chance of saving him." I figured that man was proof.

We toured the Montagnard village next, and I took a picture of a small, brown man who wore nothing but a loincloth. He carried an axe on a curved, homemade handle. Some of the thatch-roofed huts had tin walls. Back at the mess hall we visited with the soldiers. I noticed that one man talked on a telephone. I asked, "Who were you talking to?"

He answered, "My mother," and gave me a sly smile.

Another man complained, "I didn't get a letter today. No letters, no phone calls. . . ."

At the fifth stop, an escort officer with "Pray for Peace" hand-lettered on his helmet band took us to a nearby Army compound. Camilla and I split up, as usual, and toured the camp with separate escorts, so we could see more people. The officer in charge told me that this camp housed Viet Cong prisoners of war, *Chu Hoi* (the name for an amnesty program meaning "open arms"). We stood in the middle of an ordinary Army compound with no extra, armed guards that I could see.

My escort told me, "The Army gives the POWs work to do, gives them tools to do the work, such as hammers and nails and saws, and pays them for their work." I thought, *The part about the hammers might not be such a good idea*, but nobody seemed worried about it. The officer

Joann with Prisoners of War.

called out and motioned for the prisoners to gather around. They came from various directions nearby. I'm sure they had been watching us, as curious about me as I was about them. I had expected prisoners to be locked up. I posed for a picture with eight Vietnamese men in civilian clothes. I'm sure the Army wanted to show their prisoners that we were better friends than enemies. I hoped it would work.

Years later I learned that, in the use of spies, Sun Tzu said: "The enemy's spies who have come to spy on us must be sought out, tempted with bribes, led away and comfortably housed. Thus they will become converted spies and available for our service."[4]

It began to get late, and soon it would be dark. We would have to skip the last stop. Even when danger from the VC wasn't as obvious as it was there, no one flew at night.

Our helicopter headed out over the sunset jungle toward Bien Hoa. Patches of monsoon-season rain laced with lightning blocked our route like land mines. We dodged between them and around them, but the storm closed in on all sides. We started to come down. I couldn't see anything but jungle below, but I could tell it was not Bien Hoa. Then we landed. I was alarmed. In a few moments darkness would close in. We had landed at one of the Special Forces camps we had visited earlier. *What are we doing here? This isn't safe.* The pilot explained, "I landed because of the lightning. Between the lightning up there and the VC down here, I prefer the VC." I thought, *That seems clear enough.* The men at the camp welcomed us in out of the rain. My watch said 7:00.

The commander offered, "We can give you cold roast beef sandwiches, lots of cheese, and fried rice. The interpreter is in the kitchen. Since it's Sunday, it's the cook's day off." The commanding officer, a captain, looked like he could have been a young suburbanite. He chided the interpreter, "If this is good, I'll make you a cook. If it's no good, I'll make you a mechanic."

I finished my sandwich and the fried rice, which *was* good. Ever since November, when I had eaten that big plate of fried rice in the sidewalk café in Singapore at 2:00 in the morning, I had loved fried rice. Our escort officer Captain Goodwin came and sat beside me. He informed me, "The weather is getting worse. We might have to stay the night." I set down my chocolate milk. The two pilots came over, and then the commanding officer joined us. Captain Goodwin explained, "The ceiling over Bien Hoa is dropping fast. If we don't get there within half an hour, we won't be able to land." The A Team Commander offered, "There is room for all of you to stay. We can set aside a separate place for you two girls." He nodded at Camilla and me. "My men can secure and guard the helicopter. We are in a secure area where there is little danger of attack." I thought, *That's what they said about the Delta just before the ambush.* He continued, "You wouldn't be a burden. You're welcome to stay the night. We would be glad to have you." Everyone looked at *me*. They wanted *me* to decide whether we would go or stay. It stunned me at first. *With all these trained men around, why should I be the one to decide?* Then I realized that because I was a civilian, everyone treated me as though I out-ranked all military people. That was why the A Team commander earlier in the day had told me, not the pilot, to keep our altitude high on approach.

Years later, a neighbor who was a former Navy officer, told me, "Technically, no military officer could order a civilian to do anything. As a practical matter, any military commander would be reluctant to tell a civilian what to do, especially in a situation that involved significant risk. You had to make the decision for yourself, whether you would go or stay. Whatever conclusion you came to would be the choice for everyone."[5] I would make the life-or-death decision.

I didn't know what to do. The decision involved the lives of two pilots, highly trained personnel; a huge piece of valuable equipment, the helicopter; two enlisted men, the crew chief and the gunner; Goodwin; and the life of another girl, besides my own. The pilot added urgency. "Every minute we sit here talking we lessen our chances. The weather is getting worse and worse. If we don't start now we won't make it back at all."

I asked, "What would the Special Forces headquarters in Bien Hoa say? Would they say the area is secure enough for us to stay through the night?"

The Special Forces commander answered, "The authorities would leave the decision to your party." *No help there.* My mind was not going click, click, click. I was not confused. I was feeling and thinking intuitively, rather than dispassionately. I knew that if two Red Cross girls were forced to spend the night at a Special Forces camp, the Red Cross would be upset, especially if the VC decided to attack. Only a large force could over-run the camp, but just to get caught in an assault would cause a stir in Saigon. As a non-combatant, my job required me to stay out of danger, not cause it. Besides, the helicopter parked outside would attract every VC within miles. I doubted that they could resist sniping at it and they might be able to destroy it. Would the VC attack? I remembered last Thanksgiving, when it took a sniper less than 20 minutes to find three helicopters parked on the ground, in the afternoon. And the VC operated at night.

On the other hand, I asked the pilot, "What are the chances we could crash in the jungle?"

He replied, "I can't answer that."

Captain Goodwin offered his opinion. "I think we should stay."

I asked the pilot, "Are you willing to try it?"

He said, "Yes." *I didn't expect that.* I had spent a lot of time with pilots. I knew they hated bad weather. Some fixed-wing pilots would fly in mildly bad weather, but if chopper pilots thought the weather was too severe, nothing could get them to go up. Pilots knew almost as much about the weather as a weatherman. They had enormous amounts of highly technical training and knew their ships. I thought, *If the pilot is willing to fly through that storm, I'm willing to go with him.*

That did it. I said, "Let's go." I got up and left my chocolate milk sitting on the table; and I love chocolate milk. In military fashion everyone reacted. The co-pilot, crew chief, and gunner got up without a word. I had made the decision, and now they had a job to do. They were aware of the danger. In civilian life each man decides for himself whether he will go or stay. Not here. Such remained the discipline and dedication of those teenage warriors. For the group to make it out, everyone had to work together. The Special Forces commander shrugged. It was risky, but it was our decision. Captain Goodwin didn't like the looks of the weather, but he would escort us and do his best to protect us. It might come down to that. Camilla, as new as she was, probably didn't understand everything that happened. I thought, *She's the only one who's not afraid.*

We dashed outside. No more time to think. The night hung black and blood-warm. Tropical air folded heavily around us. The rain had stopped. A quick jeep ride brought us the few hundred feet to the helicopter. I jumped off the vehicle. The ground was rough. *Don't turn your ankle,* I said to myself. *If we crash in the jungle, I won't make it out on a bad foot. I wouldn't make it out anyway.* The ship sat on a rise, too high. I couldn't step up into it. That happened often. The men were all busy readying the aircraft. No one had time to help a sissy girl. I climbed up on one knee. *Nobody pays any attention to a skinned-up knee.* I felt my way to a seat and fumbled for a seatbelt.

"Lighten the aircraft," someone said. Everybody passed the PX boxes out. Dark forms climbed into the seats around me and pulled at seatbelts. The pilots began to strap in.

Suddenly a blinding flash of tropical lightning flooded the skies, making everything brighter than day. The world was on fire. The co-pilot looked at the pilot and said, "Oooh!" His voice wavered. He hesitated. The pilot never faltered. "Don't sweat it," he said, and continued to check his instruments. He was a brave man. At that moment I changed my definition of bravery. The old one that I had brought with me on that first night in Vietnam was, "You're brave if you're scared, but you do it anyway." Now I added, "And you don't let anyone know you're afraid." I knew that trip was going to be bad if the co-pilot was so scared. I tried to follow the pilot's advice, "Don't sweat it." Everything was ready. The rotor started to turn; the gunner and crew chief climbed in behind their machine guns, strapped in, and readied their weapons. The noise of the jet engines increased, the ship shuddered and then lifted a few inches off the ground. It hung there for long seconds.

Just as we hovered and began to rise, Camilla yelled into my ear above the noise, "We could have stayed here, nothing would have happened." Suddenly, fear seized me. I fought it. My mind had functioned on intuition before. Now the situation became stark, clear, and real. If we stayed the night, maybe the VC wouldn't find us. *I wouldn't bet on it. They already know we're here.* If we tried to fly out, the weather could tear the helicopter apart. If lightning struck us, it would destroy the rotor, and we would crash and burn in the jungle. There would be nothing left to identify. It was possible that none of us would make it back. Fear began to take hold of me and I started to lose the battle. The pilot never turned on the landing lights. The invisible ship's tail lifted. We began to rise and spiral fast, climbing higher and higher. My ears popped and gravity clawed at me as we raced to safety. Even when we reached cruising altitude, the red blinking identification light on the top of the aircraft never came on. We flew without lights, even though we were out of range of ground fire.

Rain exploded on the windshield. I thought it would blast the paint off the helicopter. Inside the ship everything was dark except for the green glow of the instrument lights. The pilot and co-pilot faced front behind their windshields, anonymous in their green flight helmets. Their armor-plated seats hid all except their heads. Below us spread a sea of black velvet. Here and there tiny lights sparkled. We crawled past them. Lightning struck around us. My fear grew. The windshield wipers began to lose their struggle to keep up with the torrent. To put a thought out of your head, you have to replace it with another. I started to talk to Camilla. I remembered the lieutenant who had talked about his mother's barstool in the bunker in that first mortar attack back at An Khe. He needed to fight his fear the day before he would go home. Now, it was my turn, with ten days to go.

The noise of the helicopter made conversation difficult. I had to yell at the top of my lungs into Camilla's ear and pronounce everything carefully before she could understand me. Then I had to listen hard and concentrate on what she said. Her Southern accent added another layer to our communication. We compensated by simplifying our sentences. I yelled, "It was great to see the Montagnards today. What level do you think they are in the scale of civilization?"

She hollered back, "I'm not sure how to compare them in anthropology. They are primitive tribes."

I forced my brain to scour my memory, "Do you think they belong to the Stone Age?"

"I don't know. Maybe." Our small talk chewed up the time. Then, we discussed the places we had visited and what an enthusiastic reception we had received. After about 20 minutes we could see the lights of a large town or military base. We tried to figure out where we were. The weather had not been bumpy, and the lightning had lessened by now. It looked like we would make it.

Out of the calm, a monstrous flash of lightning streaked toward us across the width of the sky. The bolt slammed us from the left front. The helicopter wrenched to the right. Fiery forks shot all around the ship. Dozens of fingers clawed so close I couldn't believe we would escape. I knew the flash would tear us apart. Everything went black. Then the ship righted itself and flew on through the night. The windshield wipers slapped back and forth. The instruments glowed green. Small streaks of lightning marked the sky. I sat dazed. It took me a moment to realize that the lightning had not destroyed the ship. We were not a falling ball of fire. We were almost home. However, even though we had dodged one bolt of lightning, others were still out there. Until we came down, we were in danger.

I looked behind me at the gunner on my side of the aircraft. His bench seat faced outward behind his machine gun. He had shifted to sit crosswise with his legs stretched out, arms crossed over his chest, his head nodded. He was dozing. *Nerves of steel*, I thought. *He probably does things like this every day.* The gunners were on a break as long as we continued to fly out of range of ground fire. I remembered when I was in 1st Infantry Division I had heard one lieutenant say to another, "You give these men a ten-minute break, and they get nine minutes of sleep."

Camilla spoke to Captain Goodwin beside her. Then she yelled into my ear, "Those are the lights of Bien Hoa." We looked for landmarks. We scoured every light for familiar patterns. I spotted a radio tower that

I knew was near our house. We started to come down. I said to myself, *Oh please, please, lightning, don't hit us now. We made it this far. Let us get home.* We came closer, closer. The lights got bigger. Then I saw the place where we would land. We came down over the town. I remembered in July at An Khe, Capt. Wayne Halpern had told me that one of his best friends, a medical service corps (MSC) pilot, had gone down in a medical evacuation chopper.

Captain Halpern had said, "You can't always tell why the ships go down. They could have taken a round from one of the villages and you would never hear it." *Please, snipers in the town*, I said to myself, *please don't shoot us down. I know the night is yours, but just let us get down.* We passed the town and left it behind. Finally we crossed over the air base perimeter. I could see all the other helicopters tied down safely long before dusk. We returned like the last sheep. A truck sat next to the helipad. I could see the ground crew. *How long had they been waiting?* Our landing light came on as we neared the ground. We descended slowly, and then the tail went down. The circle of light passed over a mud puddle. The ship settled, turned around a few feet off the ground, slipped to the side to come down dead center, and landed with a little bump. We had made it.

I sat for a minute to get used to the idea. I felt like the celebration I remembered one day last April. The Cowboys, 335th Aviation gun ships, sent 15 choppers out in formation in the morning. At the end of the day only two were still flyable. All the others had suffered hits or engine trouble. The last two ships came home in formation, the second one with smoke grenades taped to both skids, leaving a double trail of yellow smoke. I felt like having that kind of celebration.

My watch read 9:00. It had been just two hours since we had first landed at the A Camp to avoid the lightning. The helicopter's engine stopped; the big rotor blade turned slower and slower. It made a *swish* sound. I heard the snap, snap as people unbuckled their seatbelts. I freed myself and stuck my head up into the cockpit. I asked the pilot, "Now that it's over, really, how much danger were we in?"

He answered confidentially, with a smile, "I'd rather not say." I smiled back. He had told me what I had suspected: it had been a dangerous trip. Captain Goodwin, Camilla, and I piled into the truck ready for the 20-minute ride across the base to our house. The aircraft and ground crews worked to put the helicopter to bed.

As we were about to pull away, the boy-faced co-pilot stuck his head in the window and laughed, "Have a safe trip home." We laughed as we drove off.

We rode back over the bumpy road to our house. Captain Goodwin told us, "During the flight the pilot and co-pilot were singing a duet over the inter-com, '*I wanna go home, I wanna go home. Oh, how I wanna go home.*'"

Every detail of that trip remained in my memory, undimmed, for 40 years. Then I recounted it in a videotaped interview for the Smithsonian Museum's Veteran's History Project. Within days some of the details began to fade. Within weeks I could not tell the story without referring to my diary. I concluded that my memory could let go of the story because it had been preserved.

Years later I wondered how dangerous that helicopter flight through the thunderstorm was. I found that our trip was suicidal. When lightning strikes a tree, the sap flashes into steam and the tree explodes.[6] Lightning can throw a person several yards, or worse, kill him.[7] A bolt from above would strike the highest point on a helicopter, its whirling blade, and destroy it. The ship would crash.[8] Even an air ambulance won't fly through thunderstorms and lightning.[9]

In 1966, helicopters had an all-metal fuselage.[10] In the extraordinary situation when lightning might hit the body of the helicopter instead of the rotor, the bolt would not surge through the electrical system and short it out, as Bob guessed. The all-metal body would protect the occupants because the shell of the helicopter would form a "Faraday Cage." The lightning would be conducted around the outside of the helicopter, engulfing it, but leaving it unharmed.[11]

I wrote in my diary that the lightning seemed to surround the helicopter. I felt a jolt as if we had been hit. On that night, the impossible happened. The lightning hit the body of the helicopter instead of the rotor. We all should have been dead. A miracle? Maybe God had some higher purpose for my life. I don't know what it is. On the other hand, maybe the higher purpose wasn't for me. Maybe it was for someone else on that helicopter. Maybe for the door gunner, who slept through it. Or, maybe for all of us.

Friday, May 6, Long Binh

Four days left before I go home. I sweltered in the parking lot of II Field Force, the high-level III Corps headquarters just north of Long Binh. All around, drivers waited for captains and majors who took care of business inside. The drivers sat in their jeeps. Some leaned out the sides and talked with each other. One large two-and-a-half-ton truck with a covered cargo area probably had stopped on a supply run. The passenger door stood open with the window rolled down to catch any stray breeze. A pair of legs rested on the door, not moving, the man slumped in the passenger seat, asleep. The legs wore a white uniform. White? Who wore white in a combat zone? The legs belonged to somebody who never went near danger. All the hospital people I ever saw wore green. That man had to be a cook on an airbase. They wore white.

It began to rain a little. The driver of the jeep next to ours shifted the packages in his back seat to keep them dry. The jeep next to him had no top, and the driver got out a poncho. But instead of putting it on, he covered the seat next to him where his officer would sit. The poncho placed, he sat back and smoked a cigarette in the rain. I chuckled.

Most of those soft jobs were plums. Good men earned them by exemplary service in combat, like the Private First Class I had met in the general's office in July at An Khe. I was sure he was a recipient of the Medal of Honor. While the man who smoked a cigarette had been in the field, the rain had drenched him and the sun had dried him out again and again in the same clothes. I had experienced that in October, when I went from one gate to another at Tan Son Nhut Airbase to look for my bus to Di An. This sprinkle didn't qualify as rain.

I could see why that man who smoked a cigarette in the mist was a driver for a field-grade officer. His boss could count on him to think of everything. An officer's dignity and image were not trivial. The combat veteran knew that followers had to take strength and courage from their leader. I had learned that lesson in the flight through the thunderstorm six days ago. To project courage, the leader must have confidence in himself. The driver had attended to his business. Now he could go back to his break. He could enjoy a rare opportunity to cool off on a blazing summer day. Those wet clothes would feel even better if they didn't dry out before the jeep started to move again.

Every person in Vietnam had a different experience in their last month. Some men who stayed in safe, rear positions, continued with their routine jobs. Other men were in the field in combat. They had long, fear-filled days and nights when nothing happened. Nonetheless, they had to be at high alert. When you have to wait too long, you think too much.

For myself, in my last days events crowded together. When Bob went home, I missed him. I didn't have his letters and phone calls. I made trips to isolated Special Forces camps. The change of seasons made us restless. We visited The Old Guard in the Delta, then the ambush forced us to stop. I was in a constant state of imbalance.

Jamie, the gunship pilot, took the cowboy movie as a premonition; the two helicopters crashed; I went to the memorial service; and then the pilots stopped talking to me. I lost the security of my friend, Bob, and my close group of friends, the pilots, at the same time. Finally, I made the life-or-death decision to fly through the thunder storm. I couldn't find anything to grab onto to stabilize myself.

The men in the field had tension-filled boredom and fear for their lives. My work kept me frantically busy. Most of the time the soldiers assured my security. When I first got to Vietnam, like most people, I was always afraid. That passed in a few weeks when I had enough experience to learn where the dangers really lay. During my year, I dove into a few bunkers, but mostly as a precaution. I made the trip to the foxholes at Buon Blech and the dives into the bunkers on Thanksgiving to avoid snipers and firefights. Those were decisions of commanders who believed that the benefit to their men would be worth the extra hazard. I had the brush with the ambush in the Delta, but that was an aberration, an intelligence miscalculation. I had the flight through the thunderstorm, but again, that was not the daily fare. My days were crammed with both mental and physical threats, but in safe places.

The heaviest burdens I fought in my last 30 days were fatigue and loneliness. I never recovered my strength or enthusiasm after the rabies shots. I grew weary of the pressure of parties, making conversation with strangers, surrounded by a blur of people. I missed having a sense of something familiar, of the time to relax with friends when the pilots rejected me. To share my feelings with someone was the last thing I needed. That would mean reliving fears, anticipating danger, thinking too much, inviting nightmares. We needed to do what the pilots did, what we helped the men to do: laugh together, distract ourselves, think about home, keep our minds off what might happen tomorrow, or what happened today. A good alternative was to get drunk and pass out. For me, my tolerance stopped at a beer.

I didn't have the collegiality with the girls to fall back on, because we did not develop friendships. Years later the Donut Dollies had a discussion about the phenomenon on our private email list and agreed. When we worked, we worked mostly alone. We had weekly meetings for business, two of us gave programs together, we almost always traveled with another girl, but we split up at our destination to circulate, to eat, at parties, almost everywhere, so we could see more people. When we had a day off, we had it alone. We didn't spend social time together, because we didn't have free time. If we had time off together in the evening, more often than not soldiers dropped in to talk and visit. We didn't discuss anything in front of them. Every moment of our days we spent with the men. They were the reason we were there, and we gave them all of our attention.

I felt irritable during my last days. Little problems began to annoy me. By the time my 30 days were up, I couldn't wait to get away from everybody. I think they felt the same about me. The girls and our headquarters company gave me the customary going-away party and commemorative plaque; but I had no conflict between going and staying. I just wanted to leave.

I recalled that one of the reasons I went to Vietnam was to find out what it was like to be in a war. Constant explosions; everybody gets killed; danger? I concluded that for me, it was like being in a bad neighborhood. Of the thousands of people, I only met a few people who were killed: the flying medic, the three people at the artillery compound, and Sergeant Harris in the Delta. I had heard of four people who died in a helicopter shot down near a Special Forces camp and of the two helicopters that collided.

As in a bad neighborhood, we couldn't go anywhere at night. We had to plan everything around being in a safe area before dark. Cam Ranh Bay was the only place we could go after sundown. Again, as in a bad neighborhood, there were some places we couldn't go in the daytime. We relied on commanders to assess danger everywhere we went. The threat level changed daily. Sometimes we could travel in a jeep alone, but other times we had to have an MP escort or travel in a convoy, or we flew. But, most of the time, because we were careful we could go about our business in the daytime without fear.

I had learned that war isn't as movie directors depict it.

Did I accomplish my goal to make a difference? To make it easier for the people who had to be there? I did that on the first day and on every day I was there, for thousands of soldiers. Other people could do good things, but the difference I could make was bigger than I had imagined.

I didn't learn until years later that I accomplished something I never set out to do and never thought about. General Westmoreland invited the Red Cross girls to be the first women officially allowed in a combat zone. Our success gave impetus to women's equality in work and access to responsibility and career advancement.

I was a pioneer in women's progress.

✛ CHAPTER 11 ✛

The Long, Confusing
Road Home

May 14, 1967, United States of America

After being in the combat zone, I never guessed I would be ambushed in my hometown Flint, Michigan. On this day I would fly home from the Republic of South Vietnam. I had been a civilian, non-combatant, supported and protected by the military units I served. After two years, one in Korea and one in Vietnam, I traveled to Tan Son Nhut Air Base, my departure point from Southeast Asia. From there, traveling alone, I flew to San Francisco to check in and clear at the Red Cross office.

At the San Francisco airport, I stopped at the first restaurant and told the waiter, "I'd like a glass of milk, please." It was the most urgent thing I wanted. I had some milk on the R&R plane to Singapore, but it was European, and didn't taste exactly like home. In the States, a glass of milk was an unusual order, so I explained, "I just came in from Vietnam. We only had powdered milk, and you could taste the powder. We missed fresh milk more than anything."

The waiter responded with a warm smile filled with kind sympathy: "Right away." He brought me the milk tenderly. He started to leave, then stayed to watch me take the first taste, to share in my joy. It was everything I remembered, and for him to be there with me heightened the moment.

Another thing the men looked forward to when they were short (under 30 days from departure) was television with commercials. In Vietnam we had television, but there were no commercials. To see commercials on TV would mean they were home. Someone also said that the TV program *Bonanza* had gone off the air in the States. So, when the men were three weeks from going home they would say, "Three more *Bonanza*s before I go home." When I checked in at the hotel in downtown San Francisco, it was dusk, body time. I thought I would watch some television, with commercials, maybe see if *Bonanza* was really off the air, and then go to bed. The bellboy turned on the TV. Surprise. An early morning program greeted me, not evening. It was 8:00 in the morning in San Francisco. Besides, it was Sunday. I didn't know that. I saw right away that the program had commercials, though. It wasn't nearly as exciting as I had expected it to be. I got ready to fight jet lag again. I turned off the television and went to bed.

The jet lag tripped me up. I was supposed to check in at Red Cross headquarters on Monday and fly out at the end of the day. I slept so long I missed everything except my flight. Headquarters told me they would mail me the paperwork.

I stopped in Cheyenne to see Aunt Ernestine, my grandmother's sister, and then flew to Flint, my hometown, to my parents' apartment. My mom had gone north to the family farm, our Christmas tree plantation, for the Memorial Day weekend. Dad had stayed in Flint to wait for me. When I arrived on Friday, Dad told me, "We'll drive to the farm in the morning." I was shocked. That was a 150-mile trip. Tomorrow was Saturday, Memorial Day weekend, the most dangerous time of the year to be on the highways. In the US more people were killed in traffic accidents on that weekend than at any other time of the year. To be on the road then was like Russian roulette.

I pleaded, "This scares me witless. I never did anything that bone-chilling in the last year." We had been that careful in Vietnam.

My dad ignored me. He had always said, "When the roads are slippery, that's the best time to travel. There's nobody to run into." He was never afraid of driving, in good or bad weather, and he didn't intend to stop now. We drove north. The traffic was light and sensible on that clear Saturday. It didn't matter that the family had been driving the same route all my life. I was scared for most of the three-hour trip. The more familiar the landscape, the more I settled down. On Sunday we went to our country church. The neighbors welcomed me home. They had watched me grow up. I'm sure they recalled the memories of my two-year-old sister putting my mother's white gloves on her feet and running up and down the church aisle during the sermon. Somewhere else, warriors were fighting for our freedom. But here, in small-town America, things seldom changed.

Joann with her field jacket, home at the farm, June, 1967.

The neighbors were confused about the war. That surprised me. By the time I had been home for a week, I felt that the debate was unhealthy. Discussion refused to clear the air, as it should in a democracy. Everywhere I went people ask me, "What do you think about the Vietnam situation?" "Should we get out?" "Should we stop bombing the North?" They hungered for something that sounded logical and right.

The neighbors' questions prompted random and disjointed thoughts of the war. I didn't care about politics. I knew what the soldiers had told me about their experiences, what kind of men they were, what they thought was right. Everyone I knew in Vietnam agreed that what we did there was correct. They were fighting for the people. No one talked about pulling out or questioned whether we should bomb the north. As badly as they all wanted to go home, they all agreed, "How can anyone look at those little kids in the village and have any doubt what we are fighting for?" "Anybody can see that we didn't appreciate what we had at home." The soldiers were talking about the poverty, disease, ignorance, and terror that the people lived with every day. Children growing up had almost nothing of what youngsters in America expected. Fate and their politicians had dealt them a cruel hand. The men looked at the children and saw their little brothers and sisters, and their own loved ones. Those innocent little Vietnamese kids did nothing to bring on their bleak lives. The men felt they deserved more than this. Most of our soldiers didn't worry about the adults, but they would fight for the future of the youngsters. I remembered their faces when the orphans came to the talent show at Dong Ba Thin. Years later I was aware that a few veterans opposed the war, but I never met one in Vietnam in those early days of the conflict. As Ernie Pyle said, "I only know what we see from our worm's-eye view."[1] A discussion of the antiwar movement is beyond the scope of this book.

Our soldiers didn't complain about their living conditions, the heat, the bugs; but, they did object to the Rules of Engagement. "We're not allowed to fire unless we're fired upon," they protested. They grumbled about the periodic truces called for holidays and negotiations. "We hold our fire, but the VC don't. They fire on us and we can't fire back. They use the cease fire to bring in supplies, and reinforcements, and dig in."

I remember another conversation with several junior officers over lunch. They complained, "We make contact with the enemy, drive them out, take over their area, and then we pull out. After a little while the VC come back. Before long we retake the same ground." It was discouraging and added useless risk. I was aware that Rules of Engagement were different in various parts of the combat zone, just as the levels of security were different for us girls under different commanders.

Years later another soldier confirmed the conclusion we girls came to at Dong Ba Thin, that soldiers were aware of forces beyond their control. He said many men encountered "spooky" coincidences and close calls when their lives were saved by inches, or for unexplained reasons. "Once, someone grabbed my collar from behind and pulled me away from a booby trap. I never could find out who did it, or if it was 'the hand of God.'" I knew that he believed it was "the hand of God." He is angry because, "We didn't lose any battles. They wanted us to get out of Vietnam. Then, when we did, they said, 'You lost the war.'"[2]

These soldiers' sentiments echoed in the movie, *Rambo: First Blood*, when the character Rambo said, "And I did what I had to do to win! But somebody wouldn't let us win!"[3]

Back home, the media seemed to confuse the picture rather than clarify it. The Bible says, "And ye shall hear of wars and rumors of wars" (Mathew 24:6). On the news it sounded as if most of our soldiers were dying. I knew that was because there were so few deaths compared to the number of people involved, that we heard about each one. Walter Cronkite, CBS network anchor, read the figures on television every day like a scorecard. Reporters splashed a battle across the newspapers like a sex crime or a traffic accident. They covered the war under a microscope. One day in Vietnam I flew in a nine-seat helicopter with six news correspondents. There might be one battle, or less, a day worth mentioning in the whole war. Newsmen swooped down to cover it. The reporter with the bloodiest story won the race. If there were many, many battles, and thousands of our boys being killed every day, the newsmen wouldn't have time to cover all of them. I moved around the jungles and villages a great deal in my time in Vietnam, surely more than most of the men and it was usually boring. So when something did happen, the newsmen had to latch onto it to earn their pay. And they did a competent job, as the front pages testified.

After I had been home for a while, I could see why the neighbors were confused. I couldn't understand the war anymore, either. The news didn't give me enough information to figure out what was going on. I realized why people were confused about the war and why many were against it. They had no way to know what was going on. Worse, nobody seemed to think it was important to tell them. I thought it should be the responsibility of the people reporting the news to give a true picture of what was happening, to do objective reporting, but no one seemed to do that. I felt as though the public was being cheated, lied to. How could people know what to believe? Wasn't that why we had a free press in the first place? Why we had free education? Why we had a democracy? Why our soldiers and heroes before them, had fought to preserve our republic and our liberties? And why our country had helped to free our allies from lies? Misleading the people didn't make sense to me. I was angry.

Reporting on the Tet Offensive and on the My Lai (pronounced "Mee Lie") Massacre is one of the illustrations of media bias. The year 1968 was frustrating and violent, both in Vietnam and in the United States. In January the VC launched the Tet Offensive. The My Lai Massacre occurred in March. In April of 1968 Martin Luther King Jr. was assassinated. Two months later, in June, Bobby Kennedy was assassinated. In August, riots erupted around the Democratic National Convention in Chicago.

On January 31, 1968, during the Tet Truce, the Vietnamese New Year, the VC simultaneously attacked more than 100[4] targets throughout the country, including the American embassy in Saigon. The strikes inflicted "a stinging psychological shock to the American public," catching everyone off guard and leaving thousands of casualties. At home in the United States, I saw news accounts of a powerful, continuous, VC offensive. Though still only eight months away from the war, I was confused. I knew we out-gunned and out-manned the VC. How could we lose? Years later I learned that our forces launched overwhelming counterattacks that threw back every assault. Inexplicably, the press refused to report that the Tet Offensive was crushed. "Even though it was a tactical disaster for the Communists, for most Americans and many of the country's leaders, hope for a military victory evaporated."

Trumping all the incidents of that year was the My Lai Massacre. "On March 16, 1968, a platoon lead by 2nd Lieutenant William Laws Calley, Jr. killed a large group—some say 20, some say 100, some say 500—of unarmed old men, women and children in a horrific display of inhuman conduct." As I watched the court martial I was aggravated that correspondents slanted their accounts. Some news stories said that Calley was a victim bravely serving his country. Others said he was following orders, or he was a scapegoat.

"The evidence at trial was conclusive beyond a reasonable doubt that Lieutenant Calley deserved to be court-martialed and punished for his actions at My Lai." Calley was sentenced to life imprisonment and hard labor at Fort Leavenworth.[5] Even after the verdict came out, controversy swirled.[6] Later in 1974, President Nixon tacitly issued Calley a limited Presidential Pardon.[7] At the time, as part of the public, I didn't know what to believe. Opinions and agendae are appropriate in editorial discourse, but they should never be intertwined with hard news.

When I was in Vietnam the soldiers I talked to throughout the country were clear about why we were there: we were fighting for the oppressed, to stop the spread of Communism. The soldiers believed that the Communists were committed to world domination, just as Hitler before them had been. If they could take over Vietnam they could go on to take over the rest of Southeast Asia.

Some time in July or August I went to my cousin's wedding on the west side of the state near Grand Rapids. At the reception I had a chance to see all the aunts and uncles and cousins whom I hadn't seen since I was a child. I became aware that I wasn't participating emotionally in the wedding. I felt detached. I realized that I had learned this detachment to protect myself from the emotions of some of my Vietnam experiences. When friends died or were in danger, or I was in danger, that detachment allowed me to continue to function for those who depended on me. Not long after the wedding, when I had recognized what was happening, my *humanness* returned.

Shortly after I arrived home in the summer of 1967 I began receiving infrequent letters from Bob. It was good to hear from him. On Labor Day weekend I flew down to see him in Savannah, Georgia. He met me for dinner at the Pirate's Cove restaurant. He was gracious and thoughtful, but he smiled less, and he had a far-away look in his eyes. I thought the demands of command in combat had changed him. My mind recalled the image from Korea of my married pilot friend, my amiable dinner companion. He had left, the same as Bob, to become a company commander. When he returned for a visit he sat stiffly and argued with me. I realized command had changed him. I had said a silent, sad goodbye to him, but I kept his warmth in my memory.

When I returned to Flint, Bob and I continued to exchange letters for several months. Then they stopped. Many years after our last meeting our paths crossed online. I asked him what happened. He answered:

Hi Joann,

Unfortunately, time and true life events have diluted my recall. I know that I was alerted for my second tour shortly after getting home from my first tour. While I don't recall my exact feelings at that time, I am aware that the pending second tour weighed heavily on my mind and played a key role in my actions/inactions. However, please know that from my perspective, our time together was true and sincere.

My best always,

Bob

I thought, *How ironic, this friendship left hanging so reflected the story of the Vietnam War, which to this day remains incomplete.*

Would Bob and I have been so attracted to each other outside the war? He may have been. I certainly would have been. He had the qualities I like in a man, but most telling is that he and my husband are very much alike.

In Flint in the summer I returned from the war, I got a job teaching math at a high school and an apartment. It turned out to be a friendly place; everyone knew everyone else. The young tenants often left their apartment doors open and wandered among them. It seemed one or two men always showed up in my kitchen when it was about time to eat. I kicked them out because I didn't want anyone to know that I couldn't cook.

For the next year I got frequent requests to speak about my experiences in Vietnam. I showed my slides and answered questions for one program after another. I addressed several local Red Cross groups in that first year. One was called "Waiting Wives," young women about my age, whose husbands were in Vietnam. I told them their men missed them, the men talked about their families and their children, and the husbands longed to see their wives. I told the young women that the men enjoyed mail and packages of cookies. I explained how cookies should be wrapped to survive the eight-week sea voyage. After I gave a speech, I always received a prompt thank-you note. The one from the Waiting Wives didn't come. I forgot about it. A few weeks later I received a letter from, not the president of the group, but the vice president. She thanked me sincerely for my talk and said she was sorry she took so long to respond.

She wrote, "A few days after your visit, our president received the news that her husband had been killed. We have been busy with the funeral. We apologize." I wished the earlier emotional detachment had lasted a little longer. Vietnam had followed me home.

A church group came after the Waiting Wives, as we moved into 1968. It was the lady's club of a Unitarian Church in Flint, about eight middle-aged women. Their business meeting revealed that they did an impressive amount of work. They made big donations and baked quantities of food for fundraisers. They functioned like the ladies' groups I had attended with my mother at the Methodist church near the farm. I showed my slides and proudly told the women all about what I had seen and what I had done in Vietnam. Then I invited questions.

Those sweet ladies ripped me to shreds, all eight of them. They condemned the war. It was wrong. We should get out of Vietnam. It sounded as if they blamed me for the whole war. I had walked straight into an ambush in my hometown. Why would they invite me to be their guest, to donate my time to prepare a presentation for them, then punish and insult me? I was so shocked I didn't have anything to say. I think I mumbled something lame like, "I thought you wanted to learn about what it was like in Vietnam." I just sat there stunned. I had never known anyone so crude. Was that what their church represented?

Years later a friend learned what I had done in Vietnam. She said to me, "That was a great thing that you did. You had to listen to the soldiers. You had to feel their pain." I smiled to myself, *No, it was the opposite. You have the wrong idea. One of the first things I had to learn, as I sat in a bunker while artillery shells flew over my head, was how to fight fear and* *worry, how <u>not</u> to feel. Otherwise I couldn't function. I might as well pack up and go home. The big test came at the end of my tour at the Sunday Coffee Call when I learned about the ambush in the Delta. Had I been less experienced, I may not have been able to take such a crushing revelation.*

One of the former Donut Dollies recently wrote in an email: "In 1985 I met a WWII WASP (civilian Women Air Service Pilots)." Those were pilots who ferried planes, towed targets for practice with live ammunition, flew reconnaissance, and performed aviation administrative duties to release male pilots for combat flying.[8] "She [the WASP] had served on the Pentagon's DACOWITS (Defense Department Advisory Committee on Women in the Services) commission—regarding roles for women in the military.[9] She told me how glad she was to have the opportunity to meet me, and to let me know that one of the arguments they used to the Pentagon was, 'If the Red Cross girls can do it (serve in forward areas), why can't other women?'"

My fellow Donut Dolly couldn't remember the WASP's name, but I have no doubt she was telling the truth. We Red Cross girls were the first women officially allowed in forward areas. The only other civilians allowed forward were reporters and photographers. Even the Army nurses couldn't go where we went. I strongly believe we were a contributing factor that helped pave the way for the opportunities in diverse careers open to women in society. The Red Cross imposed only one restriction on where we could go, and that was, we had to have a commanding officer's permission. In retrospect, our performance record had to be evidence that women could function effectively in a combat zone. At that time, military women were prohibited in combat zones and few went overseas.[10] My sister Phyllis, a WAC captain, was a rarity. She served in Saigon in Army Intelligence, Company A 519 Military Intelligence Battalion, MACV J2, and told me she was "in the Man's Army." As I recall, she was issued a weapon. To be excluded from forward areas effectively eliminated women from all but a narrow range of jobs. As a result, few women could earn progress in rank, responsibility, and career advancement. During the war and after, the debate continued at home and abroad: should we send women soldiers into combat? After the war, the restrictions disappeared.

Before Vietnam, women had served close to combat areas. Because of the unpredictability of combat, women became involved and some lost their lives. The Red Cross girls were not prohibited from any areas in Vietnam, but caution guided us. Any woman could look at us and ask, "If the Red Cross girls can serve in life-threatening situations, why can't we?" Our example served to add impetus to the movement to open up formerly unavailable military career choices for women. "Today, women still aren't in combat but can work in 161 of 181 military jobs."[11]

I went to Vietnam because I wanted to make a difference. I had no idea.

* * *

Late one Sunday evening in early October after I returned home from Vietnam, someone rang my doorbell in the apartment building. "You remember me, Dave Kotcher? From across the hall? Will you go for a walk with me?"

"It's kind of late."

"Over by the water treatment plant? It's not far."

"It's really cold outside."

"We won't be gone long. I just got a big promotion. I start my new job in the morning, and I need someone to talk to. . . ."

"Just a short walk?"

"We'll come right back."

"Well, I guess so. Let me get my coat."

He was assertive and authoritative, but I figured he had to act that way to be a successful auto executive. He had many other great qualities. That was a longer walk than we expected. We continue our walk for the rest of our lives. We were married the following year.

Epilogue

Soon after I returned from Vietnam, outside the window of my apartment I could see young people going on with their lives. They didn't do anything remarkable. They swam in the pool. Washed their cars. Talked to each other; everyday activities that were normal to them, but that had become foreign to me. I had been in Vietnam for a year, during the intense beginnings of the conflict. Soldiers my age, the same age as the people I now watched, engaged an enemy. That was a lofty assignment for kids out of school. How different were the young men I now watched from the soldiers I had left? Not much, except the military had trained the soldiers to react to war, to defend themselves and others. But sooner or later, everyone in the military goes home. They return to buying groceries, worry about paying bills, and getting their dreams in order, the same things the people I looked at were doing.

As I unpacked my memories of the last year, I thought how different my life was in Vietnam. How quiet it was here. How I now had the right to make my own decisions, to drive my own car, to choose what I wanted to eat, to shower when I wanted to. All this, because soldiers 10,000 miles away were defending my right to make my own choices. Whatever philosophers tell us, life doesn't give us many clues how to confront death. No one can ever feel another's pain. No one can predict how they will react in a war zone, a war zone that in one minute is bone-rottingly boring, and in the next, life-threateningly dangerous. But even more, no one can repay those who sacrifice every day, to protect our rights to swim, to wax our cars, or do the little and big things we take as our rights. I had heard that some of the first soldiers who returned from the war had suffered insults and threats. Some people had called them murderers. These were men I knew. Did they kill people? Only if they shot before someone shot them. Kill women and children? Collateral casualties are unfortunate, and inevitable. War is never precise; war is never fair; war is messy and brutal.

I recall I folded my Red Cross uniform and put it on a shelf. It had held up well. I think I had, too. I would never officially wear it again. I had done my duty, and now it was time to go elsewhere. The war would continue, but for me it was over except for the memories of the people I had learned to respect and admire for their courage and their humanness. The soldiers I had worked with had taught me not to complain. We lived with scorching weather, uncomfortable conditions, and an enemy intent on killing us. All the soldiers I knew faced each day with a sense of duty and commitment. They understood that what they did was honorable. I did go on. I settled into a life that many would consider normal: marriage, a home and mortgage, a family, moves from here to there. Typical of so many people, yet fought for so gallantly by others, I lived the American Dream. But inside me I knew that the American Dream was so much more. The young soldiers I had been honored to work with and to serve in Vietnam had earned it for us.

To this day, I meet many of them. They all have their stories of quiet bravery and valor beyond what they had known was inside them. To dedicate this book to them would be insufficient and would diminish their contributions to our freedoms. I, and I mean "we," must thank and honor them for their profound gift to our nation and to us: the right to do all the things we take for granted. But they've also given us the obligation to remember and honor their sacrifice.

✦ APPENDIX 1 ✦

Let Us Remember

The first Red Cross units in Vietnam opened in 1965. In the peak year of 1969, 110 young women operated 17 SRAO units. It was estimated that they reached nearly 300,000 servicemen each month. (American Red Cross Press Release, May 26, 1972.) Maggie Hodge[1] calculated that each pair of girls "might easily see 200 troops a day."

The last unit closed in May 1972. In a Certificate of Appreciation sent to American Red Cross President George M. Elsey when the program ended, Gen. Creighton W. Abrams, Commanding General, US Military Assistance Command, Vietnam, wrote: "The young women who were the core of this program's success contributed materially to the improvement of the morale of the servicemen assigned to Vietnam. Their personal dedication and attitude reflected favorably on the American Red Cross and assisted the commander in the field in the accomplishment of his mission." (American Red Cross Press Release, May 26, 1972)

Three Donut Dollies lost their lives in Vietnam and one was wounded. These four young women deserve to be honored and remembered.

Red Cross Recreation Aide **Hannah Elizabeth Crews**, age unknown, from North Carolina, died at the 24th Evacuation Hospital at

Long Binh, South Vietnam, on October 2, 1969, due to injuries sustained in a jeep accident. She was traveling to visit servicemen in a base camp area. She died in the first months of her tour in Vietnam.

Red Cross Recreation Aide **Virginia E. Kirsch**, 21, from Brookfield, Ohio, was killed by a US soldier on August 16, 1970, in Cu Chi, South Vietnam. Ginny had been there one week. She died of multiple stab wounds, in her billet at the headquarters of the 25th Infantry Division near Saigon. Her Red Cross billet was less than 200 yards from division headquarters. It was guarded by Military Police at night. Ginny was the first Red Cross worker to be murdered in the 17-year history of overseas service. Officials were silent about the death, but one said soldiers at the base camp were angered by the slaying. Authorities used tracker dogs and offered a reward to search for a 23-year-old white man in civilian clothes. Pathologists found no evidence Miss Kirsch was raped.[2]

The murderer was caught and found to have been in Vietnam for three days. He admitted to killing Ginny, revealing that he broke into the billet through a side door. He was judged incompetent to stand trial and was sent to a psychiatric hospital. He received honorable retirement upon release. He later killed a friend and was returned to confinement in a psychiatric hospital.[3]

Red Cross Recreation Aide **Lucinda J. Richter**, St. Paul, Minnesota, died at the age of 21 on February 8, 1971, from Post Infectious Polyneuritis, complications of Guillain-Barre Syndrome. She was stationed at Cam Ranh Bay. Guillain-Barre Syndrome (GBS) is a rare disease of unknown origin that causes progressive muscle weakness and paralysis. It often follows a common viral infection.[4]

The names of these three women are preserved on a memorial in the Red Cross headquarters' garden, along with the two Red Cross men who died in Vietnam, **Vernon M. Lyons**, August 29, 1967, and **Paul E. Samuels**, January 25, 1968.

Red Cross Unit Director **"Dusty" Hall** from Little Rock, Arkansas, was shot in the hip by a sniper while flying in a chopper outside Pleiku in 1967. She was medevaced to the States and did her healing in an Air Force hospital.[5] One Donut Dolly recalls, "And when I talked to the gal who was wounded flying in or out of Lai Khe, she told me the two things she remembers the most were the other Red Cross girl taking off her harness to move next to her and hold her as the chopper crashed, and also running BACK to the Huey for the first aid kit after they had all moved far away in case it blew. Also, it was my understanding that Dusty was hit in the thigh from the bottom of the chopper and the bullet went up through her leg."[6]

All women who died in Vietnam of various causes:

67 Civilians, including 4 Australians, 1 New Zealander, 2 Volunteers with the Knights of Malta, and one former Red Cross girl working in another program.

8 Military Women totaling

75 Women, and one baby girl, who should be remembered.[7]

✚ APPENDIX 2 ✚

Some Questions Answered

S tatistics compiled after the war tell us more of the story. We know that 2,600,000[1] Americans served in Vietnam, and 58,000[2] Americans lost their lives there. Compare that to 117,000 who lost their lives in WW I; 407,000 in World War II; and 54,000 in Korea. It is sobering to learn that there were 43,000 people killed on the highways in the United States in each of the years 2002, 2003, and 2004.[3] The percentage of people who died in Vietnam was similar to other wars: 2 percent.[4] For every 100 people who served in Vietnam, two would die. That's a lot less than *everybody*, which was what I thought before I went.

In 2007 I ran into a man at a party who said he was a Vietnam veteran. He told me that the Red Cross girls sold their favors. He knew of commanders who would not let us visit their men because of it. I never heard that rumor in Vietnam. I am sure that, of all the girls I ever met, not one behaved immorally. Moreover, I am sure not one of them slept with or got too friendly with individual soldiers. Those who would assert otherwise are ignorant of our commitment and of the times.

I wanted to put this rumor to rest permanently. I posed the question to a group of former Red Cross girls, spanning the seven years of our service. The replies came flying back. Not one could say that she ever knew of a girl who behaved improperly. One or two said they were suspicious of someone, but had no personal knowledge to prove it. Another said she attended meetings where such a problem would have been discussed. It never was. Several said they, themselves had tracked down a few rumors that evaporated under scrutiny. Did it happen? I'm sure it could have. But, if any Red Cross girl in Vietnam behaved improperly, no one can verify it. As one girl remarked, "Such rumors are bar room talk from some clueless nitwit." A legal maxim says: That which can be asserted without proof can be denied without proof.

Much of the attention on us in Vietnam would be considered sexual harassment by today's standards. Sexual harassment is persistent, unwanted sexual advances. Both men and women dislike harassment. I enjoyed the attention I received, and I did not consider it harassment. I felt the soldiers appreciated my presence.

As a worker in the United States, I have experienced harassment in three incidents. In my 26 months overseas, I met thousands of men of all ages. They were homesick, lonely, and could have forgotten about appropriate conduct. I experienced one incident of sexual harassment in Korea and two in Vietnam. In Korea, I was lured away from a party by a handsome Russian captain. A lieutenant from Louisiana rescued me. He stood up to a superior officer. In Vietnam the captain at the 9th Cavalry party persistently put his arm around me. I handled him appropriately according to the training I received in 1964. The third incident was when the supply sergeant abducted me as I tried to travel alone from Saigon to Di An. Armed MPs burst into the room, surrounded me, and escorted me out. To be aware of the problem is good, but one can be too cautious.

Professor Dave Kotcher weighed in. "Women who are fixated on the supposed obsession men have with sex are themselves overly concerned with one aspect of a person's personality. In short, their tunnel vision often obscures the problems and creates false ones. My experience is that this is based in self interest, not scholarship." He suggests they read Christina Hoff Sommers, *Who Stole Feminism?: How Women Have Betrayed Women* (New York: Simon and Schuster, 1994), and *The War Against Boys: How Misguided Feminism Is Harming Our Young Men* (New York: Simon and Schuster, 2000).[5] Professor Kotcher teaches behavioral sciences in business programs in Europe and North America.

I saw sexual harassment more often in the workplace than in the war. Since I was always in physical public view, with the military's vigilance and discipline, men restrained themselves from improper conduct. We were told never to be alone with a man. At the time, I thought it was to protect our reputation. Now I know that it was also for our physical safety. Always being with another woman, or in the company of more than one man, gave us protection.

In general, a determined man can find a way to be alone with a woman. Coworkers are not as aware of danger as are men at war. A woman at work could more easily be caught off guard. The war-time situation and our celebrity status worked to protect us.

Sergeant Charles Murray put it insightfully:

> If the men disrespected the [Red Cross] girls, it was because they were not removed from their [war] environment totally, and that when they visited the red light district, hometown respect rules were disregarded. . . . I made sure that my men wrote home at least once a week, just to keep communications open.[6]

Kammy McCleery, class of '67, believed that after Tet, January 1968, the men didn't treat the girls as well, and times were not as safe as before. She expressed the girl's view: "Many of the guys in the field thought of us as snobs because of our education and the 'don't hug, don't touch' rules of the ARC. . . . We were Snow White and they were the dwarves . . . look, but don't touch . . . Many times people asked me what ARC expected of us in Nam. My answer was they expected us to be Snow White, and there better not be any damn little dwarves follow-ing us home!"[7]

My attempts to verify facts, answer questions, and supplement information in my diary took me to books, magazines, and internet searches. I encountered people, men and women, veterans and civil-ians, who shared everything they could remember. Their kindness and generosity was beyond anything I have ever experienced. They accepted me as a fellow veteran and comrade. They guided me to resources of all kinds and introduced me to other veterans as cooperative as them-selves. Through them I uncovered information not found anywhere else, that would otherwise have been lost. And, I found some colleagues whom I had known in Vietnam.

Every soldier I saw in Vietnam knew who the Donut Dollies were. Every veteran I have met since I left Vietnam, who served in Korea or Vietnam, knew about the Donut Dollies. Did everyone in Vietnam know about us? Were there some people who never saw a Donut Dolly? Yes, some people spent all their time in areas that were too isolated for us to visit. How did the men understand the Donut Dollies and their recreational work? And, what kind of men did we work with? I have provided contextual information about the men's background and work in the war. We can judge from their own words:

James Manning, said, "I was in Da Lat. I didn't know anything about Donut Dollies."[8]

Capt. **Wilmer K. Benson**, USA-Ret.: "I was a Squad Leader in B Company 2nd Battalion, 2nd Infantry under Captain **Wheatly**. I received the first 'Direct Commission' to 2nd Lieutenant in the 1st Division. The Battalion Commander, LTC **Jack Conn**, swore me in as an officer on October 20th [1966]. I went to Di An for lunch with General **DePuy**, visited the Red Cross tent, and saw a few of the 'girls.' You were the first 'Round Eyes' I had seen in 10 months. I enjoyed the coffee and the visit! That was my only experience with you folks, but one I have never forgotten. I left Di An the next morning for Phouc Vin as a Platoon Leader in Company A, 1st Battalion, 28th Infantry. I was in the field during this year, and not in any of the large base camps. The only shelter I had was a poncho hooch, and I slept on the ground in a foxhole most of the time. From my personal experience from my three tours, I would say that only the rear area folks would know about the Donut Dollies."

Bob Fulps, the sergeant who knelt in the bunker door during the sniper attack on Thanksgiving: "It would be hard to find someone who served in Vietnam who was not aware of the Donut Dollies and their invaluable contribution to the morale of the troops." He has the Combat Infantry Badge and the Bronze Star.

Ray J. Smith Co C 1st Battalion 69th Armor 4th Infantry Division/173rd Airborne Brigade Vietnam, 1968, who made the map of Vietnam for this book: "Our job was to keep Highway 19, which ran from Qui Nhon on the coast to Pleiku in the Central Highlands, open and free from attack by the NVA. The Donut Dollies visited us at LZ Schueller, about 15 miles west of An Khe on Highway 19. For the record, we saw Red Cross Donut Dollies once during my tour. We gave them a ride in our tank. I admired their courage for coming out to visit us in the boonies. Even our commanding officer was afraid to come out where we operated.

"The picture you sent came through just fine. You are one good looking round eye.

"Welcome home."

Mike McGhie, D 2/8 Cavalry "Angry Skipper" said, "Don't think for one second that we do not think of you girls as heroes too. It had to take a lot of guts to travel 12000 miles into a war zone to support the troops. No one ever says anything bad about the Donut Dollies."[9]

A few people have suggested that some vets thought poorly of the Dollies, but everyone in Vietnam always treated me like a celebrity. I was there at the beginning, however, and maybe attitudes changed in the later stages of the war when morale was low. I searched everyone I knew for veterans who had served more than one tour, who might have noticed a difference in how the Dollies were viewed or treated as the war progressed. I found only 14 men, but I got a response from everyone I asked, mostly during June and July of 2008. Several forwarded the question to others who answered, as well. Three people actually saw Red Cross girls on more than one tour in Vietnam, so I also relied on rumors and jokes as a measure of what troops thought of the girls. No one reported noticing any change in the way the girls were viewed or treated. Here is more from their own words about how they understood the Donut Dollies and our work:

The most telling statement came from **Wilmer Benson**, who served three tours. He said, "I think most of us joked about you ladies looking for an officer husband (think of the movie an *Officer and a Gentleman*.) or, someone who was making a lot of money selling your services, although I did not feel this way personally.

"During my last tour, the morale of the troops was very low. . . . No one wanted to be the last one killed in Vietnam . . . As to a change in jokes when morale was low, I can't say that I really noticed much, but less joking around was happening on my last tour."[10]

Charles Murray also had three tours. He had some good insight: "I have never encountered the Donut Dollies, although many of my fellow soldiers had nothing but praise and appreciation for them . . . Between 1965–70 there was only the gratitude of seeing a female (round eye) from the States to talk to and remind them of the girl they left behind. That attitude stayed the same."[11]

Jake Hargis, a Caribou pilot with two tours, wrote, "If you consider at An Khe there were probably around 10 or so Dollies whose job was to mix with the troops, improve morale, bring thoughts of home, etc. you were in the middle of about 15–20,000 young men between the ages of 17–40. Of course, you (me) heard all sorts of things. Have you ever heard a high school football team in their locker room? Multiply that and you've got the Army. I never ever saw anything or heard anything that I would give credence to . . . I never heard anything bad about Donut Dollies. I heard a lot of comments about how good those 'round-eyes' looked, etc-etc.-etc!! Just your presence did a great service to the young troops. I mean that sincerely."[12] This guy nailed it. It was locker-room talk from barely post-pubescent jocks.

Jim Brigham had two tours. He observed, "The rear guys may have enjoyed playing games and such as something to pass the time. But, those fighting troops most saw it as a time to relax—talking to a real live American girl would lift their sprits. But, some of those that had a chance to be around the girls for awhile may have had other things on their minds."[13]

Bruce Silvey, two tours, said, "I think for the most part they were welcomed and treated well by the troops . . . everyone seemed to like having them around."[14]

Serge Olive, two tours, didn't know what Red Cross girls did—thought Army Special Services did recreation. He observed the opinion of soldiers from previous wars:

"The Battalion Command Sergeant Major [CSM] was a crusty, multi-war veteran, who had been a semi/pro boxer, whom I understood had been in country for years and refused to take R&R or go home. During a stand-down the battalion commander told the CSM to pass the word about a cookout and games sponsored by Special Services (?). The instructions were passed in the presence of the Special Services (again, ?) team. The CSM turned red, raised himself up to his 5' 5" barrel-chested stature and proclaimed, [excuse language], ' . . . Sir, the troops don't need any f'g games . . . we need to set up a bunch of f'g boxing rings so they can f'g beat up on each other . . . ' The commander prevailed and I recall the troops enjoyed the games and didn't seem to miss not having the slug-fests!"[15]

Jerry Griffin, three tours, probably expressed the men's opinion:

"The troops loved having them visit before going to the field or after getting back. Seeing real 'round eyes' was great for them . . . I really have never heard of any soldiers really disliking the girls. Soldiers and Red Cross ladies have comforted each other for more years than we can count. Those that talk all the trash about either have no idea what the hell they are talking about, or just wished they had been able to experience what a few fortunate others did."[16]

Elizabeth (Arant) West observed, "What the men said to us, and the way they treated us while we were there, and what we experienced personally from them was probably much different than what they said among themselves when we were not around.

"Two of us went to an LZ by helicopter one day. We presented two programs, served chow, stayed half a day and then got picked up. We were a hit. About a month later, I saw the Commanding Officer of this group in Bien Hoa at the PX. I barely remembered him. We went to the Officer Club and had a drink. He talked about how much that day meant to his men. I asked him, 'What kinds of things do they say after we leave?'

"He blushed and said, 'You don't want to know.' I insisted he tell me. He sheepishly related that they all gathered around him and many asked if we were just high class whores and did we go down for $65–$100 a trick, which of course only field grade officers could afford. I remember feeling physically ill. I really thought I was going to vomit. I told him that was the most horrible thing I'd heard, told him about our training and about the Red Cross sending girls home who broke the rules about sleeping around, etc. and how we all worked so hard to not have that kind of reputation, etc, and that here I thought we were actually helping morale when apparently we were just making them sexually frustrated and they hated us for it and thought the worst of us. I swear I was almost crying.

"He just laughed gently and said, 'HEY, you are raising their morale.'

"And I said, 'I guess I just don't get it.'

"Then he said, 'Believe me, it makes those guys feel great to think that somewhere, somehow, in this hell hole, somebody's gettin' laid by a round-eye.'"[17]

This sample of the 14 responses seems to indicate that not much changed from 1965 to 1970. If anything, the first response, from Wilmer Benson, might show that when morale was lower, respect for the girls might have been higher. He noted that there was less joking around in general when morale was lowest. Jim Brigham's response could indicate that respect for the girls might correlate better with the men's assignment. The remote combat troops valued the girls' visits more than the rear echelon troops. In statistics, three points in a row indicate a trend. This trend line, the way troops viewed and treated the Red Cross girls, probably does not correlate with morale.

What kind of men were these? I'd say normal, American men.

I have been asked, "Did the war increase your sexual desires?" In 1967 this was hardly discussed. As years went on and mores changed, much of what was considered grandly inappropriate has become accepted. Innocence was the standard expectation in 1967. The DDs were "nice girls." "Nice girls" controlled their desires. I was not involved in combat as the men were, and I never noticed that the war increased those desires. To assert that war increased sexual desires is short of inane. As the maxim goes, there is no art during war. My experience is that there is seldom romance as bullets crease your khakis. The years when I grew up were a time when a man's honor was his word, and a girl's honor was her virtue.

I have also been asked, "Why did the Red Cross send young women to be ogled by men?" The purpose of the service of the Red Cross was to support and to lift the men's spirits. They missed their wives and mothers and other women. We were there to remind them of those they loved, to improve morale. Looking at a pretty woman makes men smile.

Whatever Happened To . . . ?

I researched online to see if I could find out what happened to some of the people I knew. That search gave me more understanding of the kind of men I worked with in Vietnam and how the war affected their lives. I found **J. S. Brigham, Jr.,** Lieutenant Colonel, USAR Retired, President of the 7th United States Cavalry Association. He observed, "You must have been there with the Red Cross girls up by the 15th Medical area. The girls had been to our officers club at the 2/7th. I was with **Myron Diduryk** when we came over there one night to pick some of the girls up to come down. Just to get a look at an American girl was always great."[1] He was the scary, tall 1st lieutenant with the big mustache in the faded fatigues. He came to pick us up to go to their party only a day or two after I arrived in country. 1st Lt J. S. Brigham, Jr., retired from the Army Reserve in 1983 as a lieutenant colonel. He lives in North Carolina with his wife, Judy. They have three grown children. **Brigham** received the Bronze Star with "V" for Valor.

Brigham gave me more information. "Captain **Myron F. Diduryk** was a very good friend," commander of Bravo Company, 2nd Battalion, 7th Cavalry. He continued, "We all thought he would be a general one day. Sadly Major **Diduryk** was Killed in Action during his second tour with the 1ˢᵗ Cavalry on April 24, 1970.[2] Myron was Ukrainian and had come to this country at the age of 12 from Germany with many others and settled in New Jersey." Ukrainian American Veterans Post 30 in New Jersey is named for Major **Diduryk.** He received two Silver Stars, three Bronze Stars, 24 Air Medals, and a Purple Heart.[3]

Brigham told me what happened to **Cyril Richard "Rick" Rescorla**, the Englishman who wrote the songs and led the singing at the party. He left active duty in 1967, but continued in the Army Reserves until retirement in 1990 as a colonel. He had a wife and two children. He earned a master's degree and a law degree, and became head of security for Morgan Stanley in the World Trade Center. Following the attack of 9-11 he saved nearly 3,000 people, and then went back looking for stragglers. The building came down on top of him. Rescorla received the Purple Heart, the Silver Star, and two Bronze Stars for his Vietnam service.[4]

Also, through Brigham, I learned that **Captain Windsor** is married and has three sons. **Rolando A. Salazar** served under Windsor, maintains the D Company 2/7ᵗʰ Cavalry web site, <http://www.delta2-7.org> and has posted a journal of his year in Vietnam at <www.rsalazar.net/journal.htm>. Salazar says Windsor served in the Delta in '69–'70 as the S-3 (operations officer) of the 214th Combat Aviation Battalion and later commander of the 175th Assault Helo Company "Outlaws." **Alec Lyall**, one of Windsor's RTOs, declared, "The captain had my highest respect. When he gave an order it was always the right thing. The sergeants respected him." Colonel **Windsor** retired from the Army, worked with US industry for eighteen years, and retired in Florida. He received two Distinguished Flying Crosses and three Bronze Stars.

Alec Lyall became a pilot for US Airways and retired as captain in command of a twin engine, 200-passenger Boeing 767. He lives in Vermont, is married, and has three grown sons. He received the Purple Heart and the Army Commendation Medal.

Recently, Lyall has written a memoir. Of his year in Vietnam, he confessed: "It may have been a common if not practical solution to a thorny situation. Considering the record, backed by anecdotal evidence, I came rapidly to an unmistakable conclusion. I would not live out the year. . . . In fact, the sudden encounter with reality allowed me to move past anything morbid or depressing, and merely get on with an unencumbered existence, freed from distraction . . . I would skip the whole dying process, the burden of self-mourning . . . and take twenty-four hours at a time as if I worked for the Conservation Corps, clearing trails."[5]

Of his commanding officer, Captain Windsor: "A man easily remembered. We would, as they say, follow him anywhere."[6]

Jim Brigham put me in touch with **Nancy Kelly**, one of the three other girls at An Khe when I arrived. She introduced me to a number of former Red Cross girls, and put me in touch with **Larry Gwin**. He was the lieutenant who was a patient at the hospital when I was there and author of the memoir, *Baptism*.

Nancy also told me that Major **Paul "Woody" Hayne**, Executive Officer of 2/8th Cavalry, who showed me how to wake the sleeping soldier, died in Korea of a massive heart attack in 1971.

Nancy Kelly earned a Ph.D. after her tour in Korea and Vietnam. She is married, has two grown sons, and works as a readjustment counseling therapist in western Pennsylvania.

Larry Gwin's Alpha Company 2/7th Cavalry arrived in Vietnam with 146 officers and men. At the end of a year only fifteen of the original contingent were still there, Gwin included.[7]

> . . . to celebrate that dawning realization, that we were indeed going home in one piece? Raid the Red Cross compound. I remember finding Nancy Kelly somehow, and asking her if she'd like to come back to our O-club and have a drink with us. And she accepted. Just like that! She was so lovely, so gentle, so nice and kind to us.

And Jim and I were so love-struck, so shy that we just sat around and sipped our beers.

There was a star-lit moment, when [Nancy and I] were sitting in the jeep together all alone, when I thought fleetingly of kissing her. Just kissing her. She was too sweet, too precious, and I was too scared to try. (Years later I have kicked myself in the ass several times.) But I was also too shell-shocked by what had happened to us that year, and I couldn't have made a pass at her.

For months after coming home—more months than I care to admit—I was totally sexually dysfunctional.[8]

It wasn't because of her, but because he couldn't get the war out of his head. Gwin's description of Nancy is accurate. She was also sensitive and pretty.

Nancy told me that she received death threats because Gwin mentioned her in his book.

Gwin left the Army, graduated from Boston University Law School, and practiced law in Boston for ten years. He dropped out to write, teach, and practice arbitration. He has two grown sons and resides north of Boston. He was awarded the Silver Star for his extraordinary heroism in the Ia Drang Valley.[9]

I believe the tall, shy private in General Norton's office when we went to dinner there was PFC **David C. Dolby**, who received the Medal of Honor for actions on May 21, 1966.[10] General Norton had introduced him saying, "He did a fine job in the field for us." **Nancy Kelly** said she had talked to Dolby at reunions, but wasn't sure he was the same man. Everyone guards the privacy of these heroes, so no one would confirm his identity.

RIP Sgt. David C. Dolby, USA

August 6, 2010, David C. Dolby passed away in Spirit Lake, Idaho, at the age of 64. Mr. Dolby had lived in seclusion in the town of Barto, Pennsylvania, since the passing of his wife in 1997. Mr. Dolby's passing went so unnoticed that even his hometown paper didn't acknowledge it. His passing was announced by an organization to which he belonged. ("The Congressional Medal of Honor Society.")

During the Vietnam War, on May 21 1966, Dolby's platoon had come under heavy fire which killed six soldiers and wounded a number of others, including the platoon leader. Dolby led his platoon in its defense, organized the extraction of the wounded, and directed artillery fire despite close-range attacks from enemy snipers. He attacked hostile positions and silenced three machine guns, allowing US forces to execute a flank attack.[11]

A funeral service will be held at Arlington National Cemetery. There won't be any press there and likely only a handful of mourners who had the privilege to know David Dolby. Let us all mourn the passing of a quiet hero.[12]

Bud Alley, who took us to the perimeter at An Khe, served two years on active duty, earned an MBA in 1974, and spent his career in the packaging field. He married his fiancée two weeks after returning to South Carolina. They have two children and three grandkids. He earned an MA in Public History in May 2011.

Jake Hargis, the Army captain Caribou pilot at An Khe, returned to his home town, Tahlequah, Oklahoma, and became director of a three-county Head Start program. Over the next fourteen years, he served several terms as president of the Oklahoma Head Start Association as well as serving on the five-state Regional Head Start Board of Directors. In 1996 he moved to Texas and worked for the Institute for Child and Family Studies at Texas Tech University until his retirement in 2003. Jake has done consultant work with Head Start programs all across the

United States. He and his wife, Dr. Michelle Hargis, an associate dean at a university, live in North Carolina.

Jim Huggins was the 1st lieutenant at Company A 2/2 on Thanksgiving, who thought the Red Cross girls were "the most beautiful women I ever saw in my life." The war affected his life in a positive way. He started a correspondence with his best friend's sister-in-law, Phyllis. He spoke to her from Tokyo on R&R, and the friendship deepened. "In fact, my driver and I ran the roads from Saigon to Lai Khe several times after dark so that I could check the mail . . . this was very dumb in retrospect." When he received a picture of her, "she was very cute," but he was suspicious that it wasn't her. When he arrived home in Kentucky in May, Phyllis invited him to Maryland for her family's annual picnic. He agreed to go, and "left after being home for three days. Mom was not happy, but Dad understood." When they finally met, the girl he saw was unattractive to him. He was "about ready to turn around and go home," when he discovered he was looking at the wrong girl. The right girl arrived, and he found her "very cute, dainty, and attractive, and I decided to stay." They corresponded over the summer, visited each other, and talked on the phone every day. After six months they were married—42 years ago. They have five children and five grandchildren.

I believe, whether the war pushed them together or not, given a chance to know each other anywhere, these two would have fallen in love. Asked how the war affected him, Jim answered, "I found my life partner, Chaplain Carter baptized me as a Christian, I found that I could lead men in and out of combat, my self-confidence grew tremendously, and I 'grew up.'"[13]

Gerald Burns, who told me about the **VC torture**, was a Special Agent, Army Counter Intelligence with the 1st Military Intelligence Detachment at Phu Loi in 1966–67. "Our rank was classified. The only thing that showed on our military ID card was 'Special Agent.' We lived and messed in the officers' area and saluted Field Grade and above. We wore an officer's *US* insignia on each collar. We were a different breed. No one knew much about us and we liked it that way." After Vietnam Burns earned an MBA and worked for the US Treasury Department. Today he owns a private investigative agency and bonding company. He has two children and three grandchildren.

Tom Carter was the **chaplain** on Thanksgiving, whom everyone admired just before the sniper broke up the champagne celebration. On line he told me his year there had a big effect on his life. He went to Vietnam with the 2/2 Infantry, engaged in regular combat. "My own strong faith and trust in God helped me minister to the troops and also with the surviving family members back home. I conducted regular worship services with each of the companies weekly, accompanied them on combat operations, and visited the wounded in the hospitals. In combat, men share honest faith. They detect pretense, and reject it. I lived my faith to the fullest."[14]

Carter's code name was Celestial Six. One soldier reported proudly, ". . . suddenly a VC machine gun opened up. Me and a buddy jumped in a foxhole and right behind us, here comes Celestial Six. We asked him what the deuce he was doing up there. . . . said he heard there was an atheist in our foxhole. Said he'd always wanted to meet one."[15]

As a Red Cross girl, I observed that the combat zone was full of incomprehensible events. Men responded to them with superstition, myth, rumors, songs, bonds of mutual support, anything that would get them through. Our chaplains guided our young soldiers to a faith that would give them the true comfort and strength they sought.

The sergeant **in the doorway of the bunker** during the sniper attack, was **Robert C. Fulps**. He was a squad leader in the 3rd Platoon. He is now a retired first sergeant.

My sister, **Phyllis Puffer,** earned a Ph.D. and teaches sociology at a college in the southern United States. She received the Army Commendation Medal.

Maj. Gen. **John R. Norton** commanded the 1st Cavalry Division (Airmobile) from May 6, 1966, until April 1, 1967.[16] After two years as an enlisted man, he won an appointment to the US Military Academy at West Point, and parachuted into Normandy on D-Day. As a colonel, he was part of the research team that developed the helicopter to carry the infantry into battle.[17] He received the Silver Star and two Bronze Stars and reached the rank of lieutenant general. He died in 2004, and is buried at Arlington National Cemetery.[18]

Former Air Force Sergeant **Adrian Cronauer**, the DJ who woke us with "GOOOOD Morning, Vietnam!" was the inspiration for the motion picture of that name, starring Robin Williams. He stayed in broadcast management and advertising for many years. In the mid-1980s he went to law school and then practiced communications law in Washington, D.C. He is now the special assistant to the director of the POW/MIA Office at the Pentagon.[19]

Among the group of Donut Dollies a short time back, a veteran was trying to locate a girl named **Linda from Kansas**. One of the girls whom I have never met said she "knew a girl by that name, tall, blonde, responsible, dated a general's aide, and might have married him." I asked her if there were two of us. I was tall, blonde, hopefully responsible, dated a general's aide from An Khe, didn't marry him. She didn't answer me. I think I had become a rumor. Gossip was rampant in the combat zone.

Among the medals presented at the ceremony at Phu Loi when I was there that Thanksgiving Day, the Republic of Vietnam National Order Medal Fifth Class went to 1st Infantry Division G-3 (Intelligence), Lt. Col. **Alexander M. Haig, Jr.,** from Oderbrook, Pennsylvania.[20] Haig had received two Silver Stars in Korea, and later in Vietnam he received a Purple Heart and two Distinguished Service Crosses. Finally, he served as Secretary of State under President Reagan.[21]

What kind of men are these? Good men I am proud to know.

Every once in a while something reminds me of **Sergeant Harris**, the supply sergeant NCOIC on the supply truck who was killed in my place in the ambush in the Delta. I'm here because he isn't. My life is a gift he gave to me. When I remember him I think, "What would I want if I had died instead of him?" I would not want my death to ruin another's life, for them to feel survivor's guilt for having lived. I would want my death to achieve something important. For Sergeant Harris, I must use my life well. I live for both of us.

One aspect of Vietnam continues to follow me. I don't want to go on any of the rides at carnivals. I've had enough thrills.

Endnotes

Preface

1. Today we would be called "women." In 1964 we referred to each other as "girls." We wore our title, Red Cross Girls, as proudly as any soldier wore his rank. Only 627 had earned the right to call themselves that in Vietnam. Politically correct? No. Historically correct? Yes. We always wrote the name of the country as two words, Viet Nam, during my time there, but I have changed it to modern English rendering, Vietnam, for this publication.

2. Jeff Foxworthy, *Redneck Comedy Tour 2009*, Comedy Central, 18 Dec. 2009.

3. Ernie Pyle, *Here Is Your War* (Lincoln: University of Nebraska Press, 2004), 325.

4. Jill LeSueur York, Reunion Book Chair, American Red Cross Reunion Book Committee, et al., *Red Cross Reunion '93, From Saigon to DC: The American Red Cross Women Who Served* (Bowie, MD: Volunteers from the American Red Cross, 1995).

5. United States, Military Advisory Command Vietnam (MACV) Directive 930-1 (Supersedes 940-1, 24 March 1968) 14 June 1970.

6. "The Clubmobile Program is a mobile service which extends the recreation program to military personnel in any location in the RVN (Republic of Vietnam) to which the military authorizes travel and provides transportation. Priority is given to combat and combat support units in isolated areas." <http://www.red-cross.org/museum/history/vietnam.asp>.

7. "A Place on the Wall and in Our Hearts: American, Australian and New Zealand Civilian and Military Women Who Died in the Vietnam War (1959–1975)" *Women Who Died in the Vietnam War,* 2007 <http://illyria.com/women/vnwlist.html>. Margaret Hodge, *American Red Cross Reunion Book, 1993.*

8. United States Congress, Senate, Hearings before the Senate Committee on Public Lands, Reserved Water and Resource Conservation: Margaret Hodge, statement submitted to Hearings on S.J. Res. 156, also presented orally to the House subcommittee headed by Mary Rose Oakar. Senate Hearing, Oct. 29, 1985 -The Bill was S. J. Res 156. Testimony is S. Hrg. 99-424. MINERVA, Quarterly Report on Women and the Military, Vol. IV, Number 1; Pasadena, MD: The MINERVA Center, Inc., Spring 1986 (Washington, D.C.: The Congressional Record, 1986).

9. *American College Dictionary*, (New York: Random, 1967) 1242.

10. Lawrence Grzywinski, SP-4, E-4, HHC 2ND Battalion, 2ND Infantry (Mech), 1st Infantry Division, Company Armorer and Supply, July 1966-July 1967, Combat Infantry Badge, Army Commendation Medal. Emails to author, Mar. 2010.

11. The U.S. Census Bureau (2004) reports there are 8.2 million "Vietnam Era Veterans." Of these, 2.59 million are reported to have served "in country".' Vietnam Era Veterans' Readjustment Assistance Act (VEVRAA) of 1974". U.S. Department of Labor. http://www.dol.gov/esa/regs/compliance/ofccp/fsvevraa.htm

12. Pyle, 89.

13. Pyle, 90.

14. Pyle, 319.

15. Michael W. McGhie, Vietnam D 2/8 Cav 68-69; 8th Cavalry Regiment Columnist, *Saber*, 1st Cavalry Division Association, Copperas Cove, TX, Email, Feb. 2010. Passed away at Angry Skipper Reunion, May 2011.

16. Jennifer Young, Red Cross, Dong Ba Thin, Tuy Hoa, CRAB, 4th Div, Vietnam.

17. John Ahrenberg, 1st Armor Division (Old Ironsides) Feb. 68-69, Email, June 2008.

18. William P. Conboy, 25th Div Oct. 64–April 65; 1st Inf. Wounded, July 66 – Jan. 67; 1st Cav 69-70. U.S. Mail, 5 July 2008.

19. Richard C. Morris, Lieutenant Colonel, US Army, Retired, August 1962–August 1963, MAAG-Vietnam, 14th RGT, 9th ARVN Division, Phu Cat, II CTZ; December 1967–December 1968, MACV District Advisor, Thuan Nhon, IV Corps. Email, July 2008.

Chapter 1: On My Way to the War

1. <http://www.redcross.org/museum/history/index.asp>.

2. <http://www.redcross.org/museum/history/claraBarton.asp>.

3. <http://www.redcross.org/museum/history/ww1a.asp>.

4. <http://www.redcross.org/museum/history/faqs.asp#wartime>.

5. Emily Yellin, *Our Mothers' War: American Women at Home and at the Front During World War II* (New York: Free Press, 2004), 178.

6. Yellin, 175.

7. <http://www.redcross.org/museum/history/ww2a.asp>.

8. "Military and Red Cross Partnership," www.redcross.org, accessed January 13, 2011.

9. <http://www.redcross.org/museum/history/korean.asp>.
LeSueur York, 1–8.

10. The US Centennial of Flight Commission, established by the US Congress Centennial of Flight Commemoration Act, Public Law 105-389, Nov. 13, 1998. The Flying Tigers were the American Volunteer Group, assembled by Claire Chennault, a leading developer of combat tactics for pursuit aircraft. President Roosevelt unofficially supported them. They fought the Japanese for China, operating from December 20, 1941, to July 4, 1942. After May they flew supplies to China

from India on a route called "The Hump." "They became heroes back home. Americans needed to feel they were doing something to avenge Pearl Harbor."

11. Walter J. Hermes, *Truce Tent and Fighting Front, United States Army in the Korean War*, ". . . the Communists launched a full-scale attack on 25 June 1950 across the [38ᵗʰ] Parallel." (Washington: Center of Military History United States Army, 1992), 9.

12. Norman Gelb, *The Berlin Wall, Kennedy, Khrushchev, and a Showdown in the Heart of Europe* (New York: Random House, 1986), 6, 8. Curtis Cate, *The Ides of August: The Berlin Wall Crisis 1961* (New York: M. Evans and Company, 1978), 254, 255, 259. Richard A. Leiby, *The Unification of Germany, 1989–1990* (Westport, CT: Greenwood, 1999), xix.

13. Oscar Whitelaw Rexford, *Battlestars and Doughnuts: World War II Clubmobile Experiences of Mary Metcalfe Rexford* (St. Louis, MO: Patrice, 1989), 54.

14. Carl Otis Schuster, Captain US Navy (ret.), "Case Closed: The Gulf of Tonkin Incident," *Vietnam*, June 2008: 28–33.

15. "Korean Leaders Issue Peace Call," *BBC News International version*, Thurs. 4 Oct. 2007.

16. Charles Nutt, A.B., Descendants of George Puffer of Braintree, Massachusetts 1639–1915 (Rutland, VT: The Tuttle Co., 1915), 17.

17. Nutt, 39.

18. *The Columbia Encyclopedia, Sixth Edition* (New York: Columbia University, 2007). The contest centered on possession of the spot where the Monongahela and the Allegheny join to form the Ohio (the site of Pittsburgh). The French built Fort Duquesne there in 1754. Young George Washington, sent to capture the fort, was forced to surrender in July of that year. The British finally took Fort Duquesne in 1758, Quebec in 1759, and Montreal in 1760. French control of Canada went to Britain in 1763.

Chapter 2: A Blacked-Out Runway

1. "The Billboard Hot 100 Songs of the Year (1958–1969)": Jeff Kolhede. "The Ballad of the Green Berets," *Billboard*. "It also reached #1 on Billboard's Easy Listening chart, and #2 on Billboard's Country survey. It later became the #21 song of the 1960s and sold over 9 million singles and albums." "'Ballad of the Green Berets' was the top single of a year in which the British Invasion, led by the Beatles and the Rolling Stones, dominated the US charts." <*http://www.billboard.com/specials/hot100/charts/top50-no1s-60s.shtml*>.

2. Harry G. Summers Jr., Colonel of Infantry, *The Vietnam War Almanac* (New York: Presidio, Random House, 1985), 59.

3. Sun Tzu on the Art of War: The Oldest Military Treatise in the World, trans. Lionel Giles, with Introduction and critical notes (London: 1910; repr. Republic of China: Ch'eng-wen, 1971), 83, 84.

4. Mark R. McNeilly, *Sun Tzu and the Art of Modern Warfare* (Oxford, England: Oxford University Press, 2001), 5.

5. Larry Gwin, *Baptism: A Vietnam Memoir* (New York: Ivy, Random House, 1999), 301. Gwin encountered this same nurse when he was wounded.

6. C. L. Barnhart, et al., *The American College Dictionary* (New York: Random House, 1967), 1336. It has been suggested that the term "urchin" is "insensitive." I can assure the skeptics that in 1966, "urchin" was not pejorative: urchin, n. 1. a mischievous boy, or any small boy, or youngster.

7. Gwin, 306, 307, 346, 347.

8. Gwin, 216–221.

9. James B. Stewart, *Heart of a Soldier: A Story of Love, Heroism, and September 11th* (Biography of Rick Rescorla) (New York: Simon and Schuster, 2002), 83.

10. AP–Saigon, "5 Dead in Saigon Melee," *The Daily Red Bank Area Register* (Monmouth County, NJ), Tues. 10 May 1966: A1.

11. Shelby L. Stanton, *Anatomy of a Division, 1st Cav in Vietnam* (Novto, CA: Presidio, 1987), 79–83. Operation CRAZY HORSE, May 16 to June 5, 1966; Gwin, 287. S. L. A. Marshall, Brigadier General, USAR-RET., *Battles in the Monsoon: Campaigning in the Central Highlands, Vietnam, Summer 1966* (Nashville, TN: Battery, 1966), 4.

12. "Red Cross Brings Troopers 'Closer to Home,'" Photos by Marv Wolf, *Cavalair, The Weekly Newspaper of the 1st Cavalry Division*, 25 July 1966: 5.

13. Gwin, 287, 296, 306.

14. Stanton, 79.

15. Summers, 112. "Table 1, Number of Deaths in Three Wars: World War II, Korea and Vietnam," Jan. 1965–June 1970. Vietnam 47,244 Battle Deaths, 10,446 Other (Accidents, Disease, etc.) totals 57,690. United States, Center for Electronic Records, National Archives. Combat Area Casualty File (CACF) (Washington, DC: Nov. 1993). (The CACF is the basis for the Vietnam Veterans Memorial, i.e. The Wall.) 58,169 names are in the Nov. '93 database. The Veteran's Administration states that 2,594,000 Americans served in the Vietnam War. The calculation is 58,169 divided by 2,594,000 gives 0.0224, or 2.24 percent.

16. Col. Chester McCoid II, deputy commander of the 101st Airborne Division, letter to his wife, Dorothy, 21 Aug. 1966, in Bill Adler, ed., *Letters from Vietnam* (New York: Random House, 2003), 101.

17. Stanton, 79–83.

Chapter 3: A Disguise to Fool a Sniper

1. Marvin J. Wolf, Sergeant (later Captain), Press Chief, Public Information Office, 15th Admin Co., First Cavalry Division (Airmobile), August '65–November '66, Bronze Star, Air Medals (3), Purple Heart, Email response to query 29 Mar. 2010. Years later I wondered what newspaper he was reading. Marvin Wolf knew: The paper was most likely *Stars & Stripes*. Less likely but still possible is *The Cavalair*, the division newspaper put out by the Division Public Information Office, of which, at that particular time, I was the press chief in charge of reporter assignments and story ideas. Editorial content came from the division and was sent to

Saigon, where a fellow from Detroit named Jim Graham edited, laid it out and took it to a commercial printer.

2. United States, Department of Health and Human Services, Centers for Disease Control and Prevention <http://www.cdc.gov/malaria/> "General Information:" There are approximately 3,500 species of mosquitoes grouped into 41 genera. Human malaria is transmitted only by females of the genus *Anopheles*. Of the approximately 430 *Anopheles* species, only 30–40 transmit malaria (i.e., are "vectors") in nature. Geographic Distribution: Anophelines are found worldwide except Antarctica. Malaria is transmitted by different *Anopheles* species, depending on the region and the environment. <http://cdc-malaria.ncsa.uiuc.edu/> Map of the world showing the distribution of predominant malaria vectors. 8 Feb. 2010 <http://www.cdc.gov/malaria/map/index.html>.

3. United States, Department of the Navy, Naval Historical Center, Washington Navy Yard, Washington, D.C. <www.history.navy.mil/> Page made 2 January 2006. New images added and page divided 28 December 2006. The civilian-manned, Military Sea Transportation Service (MSTS), USNS *General Maurice Rose* (T-AP-126) was a light displacement transport commissioned in 1945. Between August and October 1965 the *Rose* steamed from New York to the Far East to support US forces in Vietnam. A second such trip was made between September 1966 and January 1967.

4. The communications officer was a position normally filled by a captain. J. S. (Jim) Brigham, Alley's roommate on the USS *Rose,* Headquarters Company, 2/7th Cavalry An Khe 65–66; MACV Phan Rang 69-70, received Bronze Star with V for valor. Email Mar. 2010.

5. J. L. "Bud" Alley, First Lieutenant, Communications Officer, 2nd Battalion 7th Cavalry, An Khe, July 1965 to August 1966, was in the fight of LZ Albany in the Ia Drang, November 17, 1965 and the Bong Son battles in January and May along with numerous other skirmishes. "One lucky SOB to have come back alive." Received the Combat Infantryman's Badge, the Purple Heart, the Bronze Star, and the Silver Star. Email 26 Aug. 2009.

6. Alley, emails, 19–22 Feb. 2010.

7. Stanton, 46.

8. Summers, 202, 203.

9. McGhie, Email Sept. 2008.

10. William O. Taylor, *With Custer on the Little Bighorn: A Newly Discovered First-Person Account* (New York: Viking, 1996), 121, gives the day as June 25, 1876.

11. The noon meal. In the combat zone this was the main meal of the day. The night meal was often called supper.

12. B Company 15ᵗʰ Medical Battalion, the staff of the hospital.

13. Company C, 2nd Battalion, 35th Infantry of 25th Infantry Division's 3rd Brigade.

14. Barrie E. Zais, Thomas R. Wissinger, a Lieutenant Davis, and Charles Brown.

15. Charles Brown, Lt. Col. US Army (Ret.), "How the Ace of Spades Became One of the Enduring Legends of Vietnam Psychological Warfare," *Vietnam,* Oct. 2007: 13–15

16. Summers, 280.

17. Dr. Seuss, *The Cat in the Hat* (New York: Random House, 1957). The whimsical, rhymed children's book featured Thing One and Thing Two.

18. The Socialist Republic of Vietnam, Military History Institute of Vietnam, *Victory in Vietnam: The Official History of the People's Army of Vietnam, 1954–1975,* trans. Merle L. Pribbenow (Lawrence: University Press of Kansas, 2002), 68. In the context of the Vietnam War (1959–1975), the army was referred to as the North Vietnamese Army (NVA) or the People's Army of Vietnam (PAVN). This allowed writers to distinguish northern communists from the southern communists, or Viet Cong. However, northerners and southerners were always under the same command structure. According to Hanoi's official history, the Viet Cong was a branch of the PAVN.

19. Summers, 35, 203. Harold G. Moore, Lieutenant General (Ret.) and Joseph L. Galloway, *We were Soldiers Once . . . and Young: Ia Drang—the Battle That Changed the War in Vietnam* (New York: Presidio/Random House, 1992), 59. Jack P. Smith (son of Howard K. Smith, anchorman and TV news commentator at the peak of his career in 1965), "Sandbag for a Machine Gun: The Battle of the Ia Drang Valley and the Legacy of the Vietnam War," Speech, Ia Drang Survivors Banquet, Crystal City, VA, 8 Nov. 2003.

20. Name withheld by request, Sergeant, United States Marine Corps 1959 to 1966. Special Operations, counter insurgence, intelligence gathering. Email Mar. 2010.

Chapter 4: Hot Landing Zone

1. Melborne C. Chandler, *Of Garry Owen in Glory: The History of the Seventh United States Cavalry Regiment* (Annandale, VA: Turnpike, 1960), 2.

2. United States, United States Army, *Regulation AR 670-1 (Feb. 2005),* 28-21 242 ". . . while in close proximity to the enemy it was advisable to remove symbols of rank, and the green tab, . . . was adopted as a substitute . . . to identify the leaders." <www.armystudyguide.com/>.

3. <http://en.wikipedia.org/wiki/S.L.A._Marshall>.

4. Summers, 38

5. Marshall, 178–185.

6. Marshall.

7. *Colt Safety and Instruction Manual, Colt WWII Reproduction Pistol Model M1911A1* (Colt's Manufacturing Company, 2001) Figure 1 p.1, Figure 2 p. 15.

Chapter 5: Poison Booth at the Carnival

1. "25th anniversary of the fall of Saigon, April 26, 2000," CNN chat interview (*Air Force Print News Today: Air Force News from Around the World,* 4 Oct. 2008).

2. Name withheld by request, Marine, combat veteran, Special Operations. Email Mar. 2010.

3. Gwin, 127. Moore and Galloway, 260. Note: Moore and Galloway report 26 killed; the Delta 2/7 web site lists 31 names and locations on the Wall. <http://www.delta2-7.org/kia65.htm>.

4. *Florence Times Daily* (Florence Alabama, Tri-Cities Publishing) 15 Dec. 1955: 2:5. I assumed she had worked at a Red Cross recreation center in Morocco. The Red Cross had three there in 1955.

5. Name withheld by request, M.D., Fellow American Board of Obstetrics and Gynecology. Conversation in doctor's office, Mar. 2010. "I never heard of milk having anything to do with breast volume. Weight loss and dehydration could affect volume. As far as different men's sperm causing infection, I have never heard anything about that, either. Douching won't prevent infection. Who knows what myths might be floating around among people who are not educated?"; Izora Baldwin, Certified Medical Assistant (CMA), Conversation in doctor's office, June, 2011. "Different men's sperm will not interact and cause infection."

Chapter 6: Bring a Case of Beer

1. Summers, 35.

2. Robert C. Johnson, US Army Basic Training-101st Airborne Infantry, Private; Korea, 3rd Division, 7th Regiment, "L" Company-Infantryman, 57 mm. Recoilless Rifle, Private and Private First Class; 558th Military Police Company, 8th Army Headquarters, Seoul, Korea-Military Policeman, PFC and Corporal; Parts Supply Motor Pool, Corporal; Motor Pool Motor Sergeant SGT(T)31, 1952–54. Combat Infantry Badge; United Nations Service Medallion; Commendation Ribbon with Metal Pendant; National Defense Service Medallion; Merit Unit Commendation; Foreign Service Medal with 2 Service Stars. Telephone conversation with the author, Sept. 2007.

3. Summers, 39.

Chapter 7: A Veteran under the Desk

1. Name supplied by William T. (Tom) Carter, Chaplain (CPT), HHC 3rd Bde, 1st Infantry Division attached Chaplain to 2nd Battalion, 2nd Infantry (Mech), September 1966-1967. He's the most decorated soldier I knew from Vietnam: Army Achievement Medal, Meritorious Service Medal 5th Oak Leaf Cluster (OLC), Air Medal 12th OLC, Bronze Star Medal 3 OLC, Bronze Star Medal for Valor 2 OLC, Legion of Merit 2nd OLC Retired after 28 years at Colonel. Grzywinski; and James F. Huggins, 1Lt. 1st Infantry Division, RVN, June of 1966 to May of 1967. 1st Platoon Leader, A Company, 2/2 Infantry Battalion; Liaison Officer, 2/2; and Executive Officer, HHC, 2/2. CIB, Parachute Wings, Bronze Star, Purple Heart, Meritorious Service Medal, Air Medal, Army Commendation Medal. Retired as colonel in United States Army Reserve. Carter, Grzywinski, and Huggins. An S-1 is the Unit Personnel/Administration Officer. He is also designated as the adjutant who has the authority to sign for the commanding officer. Emails to author Mar. 2010.

2. "Special Awards Ceremony Held," *The American Traveler* (1ˢᵗ Infantry Division Information Office) 3 Dec. 1966: 3.

3. Carter, Sermon outline and attendance record, 24 Nov. '66. Emails Mar. 2010.

4. Grzywinski, presently Historian, 2ND INF REGT ASSN. Researched and supplied names; also wrote 75 to 80 percent of the Wikipedia site on the regiment at <http://en.wikipedia.org/wiki/2nd_Battalion%2C_2nd_Infantry_Regiment>. Jason Mitchell, who served with the 2nd Battalion in Bosnia, did the basic outline and history and inserted the pictures. Emails Dec. 2008 and Mar. 2010.

5. Huggins, Phone conversation Mar. 2010.

6. Rolando A. Salazar, SP4, Chief, Fire Direction Control (FDC), June 1967 to December 1967, Mortar Platoon, Co. D, 2nd Bn. 7th Cavalry, 1st Cavalry Division, Bronze Star Medal, Army Commendation Medal, Air Medal, Combat Infantry Badge. Email Dec. 2009.

7. Salazar, "When 'fire mission' was called out, everyone in the area immediately went into position and the gun crew got ready to execute the mission. This all happened within seconds, and certainly within less than a minute, the gun crews and FDC would have reacted and started to get into position. How quickly the first round went out of the tube depended on the FO [Forward Observer] calling in the information and it's being computed by the FDC. It was always very fast. However, I don't think we ever timed ourselves. . . . We typically would have three mortars set up. " Email Dec. 2009.

8. Huggins: "The mortars would have fired non-stop only if there had been a major fire fight. We did try to conserve ammo. I suspect that it would have only been five to ten minutes." Email Mar. 2010.

9. Carter, sermon outline and attendance records, Email Mar. 2010.

10. Carter, Email Apr. 2010.

11. Giles, 38. Sun Tzu says: "Amid the turmoil and tumult of battle, there may be seeming disorder and yet no real disorder at all."

12. Grzywinski, Email to author Mar. 2010.

13. Carter, Email to author Oct. 2010.

14. Robert C. Fulps, Rifle Squad Leader, 3rd Platoon, Charlie Company, 2/2 Infantry. Feb. 1966–Jan. 1967. Bronze Star, Army Commendation Medal, Vietnamese Cross of Gallantry. Plus a bunch of "thank you for coming" ribbons. "I was a professional Soldier and was proud to serve. . . . I am a retired First Sergeant and had occassion to meet many 'Donut Dollies.' In Korea for two winters, we really looked forward to your visits there. I have always admired your courage and fortitude as you pursued your mission of contributing to the morale of the troops. Thank you for your service. We appreciate you very much. May God bless and keep you safe." Emails to author Nov. 2007 to Jan. 2011.

15. Justin Fishel, "First Living Soldier Since Vietnam Awarded Military's Highest Honor," (The Medal of Honor) *FoxNews.com*, 14 Sept. 2010. Jennifer Griffith, at the Pentagon, "Salvatore Giunta (Joon ta) Video report," minute 1.2, WASHINGTON, D.C. *FoxNews.com*, <http://www.foxnews.com/politics/2010/09/14/living-soldier-awarded-militarys-highest-honor/>.

16. Fulps, Emails Oct. 2010.

17. Alec Lyall, Specialist 4th Class, Radio Telephone Operator, D Company, 2/7th Cavalry, February 66-67, Purple Heart, Army Commendation Medal, Telephone interview, 30 May 2008.

18. Andy Askew, Tech 5, 767th Tank Battalion, 7th Division, M-4 Sherman Tank #26, The Michigander, Kenworth Wrecker, The Lady Margaret, December 1942-45; Bill Grandstaff, Sp 5 E-5, 3rd Brigade Headquarters Company, 101st Airborne, Hue, April 1968-December 1969; and Jack Ryan, Sgt E-5, A Battery, 2/17th Artillery, 1st Cavalry Division (Airmobile), An Khe, July 1966–August 67; Conversation Oct. 2006.

Chapter 8: Rabies

1. Summers, 40.

2. Summers, 182, 290. The name was derived from the song "Puff the Magic Dragon," since a gunship firing at night looked like a dragon spitting fire. The WW II-vintage twin-engine C-47 Gooneybird cargo plane, redesignated the AC-47, with the more elegant name Dragonship, they were outfitted with three rapid-fire 7.62-mm multibarreled machine guns and aerial parachute flares that could turn night into day.

3. "F-100 History," Chicago: Boeing, <http://www.boeing.com/history/bna/f100.htm>; Summers, 158.

4. Summers, 40.

5. Phil Rosette, Spc4, 128 Assault Helicopter Company, "The Gunslingers," Door Gunner, GS-41, Huey B model Gunship "Happy-Happy", March 69 to Feb. 70, Hundred or more missions, Air Medal, Good Conduct Medal, Expert Badge for the auto rifle, Emails Sept. 2008–2010.

6. Rick Polizzi and Fred Schaefer, *Spin Again, Board Games from the Fifties and Sixties* (San Francisco: Chronicle, 1991), 116–17.

7. John S. Bowman, et al., eds. *The Vietnam War Almanac* (New York: World Almanac, 1985), 162. "8–12 February 1967 . . . The United States halts the bombing of North Vietnam during Tet."

Chapter 9: Ambush in the Delta

1. I went without another girl, because I was off duty. We regularly went alone to dinner at various mess halls. Going to the room with a dozen pilots was appropriate, because there was a crowd of us.

2. Ian Scott, *Political Change and the Crisis of Legitimacy in Hong Kong* (Hawaii: University of Hawaii, 1989). The Hong Kong 1967 riots were caused by pro-communist leftists in Hong Kong, inspired by the Cultural Revolution in the People's Republic of China (PRC), who turned a labor dispute into large scale demonstrations against British colonial rule These began as early as March 1967 in shipping, taxi, textile, cement companies and the Hong Kong artificial flowerworks.

3. Raymond Strait, *James Garner* (New York: St. Martin's, 1985).

4. Name supplied by Wayne Williams, 1LT, Recon Plt Ldr, E Company; Commander, C Company, 2nd Bn 3rd Inf, 199th LIB 6/66-12/67, Nhon Duc, Combat Infantry Badge, Bronze Star with "V" Device and Oak Leaf Cluster, Defense Meritorious Service Medal, Meritorious Service Medal; Joint Commendation Medal. However, the greatest award of all was that every man that deployed from Fort Benning with me to Vietnam who was assigned to the original Recon Platoon returned home alive. This remains the greatest feat I have ever accomplished in my entire life. Emails to author Jan. 2011, Aug. 2011.

5. Name supplied by Williams. Email to author Jan. 2011.

6. Name supplied by Peter J. McDermott, CW4(R), Honor Guard Company and Fife and Drum Corps, 1st BG, 3d Infantry (The Old Guard) at Fort Myer, Virginia 1960-62; retired in 2002. Past President and Historian of The Old Guard Association. Legion of Merit, 4 Meritorious Service Medals, 4 Army Commendation Medals, Expert Infantryman Badge, Master Parachutist Badge, Special Forces Tab, British Parachute Wings. Email to author July 2011.

7. Montie J. Wagner, President, The Old Guard Association; (TOGA) http://www.oldguard.org/, Sergeant, 1962 to 1964 with Company A, 1st Battalion, 3d Infantry at Fort McNair, Washington, DC (While the majority of the Regiment is at Ft Myer, Virginia, there has always been a company at Fort McNair since 1948. McDermott, Email Jun. 2011); William J. Carr, Jr., SGM, AUS, RET. SP4, rifleman and RTO, C/2/3/199th LIB, Nov. 66–Apr. 67, Combat Infantry Badge, Purple Heart, Army Commendation Medal with Oak Leaf Cluster, Army Reserve Forces Achievement Medal; Francis W. Love, LT, USAR, Platoon Leader, B Co. and C Co. 2/3/199th LIB, Nov. 66–Dec. 67, Purple Heart, Bronze Star, Air Medal, Emails to the author in 2010.

8. It has been suggested that the correct acronym might be DEROS (Date Eligible for Return from Overseas Service) I have heard the term, but we usually used EDPAC.

9. Chet "Chief" Idalski, SSG E-6, 127th Artillery, Phu Loi, Chief of Gun Section, Ammo Sergeant, 155 Self-propelled Howitzers, about 20 Infantry patrols and ambushes as RTO; 196th Brigade, American Division. March 67-68, Conversations Mar. and Nov. 2008.

10. *Operator's Manual for AK-47 Assault Rifle* (Department of the Army, 203rd Military Intelligence Battalion) Figure 3. Technical Data.

11. Neil E. Persinger, Lieutenant, US Navy, WW II, Korea, *Ticonderoga* CV14 aircraft carrier, U.S.S. *Newport* PF27 Patrol Frigate, U.S.S. *Gloucester* PF22 Patrol Frigate, Okinawa, Saipan, Guam, May 1943–1954. Was ambushed on Okinawa, almost ambushed on Guam. Conversation Nov. 2008.

Chapter 10: The Cigarette in the Rain

1. Rosette, Emails 2008-2010.

2. Rosette, Emails 2008–2010.

3. David F. Crosby, "High Tech vs. Low Tech: The striking battle of wits and ingenuity that kept about half of the war's choppers flying . . . and got about half of

them shot down," *Vietnam,* Aug. 2009: 26. "A 1968 report on the statistical success of enemy ground fire hitting helicopters found that . . . helicopters flying above 2,000 feet took only 2 percent [of the ground fire hits] . . . helicopters flying below 100 feet rarely took hits because enemy gunners had little time to react to a helicopter sighting. The report's recommendations were clear: Fly above 2,000 feet or below 100 feet to avoid enemy ground fire."

4. Giles, 172.

5. Drew Bisio, Lieutenant USN, Damage Control Assistant, qualified in Submarines, served on the nuclear submarine USS *Trepang* (SSN-674) 1991-1994, National Defense Service Medal, Sea Service Deployment Ribbon, Meritorious Unit Commendation, Navy Achievement Medal, Conversation July 2007.

6. United States, Department of the Interior, National Park Service, *Lightning Strikes* (Cedar City, UT: Cedar Breaks National Monument, 2006).

7. M. O'Keefe, and Zane Gatewood, "Lightning injuries," *Emerg Med Clin North Am, 22*(2), R. D. (2004) 369; Mary Ann Cooper, MD, Professor, Departments of Emergency Medicine and Bioengineering, Director of Lightning and Electrical Injury Research Program, University of Illinois at Chicago; Attending Physician, Electrical Trauma Program, University of Chicago and University of Illinois at Chicago, "Lightning injuries 2004" (11 Fcb. 2005). <www.emedicine.com /emerg/topic299.htm>.

8. "Passengers and crew survive lightning strike," BBC News, UK: Scotland, Tues. 9 Nov. 1999, Published at 08:52 GMT.

9. Hanover and District Hospital, Ontario's air ambulance system, "ORNGE," helicopter-based 24/7 service.

10. Gunter Endres, ed. *Jane's Helicopter Markets and Systems.* (London: Jane's Information Group, 2006).

11. *When Lightning Strikes at Site 300,* Lawrence Livermore National Laboratory, University of California, UCRL-52000-05-12 (Livermore, CA: US Department of Energy) 14 Dec. 2005.

Chapter 11: The Long, Confusing Road Home

1. Pyle, 325.

2. Name withheld by request, Corporal E-4, Company B 2 Battalion 22 Infantry Mechanized (triple deuce), Armored Personnel Carrier, Iron Triangle, Michelin Rubber Plantation, Xuan Loc, Hobo Woods, Bo Loi (outside Cu Chi), 25th Division, Tay Ninh, Nuy Ba Dinh (Black Virgin Mountain), 63 days 1st Air Cavalry, An Khe, Song Be, December '69–February '71. Two Presidential Unit Citations, Bronze Star. Telephone conversation Apr. 2009.

3. Ted Kotcheff, Director, *First Blood* (also known as *Rambo: First Blood*) 1982, starred Sylvester Stallone, Brian Dennehy, and Richard Crenna.

4. Clark Dougan, Stephen Weiss, et al., *Nineteen Sixty-Eight* (Boston: Boston Publishing, 1983), 8.

5. United Press International, "1971 Year in Review: Calley Trial, Foreign Affairs" <http://www.upi.com/Audio/Year_in_Review/Events-of-1971/Calley-Trial%2C-Foreign-Affairs/12295509436546-8/>.

6. Merle F. Wilberding, "What Really Happened in Pinkville," Cover Story, *Vietnam*, Apr. 2008: 28–35.

7. "Found: The monster of the My Lai massacre." *Daily Mail* (London). 6 Oct. 2007 <http://www.dailymail.co.uk/news/article-485983/Found-The-monster-My-Lai-massacre.html>.

8. "Wings Across America Presents: Fly Girls of WWII," Baylor University, Mayborn Museum, Waco, Texas. <http://www.baylor.edu/mayborn/index.php?id=49549>.

9. United States, Department of Defense, Advisory Committee on Women in the Services <http://www.dtic.mil/dacowits/membrs_MilStf.html>.

10. United States, Department of Defense (DOD), Inter-Service Working Group, "Study on Utilization of Women in the Armed Services," 31 Aug. 66, ODWAC Ref File, Expansion of WAC, 1966-1969, CMH. Memo, ASD(M), to Dep UnderSec Army (Manpower) [DUSA (M)], 14 May 66, sub: Study of Utilization of Military Women; Memo, DUSA (M) to ASD (M), 7 Dec. 66, same sub; Bull 13 for Chief of Naval Personnel for Women (Capt Rita Lenihan), Apr. 67; Memo, Dep Under SecAF (Manpower) to ASD (M), 29 June 67, sub: Utilization of Women in the Air Force. All in ODWAC Ref File, Expansion of WAC 1966-1969, CMH. The study group's report of 31 August 1966 recommended that the services expand their women's components and that women continue to be concentrated in administrative, communications, and medical care fields, but that the services explore their utilization in other fields. It also urged that more women be stationed overseas. The Army approved the recommendations and directed an immediate 38 percent increase in WAC strength. The Navy followed suit, approving a 20 percent increase. The Air Force approved a 60 percent increase in enlisted WAFs and a 33 1/3- percent increase in WAF officers.

11. Pat Carr, *McClatchy-Tribune*; also Peter Gavrilovich, and Martha Thierry, *Detroit Free Press*, Cover Story: "The trials, triumphs of D-day," Sun. 31 May 2009: A30.

Appendix 1: Let Us Remember

1. Margaret Hodge, American Red Cross SRAO, Vietnam 1966–67. Emails to the author.

2. Jolynne Strang, American Red Cross, SRAO, Vietnam, A Circle of Sisters/A Circle of Friends (Civilian) Denver, CO http://vietnamreflections.blogspot.com/2009/03/circle-of-sisters.html; Ann Kelsey, Army Special Services-Libraries, Cam Ranh Bay 1969-1970. Emails to author; Vietnam Women's Memorial Project Washington, D.C. *The Dedication of the Vietnam Women's Memorial: A Celebration of Patriotism and Courage*, by Diane Carlson Evans, RN, Vietnam, 1968-1969, Army Nurse Corps, 1966-72. "American Red Cross Women in Vietnam," Sharon Lewis Dickerson, ARC Vietnam: 1970-71, page 1 http://www.vietnamwomensmemorial.

org/pdf/sdickerson.pdf; Special Collections. Penrose Library, The University of Denver, <http://library.du.edu/About/collections/SpecialCollections/Circle/>, archives@du.edu;

Dr. and Mrs. Victor Westphall, Founder; Walter Westphall, Memorial Founder, First Vietnam Veterans National Memorial, Dedicated to all Americans who served in Vietnam, late summer 1968, Angel Fire, Albuquerque, New Mexico; Stephen L. Anderson, "Vietnam Diary of SP/5 Stephen L. (Andy) Anderson," A company, 25th Aviation Battalion, 25th Infantry Division, Cu Chi Base Camp South Vietnam, http://25thaviation.org/scrapbook/id988.htm; *Stars and Stripes* Vietnam Bureau, 20 Aug. 1970; American Red Cross Vietnam Memorial, <http://72.14.205.104/search?q=cache:WApVaCq-sskJ:www.flickr.com/photos/sheenachi/2185748045/+Virginia+Kirsch&hl=en&ct=clnk&cd=5&gl=us&client=firefox-a>.

3. Susan Bradshaw-McLean, American Red Cross, SRAO Vietnam, August 1970–71, classmate and friend of Virginia Kirsch. Interview with the admitted killer on Sat. 4 Mar. 2006, at Winnebago Mental Health Institute, Oshkosh, Wisconsin. Telephone interview 10 June 2008.

4. Rosalyn Carson-DeWitt, MD. *Gale Encyclopedia of Medicine*, Dec. 2002 ed.

5. Kammy McCleery, American Red Cross SRAO Vietnam 1966–67, Email to author Apr. 2008.

6. Barb Lilly, American Red Cross SRAO Vietnam 1966–67, Emails, 14–16 Oct. 2008.

7. Strang; Kelsey; Vietnam Women's Memorial Project 2001; The University of Denver, Penrose Library; Westphall; Anderson; American Red Cross Vietnam Memorial; McCleery, Email to author Apr. 2008.

Appendix 2: Some Questions Answered

1. United States Congressional Research Service, "American War and Military Operations Casualties: Lists and Statistics," 26 Feb. 2010, "8,744,000 served in Vietnam, 58,220 deaths." http://www.fas.org/sgp/crs/natsec/RL32492.pdf

2. United States Department of Defense, DOD Live, "New Names Added to Vietnam Memorial," 4 May 2010. "The changes will bring the total number of names on the Vietnam Veterans Memorial to 58,267 men and women who were killed or remain missing in action." <http://www.dodlive.mil/index.php/2010/05/new-names-added-to-vietnam-memorial/>.

3. United States, Department of Transportation, Research and Innovative Technology Administration, Bureau of Transportation Statistics, 13 Nov. 2005 <http://www.bts.gov/>; <http://www.driveandstayalive.com/>.

4. Bowman, 358; Summers, 112; Lt. Gen. Barry R. McCaffrey, Assistant to the Chairman of the Joint Chiefs of Staff, Speech to Vietnam veterans and visitors gathered at "The Wall," Memorial Day 1993, *Pentagram*, Washington, D.C., 4 June 1993.

5. David E. Kotcher, MBA, JD, Ph.D., SPHR, Distinguished Professor, Graduate Department of Business Administration, Faculty of Economics and Administrative

Sciences, EPOKA University, Tirana, Albania. He also holds professorships (prof. dr.) at several universities in Central and Eastern Europe in both Business and Law. Email Mar. 2010.

6. Charles Murray, non-qual duty person (not Special Forces qualified, assigned to SF) logistics and supply, 5ᵗʰ Grp, Nha Trang/Phan Rang 65-66; Operations clerk, I Corp Artillery, 108ᵗʰ Intel, Phu Bai 68-69; Infantryman, Long Range Reconnaissance Patrols, Operations and Intelligence Sergeant, 1/16 1ˢᵗ Infantry Division, Lai Khe 69–70, Combat Infantry Badge, Email to author, July 2008.

7. McCleery, Phone conversation with author. 3 Mar. 2008.

8. James Manning, SP4 E-4, Field Supply Clerk Typist, 1ˢᵗ Brigade, 21ˢᵗ Signal Group, Da Lat, 21 July 1969–8 Oct. 1970. Telephone conversation with author. Nov. 2008.

9. McGhie, Email to author, 24 Aug. 2009.

10. Wilmer K. Benson, CPT USA-Retired (aka "Bill" and "Wild Bill") Fire team Leader (Sergeant), A Company, 1st Battle Group, 21st Infantry, 25th Infantry Division and TDY to MACV 63–64; Squad Leader (Sergeant), B Company, 2nd Battalion, 2nd Infantry and Platoon Leader (Second Lieutenant), A Company, 1st Battalion, 28th Infantry, 1st Infantry Division 65–66, Combat Infantry Badge, Presidential Unit Citation, Bronze Star w/"V" Device; Company Commander (CPT) C Company, 4th Battalion, 3rd Infantry and Assistant Operations Officer (Captain), Chu Lai Defense Command 69–70. Emails to author, June 2008.

11. Murray, Email to author, July 2008.

12. Jake Hargis, Cpt., Army Aviator, Korea 1/7 Cav 62, Pleiku and An Khe 66, Germany 68, Bronze Star, Air Medal (7 awards), Joint Service Commendation Medal, Army Commendation Medal. Email to author, July 2008.

13. Brigham, Email to author, Feb. 2008.

14. Bruce D. Silvey, Aviation Officer, 1ˢᵗ Air Cav and 17ᵗʰ Avn Grp, Nha Trang 65-66; 173ʳᵈ Airborne Brigade Jan. 68-69, Email June 2008.

15. Serge Olive, VN Ranger Battalion, II FF Oct. 66 Nov. 67; 101ˢᵗ Airborne Jan. 68-69, Email to author July 2008.

16. Jerry Griffin, COL, Okinawa 1ˢᵗ Group; Vietnam CAS Oct 1962; I Corps SF Cal An Diem 1964; 1ˢᵗ Div. Oct. 65-Dec. 66; Lai Khe 69, Email July 2008. Deceased, July 2010.

17. Elizabeth (Arant) West, Donut Dolly, Qui Nhon, Long Binh, Bien Hoa 68–69, Email July 2008.

Appendix 3: Whatever Happened To . . . ?

1. Gwin, 306.

2. Moore and Galloway, 380.

3. Bernard W. Krawczuk, Commander, Ukrainian American Veterans, Freehold, New Jersey, Major Myron Diduryk Post 30 http://uavets.org/Post30/Post30.html Research of National Personnel Records Center. Email to author 8 Sept. 2008

4. Stewart, 178, 141, 393.

5. Alexander Lyall, *An Occasional Hard Landing* (Manchester Center, VT: Shires, 2010), 19, 20.

6. Lyall, 21.

7. Moore and Galloway, 383.

8. Gwin, 346, 347.

9. Gwin, 353.

10. Marshall, xviii, 65-71.

11. *Medal of Honor citations*. <United States Army Center of Military History>.

12. US Army Otter-Caribou Association. Congressional Medal of Honor Society, <http://www.cmohs.org/recipient-detail/3265/dolby-david-charles.php>.

13. Huggins, Email to author, Mar. 2010.

14. Carter, Email to author Mar. 2010.

15. *Together: The Midmonth Magazine for Methodist Families* (Park Ridge, IL) Oct. 1967: Vol. 11, no. 10. It is no longer in publication.

16. Stanton, 77, 98.

17. Moore, 10.

18. Arlington National Cemetery Website, courtesy of the *Washington Post*. <http://www.arlingtoncemetery.net/john-norton.htm>.

19. *25th anniversary of the fall of Saigon, April 26, 2000*, CNN chat interview.

20. "Special Awards Ceremony Held," *The American Traveler*.

21. United States Military Academy, Association of Graduates, Citation for the 1996 Distinguished Graduate Award presented to Alexander M. Haig, Jr., Class of 1947, West Point, New York: 1996. http://www.westpointaog.org/netcommunity/page.aspx?pid=539

Works Cited

Books, Articles, and Websites

"25ᵗʰ Anniversary of the Fall of Saigon." CNN chat interview conducted 26 Apr. 2000, published in *Air Force Print News Today, Air Force News from Around the World*, 4 Oct. 2008.

Adler, Bill, ed. *Letters from Vietnam*. New York: Random House, 2003.

American Red Cross, Washington, D.C. <http://www.redcross.org/museum/history/vietnam.asp>.

———. <http://www.redcross.org/museum/history/index.asp>.

———. <http://www.redcross.org/museum/history/claraBarton.asp>.

———. <http://www.redcross.org/museum/history/ww1a.asp>.

———. <http://www.redcross.org/museum/history/faqs.asp#wartime>.

———. <http://www.redcross.org/museum/history/

———. <http://www.redcross.org/museum/history/ww2a.asp>.

———. <http://www.redcross.org/museum/history/korean.asp>.

Anderson, Stephen L., "Vietnam Diary of SP/5 Stephen L. (Andy) Anderson," Cu Chi Base Camp, South Vietnam. Aug. 1970, http://25thaviation.org/scrapbook/id988.htm

Arlington National Cemetery Website, http://www.arlingtoncemetery.mil/ courtesy of the *Washington Post*.

Associated Press-Saigon. "5 Dead in Saigon Melee." *The Daily Red Bank Area Register*. (Monmouth County, NJ), Tues. 10 May 1966: A1.

BBC News, UK: Scotland, "Passengers and crew survive lightning strike," Tuesday, November 9, 1999, Published at 08:52 GMT.

"The Billboard Hot 100 Songs of the Year (1958–1969)": Kolhede, Jeff. "The Ballad of the Green Berets," *Billboard*. <http://www.billboard.com/specials/hot100/charts/top50-no1s-60s.shtml>.

Bowman, John S., et al., eds. *The Vietnam War Almanac*. New York: World Almanac, 1985.

Brown, Charles. "How the Ace of Spades Became One of the Enduring Legends of Vietnam Psychological Warfare." *Vietnam*. Oct. 2007, 13–15.

Carr, Pat. *McClatchy-Tribune*; also Gavrilovich, Peter, and Martha Thierry. *Detroit Free Press*, "The Trials, Triumphs of D-Day," Sun. 31 May 2009, cover story.

Carson-DeWitt, Rosalyn. *Gale Encyclopedia of Medicine*. Detroit: Gale Group, 2002.

Cate, Curtis. *The Ides of August: The Berlin Wall Crisis 1961*. New York: M. Evans, 1978.

Chandler, Melborne C. *Of Garry Owen in Glory: The History of the Seventh United States Cavalry Regiment*. Annandale, VA: Turnpike, 1960.

Citation for the 1996 Distinguished Graduate Award presented to Alexander M. Haig, Jr., Class of 1947. Association of Graduates, United States Military Academy, West Point, New York. http://www.westpointaog.org/netcommunity/page.aspx?pid=539

Cole, Hugh M. *The Ardennes: Battle of the Bulge*. Washington, D.C.: Office of the Chief of Military History, Department of the Army, 1965.

Colt Safety and Instruction Manual, Colt WWII Reproduction Pistol Model M1911A1. N.p.: Colt's Manufacturing, 2001.

Columbia Encyclopedia, Sixth Edition. New York: Columbia University, 2007.

Cooper, Mary Ann. "Lightning Injuries 2004." Chicago: University of Illinois. <www.emedicine.com /emerg/topic299.htm>.

Costello, John. *The Pacific War*. New York: Rawson, Wace, 1981

Crosby, David F. "High Tech vs. Low Tech: The Striking Battle of Wits and Ingenuity That Kept about Half of the War's Choppers Flying

. . . and Got about Half of Them Shot Down." *Vietnam*, Aug. 2009, 20–27.

Dougan, Clark, and Stephen Weiss, et al. *Nineteen Sixty-Eight*. Boston: Boston Publishing, 1993.

Endres, Gunter, ed. *Jane's Helicopter Markets and Systems*. London: Jane's Information Group, 2006.

"F-100 History." Chicago: Boeing Co., <http://www.boeing.com/ history/bna/f100.htm>.

Faludi, Susan. "America's Guardian Myths," op-ed *New York Times*, September 7, 2007.

Florence Times Daily, Florence, AL: Tri-Cities. 15 Dec. 1955, 2:5.

"Found: The monster of the My Lai massacre". London: *Daily Mail*, 6 Oct. 2007. <http://www.dailymail.co.uk/news/article-485983/ Found-The-monster-My-Lai-massacre.html>.

Foxworthy, Jeff. *Redneck Comedy Tour 2009*. Broadcast on Comedy Central, 2009.

Gelb, Norman. *The Berlin Wall, Kennedy, Khrushchev, and a Showdown in the Heart of Europe*. New York: Random House, 1986.

Griffith, Jennifer. "Salvatore Giunta (Joon ta) Video report." minute 1.2, Washington, D.C. *FoxNews. com*, <http://www.foxnews.com/politics/2010/09/14/ living-soldier-awarded-militarys-highest-honor/>.

Gwin, Larry. *Baptism: A Vietnam Memoir*. New York: Ivy, Random House, 1999.

Hanover and District Hospital, Ontario's air ambulance system, "ORNGE," helicopter-based 24/7 service.

Hermes, Walter J. *Truce Tent and Fighting Front: United States Army in the Korean War*. Washington, D.C.: Center of Military History, United States Army, 1992.

Jackson, Paul, Lindsay T. Peacock, and Kenneth Munson. *Jane's All the World's Aircraft*. Alexandria, VA: Jane's Information Group, 2008.

"Korean Leaders Issue Peace Call," *BBC News International version*. Thurs. 4 Oct. 2007.

Krawczuk, Bernard W. Commander, Ukrainian American Veterans, Freehold, New Jersey, Major Myron Diduryk Post 30 http://uavets. org/Post30/Post30.html Research of National Personnel Records Center. Email to author 8 Sept. 2008.

Leiby, Richard A. *The Unification of Germany, 1989–1990.* Westport, CT: Greenwood, 1999.

LeSueur York, Jill (Reunion Book Chair), Hodge, Margaret (American Red Cross Reunion Book Committee), et al. *Red Cross Reunion '93, From Saigon to DC: The American Red Cross Women Who Served.* Bowie, MD: Volunteers from the American Red Cross, 1995.

Lyall, Alexander. *An Occasional Hard Landing.* Manchester Center, VT: Shires, 2010.

Marshall, S. L. A. *Battles in the Monsoon: Campaigning in the Central Highlands, Vietnam, Summer 1966.* Nashville, TN: Battery, 1966.

McCaffrey, Barry R. "Speech at 'The Wall.'" Memorial Day 1993; reproduced in the *Pentagram,* 4 June 1993.

McNeilly, Mark R. *Sun Tzu and the Art of Modern Warfare.* Oxford, England: Oxford University Press, 2001.

Medal of Honor Citations. <United States Army Center of Military History>.

Moore, Harold G., and Galloway, Joseph L. *We were Soldiers Once . . . and Young: Ia Drang—the Battle That Changed the War in Vietnam.* New York: Presidio, Random House, 1992.

Nutt, Charles. *Descendants of George Puffer of Braintree, Massachusetts 1639–1915.* Rutland, VT: The Tuttle Co., 1915.

O'Keefe, M., and Zane Gatewood. "Lightning Injuries." *Emergency Medical Clinics of North America* 22, no. 2 (2004).

"Passengers and Crew Survive Lightning Strike," BBC News, UK: Scotland, Tues. 9 Nov. 1999. Published at 08:52 GMT.

"Place on the Wall and in Our Hearts: American, Australian and New Zealand Civilian and Military Women Who Died in the Vietnam War (1959–1975)." *Women Who Died in the Vietnam War,* 2007 <http://illyria.com/women/vnwlist.html>.

Polizzi, Rick, and Fred Schaefer. *Spin Again: Board Games from the Fifties and Sixties*. San Francisco: Chronicle, 1991.

Pyle, Ernie. *Here Is Your War*. Lincoln: University of Nebraska Press, 2004.

"Red Cross Brings Troopers 'Closer to Home.'" *Cavalair, The Weekly Newspaper of the 1ˢᵗ Cavalry Division*. 25 July 1966.

Rexford, Oscar Whitelaw. *Battlestars and Doughnuts: World War II Clubmobile Experiences of Mary Metcalfe Rexford*. St. Louis, MO: Patrice, 1989.

Salazar, Rolando A., web site for Co. D, 2nd Bn. 7th Cavalry, 1st Cavalry Division. <http://www.delta2-7.org/kia65.htm>,

Schuster, Carl Otis. "Case Closed: The Gulf of Tonkin Incident." *Vietnam*. June 2008, 28–33.

Scott, Ian. *Political Change and the Crisis of Legitimacy in Hong Kong*. Hawaii: University of Hawaii, 1989.

Smith, Jack P. "Sandbag for a Machine Gun: The Battle of the Ia Drang Valley and the Legacy of the Vietnam War." Speech, Ia Drang Survivors Banquet, Crystal City, VA, 8 Nov. 2003.

Socialist Republic of Vietnam, Military History Institute of Vietnam. *Victory in Vietnam: The Official History of the People's Army of Vietnam, 1954–1975,* trans. Merle L. Pribbenow. Lawrence: University Press of Kansas, 2002.

"Special Awards Ceremony Held," *The American Traveler*. N.p.: 1ˢᵗ Infantry Division Information Office, 3 Dec. 1966.

Stanton, Shelby L. *Anatomy of a Division, 1ˢᵗ Cav in Vietnam*. Novto, CA: Presidio, 1987.

Stars and Stripes, Vietnam Bureau. 20 Aug. 1970.

Stewart, James B. *Heart of a Soldier: A Story of Love, Heroism, and September 11ᵗʰ*. New York: Simon and Schuster, 2002.

Strait, Raymond. *James Garner*. New York: St. Martin's, 1985.

Strang, Jolynne, A Circle of Sisters/A Circle of Friends (Civilian) Denver, CO. http://vietnamreflections.blogspot.com/2009/03/circle-of-sisters.html

20

Summers, Harry G., Jr. *The Vietnam War Almanac.* New York: Presidio, Random House, 1985.

Sun Tzu on the Art of War: The Oldest Military Treatise in the World. Trans. Lionel Giles. Shanghai: British Museum, 1910. Republic of China: Ch'eng-wen, 1971.

Taylor, William O. *With Custer on the Little Bighorn: A Newly Discovered First-Person Account.* New York: Viking, 1996.

Together: The Midmonth Magazine for Methodist Families 11, no. 10 (Oct. 1967). No longer in publication.

United Press International, "1971 Year in Review: Calley Trial, Foreign Affairs." http://www.upi.com/Audio/Year_in_Review/Events-of-1971/Calley-Trial%2C-Foreign-Affairs/12295509436546-8/

United States Army Otter-Caribou Association. Congressional Medal of Honor Society, <http://www.cmohs.org/recipient-detail/3265/dolby-david-charles.php>.

United States Army Regulation AR 670-1 (Feb 2005).

United States, Center for Electronic Records, National Archives. *Combat Area Casualty File (CACF.)* Washington, DC: Nov. 1993.

United States, Congressional Research Service, "American War and Military Operations Casualties: Lists and Statistics," 26 Feb. 2010. http://www.fas.org/sgp/crs/natsec/RL32492.pdf

United States, Department of the Army, 203rd Military Intelligence Battalion, *Operator's Manual for AK-47 Assault Rifle.*

United States, Department of Defense, Advisory Committee on Women in the Services <http://www.dtic.mil/dacowits/membrs_MilStf.html>.

United States, Department of Defense, DOD Live, "New Names Added to Vietnam Memorial." 4 May 2010. <http://www.dodlive.mil/index.php/2010/05/new-names-added-to-vietnam-memorial/>.

United States, Department of Defense, Inter-Service Working Group. "Study on Utilization of Women in the Armed Services." Washington, DC: Government Printing Office, 31 Aug. 66.

United States. Department of Health and Human Services, Centers for Disease Control and Prevention General Information, http://www.cdc.gov/malaria

United States. Department of the Interior. National Park Service, *Lightning Strikes.* Cedar City, UT: Cedar Breaks National Monument, 2006.

U.S. Department of Labor. "Vietnam Era Veterans' Readjustment Assistance Act (VEVRAA) of 1974." http://www.dol.gov/esa/regs/compliance/ofccp/fsvevraa.htm.

United States, Department of the Navy, Naval Historical Center, Washington Navy Yard, Washington, D.C. <www.history.navy.mil/>, Page created 2 Jan. 2006, New images added and page divided 28 Dec 2006. <http://www.history.navy.mil/photos/sh-usn/usnsh-g/ap126.htm>.

United States, Department of Transportation, Research and Innovative Technology Administration, Bureau of Transportation Statistics, 13 Nov. 2005 <http://www.bts.gov/>; <http://www.driveandstayalive.com/>.

United States Military Academy, Association of Graduates, West Point, New York.

United States. United States Army. *Regulation AR 670-1 (Feb 2005), 28-21* <www.armystudyguide.com/>.

United States Congress, Centennial of Flight Commission, Centennial of Flight Commemoration Act, Public Law 105-389, 13 Nov. 1998.

United States Congress, Senate, Hearings before the Senate Committee on Public Lands, Reserved Water and Resource Conservation: Margaret Hodge, Statement submitted to Hearings on S.J. Res. 156, also presented orally to the House subcommittee headed by Mary Rose Oakar. The Congressional Record, for the Senate Hearing, Oct. 29, 1985 -The Bill was S. J. Res 156. Testimony is S. Hrg. 99-424. MINERVA, Quarterly Report on Women and the Military, Vol. IV, Number 1. Pasadena, MD: The MINERVA Center, Inc., Spring 1986.

United States, Military Advisory Command Vietnam (MACV) Directive 930-1, 14 June 1970.

Van Devanter, Lynda, with Christopher Morgan. *Home Before Morning: The True Story of an Army Nurse in Vietnam*. New York: Warner, 1983.

Vietnam Women's Memorial Project, Washington, D.C. *The Dedication of the Vietnam Women's Memorial: A Celebration of Patriotism and Courage*, by Diane Carlson Evans, RN, Vietnam, 1968-1969, Army Nurse Corps, 1966-72. "American Red Cross Women in Vietnam," Sharon Lewis Dickerson, ARC Vietnam: 1970–71, page 1 http://www.vietnamwomensmemorial.org/pdf/sdickerson.pdf

Wagner, Montie J., President, The Old Guard Association (TOGA), http://www.oldguard.org/, Emails 2010.

Westphall, Dr. and Mrs. Victor, and Walter Westphall. First Vietnam Veterans National Memorial, Angel Fire, Albuquerque, New Mexico. 1968.

When Lightning Strikes at Site 300, Lawrence Livermore National Laboratory, University of California, UCRL-52000-05-12. Livermore, CA: U.S. Department of Energy, 14 Dec. 2005.

Wilberding, Merle F. "What Really Happened in Pinkville." Cover story, *Vietnam*. Apr. 2008, 28–35.

"Wings Across America Presents: Fly Girls of WWII," exhibit at Baylor University, Mayborn Museum, Waco, Texas. <http://www.baylor.edu/mayborn/index.php?id=49549>.

Yellin, Emily. *Our Mothers' War: American Women at Home and at the Front During World War II*. New York: Free Press, 2004.

Interviews, Correspondence, and Emails

Anonymous Corporal. Telephone Interview, Apr. 2009.

Anonymous, M.D., Fellow American Board of Obstetrics & Gynecology, Personal Interview, Mar. 2010.

Anonymous Sergeant. United States Marine Corps, Email to author, Mar. 2010.

Ahrenberg, John. Email to author, 2008.

Alley, J. L. "Bud." Email to author, 26 Aug. 2009.

Askew, Andy. Personal Interview, Oct. 2006.

Benson, Wilmer. Emails to author, June 2008.

Bisio, Drew. Personal Interview, July 2007.

Bradshaw-McLean, Susan. Telephone Interview with the author, 10 June 2008.

Brigham, J. S. (Jim). Emails to author, Feb. 2008–Mar. 2010.

Carr, William J., Jr. Emails to author, 2010.

Carter, William T. (Tom). Emails to author, Mar., Apr., Oct. 2010.

Conboy, William P. Email to author, July 2008.

Fulps, Robert C. Emails to author, Nov. 2007–Jan. 2011.

Grandstaff, Bill. Personal Interview, Oct. 2006.

Griffin, Jerry. Email to author, July 2008.

Grzywinski, Lawrence. Emails to author, Dec. 2007–Mar. 2010.

Hargis, Jake. Email to author, July 2008.

Huggins, James F. Emails to author, Mar. 2010.

Idalski, Chet "Chief." Personal Interviews, Mar. and Nov. 2008.

Johnson, Robert C. Telephone Interview, Sept. 2007.

Kelsey, Ann. Emails to author. 16 Jan. 2008, 6 Jun. 2008

Kotcher, David E. Email to author, Mar. 2010.

Lilly, Barb. Emails to author, 14–16 Oct. 2008.

Love, Francis W. Emails to author, 2010.

Lyall, Alec. Telephone interview with author, 30 May 2008.

Manning, James. Telephone Interview with author, Nov. 2008.

McCleery, Kammy. Email to author, Apr. 2008.

McDermott, Pete. Email to author Jan. 2011.

McGhie, Michael W. Email to author, Feb. 2010.

Morris, Richard C. Email to author, July 2008.

Murray, Charles. Email to author, July 2008.

Olive, Serge. Email to author, July 2008.

Persinger, Neil E. Personal Interview, Nov. 2008.

Rosette, Phil. Emails to author, Sept. 2008–2010.

Ryan, Jack. Personal Interview, Oct. 2006.

Salazar, Rolando A. Emails to author, Dec. 2009.

Silvey, Bruce D. Email to author, June 2008.

West, Elizabeth (Arant). Email to author, July 2008.

Williams, Wayne. Email to author, Jan. 2011.

Wolf, Marvin J. Email to author, 29 Mar. 2010.

Young, Jennifer. Email to author, 2008.

Index

Page numbers in italics refer to figures.

H

L

Linda from Kansas, 312

Liz, 32, 33, 34, 41, 53, 57, 59, 60, 63, 89, 103, 105

Long Binh, 152–157, 205, 235, 272, *216*, 291–292

Lori, 8, 194, *202, 207,* 207, 210, 211, 213, 215

Love, Francis W., 324n7

Lyall, Alec (RTO), 184–186, 211, 306–307, 318, 323n17, 329n5, 329n6

Lyons, Vernon M., 292

LZ Albany, 85, 132, 319n5

LZ Schueller, 299

LZ X-Ray, 85, 132

M

MACV (Military Assistance Command Vietnam), x, 287

Maddie, 137, 138, 142

malaria: disease, 319n2; mosquitoes, 60; pill, 38, 60

Manning, James, 298, 328n8

Mapp, Lt. Col. Jim, 60, 98 101

Marshall, Brigadier General S. L. A., 98, 100, 105, 318n11, 320n5, 320n6, 329n10

Mary in Korea, *10*

Mary (roommate), 151

Mary in Vietnam, 89

McCleery, Kammy, 297, Appendix 1 327n5, Appendix 1 327n7, Appendix 2 327n7

McCoid, Col. Chester B., II, 48, 318n16

McDermott, Pete, 324n6, 324n7

McDonald, Warrant Officer, 79, 81, 82

McGhie, Michael W., 299, 316n15, 319n9, 328n9

McKusker, chief nurse Lieutenant Colonel, 57, 59

McNiff, Joan, 225

O

P

Q

R